The Community College EXPERIENCE

Brief

THIRD EDITION

The Community College EXPERIENCE

Brief

Amy Baldwin, M.A.

Pulaski Technical College

Boston Columbus Indianapolis New York San Francisco Upper Saddle River
Amsterdam Cape Town Dubai London Madrid Milan Munich Paris Montreal Toronto
Delhi Mexico City Sao Paulo Sydney Hong Kong Seoul Singapore Taipei Tokyo

Editor-in-Chief: Jodi McPherson
Development Editor: Jennifer Gessner
Editorial Assistant: Clara Ciminelli
Vice President, Director of Marketing: Margaret Waples
Executive Marketing Manager: Amy Judd
Production Editor: Annette Joseph
Editorial Production Service: Omegatype Typography, Inc.
Manufacturing Buyer: Megan Cochran
Electronic Composition: Omegatype Typography, Inc.
Interior Design: Omegatype Typography, Inc.
Photo Researcher: Annie Fuller
Art Director: Linda Knowles
Cover Designer: Susan Paradise

Credits and acknowledgments borrowed from other sources and reproduced, with permission, in this textbook appear on appropriate page within text or below.

Chapter opening photos: p. 8: Thinkstock; p. 30: Shutterstock; p. 48: Shutterstock; p. 72: Bill Aron/PhotoEdit; p. 92: Shutterstock; p. 116: SMART Technologies, Inc; p. 138: Shutterstock; p. 158: Stockdisc; p. 180: Thinkstock; p. 200: Hola Images/Getty Images

Library of Congress Cataloging-in-Publication Data

Baldwin, Amy
The community college experience. Brief / Amy Baldwin.—3rd ed.
p. cm.
Includes bibliographical references and index.
ISBN-13: 978-0-13-248086-4 (pbk.)
ISBN-10: 0-13-248086-7
1. College student orientation—United States. 2. Community colleges—United States. 3. College students—Conduct of life. I. Title.
LB2343.32.B244 2012
378.1'543—dc22

2010052062

10 9 8 7 6 5 4 3 CKV 15 14 13 12 11

www.pearsonhighered.com

ISBN-10: 0-13-248086-7
ISBN-13: 978-0-13-248086-4

AMY'S STORY

I believe everyone has a story worth telling. My story is that I am a mother, a teacher, and a student. These three roles have been a part of who I am since my earliest memories. While other little girls played house, I played school, giving homework and telling my "students" (either agreeable neighbors or silent stuffed animals) to be quiet and pay attention. When my older sister went off to her first day of school, I begged to follow, and I gathered my "school supplies" and stuffed them into a bag. Although I was the youngest child, I mothered the neighborhood kids as early as 10 years old when I started babysitting. My teaching career started a little earlier—in 3rd grade—when I was asked to help my friend Jennifer master fractions. I continued my career throughout junior high and high school by tutoring in English, giving swimming lessons, and teaching art.

Nothing, though, prepared me for teaching at the community college. The first class I ever taught was both frightening and exhilarating. It was the first time in my life that I realized what I was doing was *exactly* what I should be doing with my life, but it was also the first time that I felt completely and utterly out of my league, ignorant, even downright dumb. I am sure my students have felt the same way—eager and excited to start a new chapter in their lives, but also concerned about the unknown. Speaking of unknown, I felt I knew nothing about how to be an effective teacher with community college students, and it was obvious that I needed to use what I knew about being a student to learn who my students were and what they really needed. Along the way, I discovered that being a nurturer for the abilities and talents that graced my classroom was a fitting role for me as well. How proud I am of the very ones who started their college career unsure of their abilities and who grew in confidence as they marked success after success.

Because I always love learning new things, I have now come full circle and am a student in a doctoral program. I am experiencing similar situations as my students—balancing a full-time job, a family, and college classes and worrying whether or not I can do it all. It's sometimes a struggle to get everything done, but I have used my experience to learn more about how my students feel and what they need in terms of content and support. I have a greater appreciation of their previous experience, their time, and even their levels of frustration when they find themselves stressed out!

It is because of these experiences that I continue to provide what I believe is the best information in the most concise way to community college students who fill a variety of roles themselves and who have to make it all work while they are pursuing a degree. I hope you find this book helps make your journey a little easier—at the very least, know that you are not alone in your experiences and that you can do it!

BRIEF CONTENTS

CONTENTS

PART TWO
Integrations

Chapter 5
Reading, Listening, and Note Taking 92

Chapter 6
Learning, Memory, and Studying for Tests 116

Chapter 9 Planning for Next Semester 180

Chapter 10 Preparing for a Career and a Life 200

PREFACE

People make a difference. As community college educators, we know that we would not be in business if people did not come to us in search of a better life through education. We also know that without the people on our campuses, those same students would not likely make it to graduation nor realize the better life they dream about. It is with this in mind that the third edition of *The Community College Experience,* Brief Edition, has been revised—to expand the opportunities for students to learn more about the people they are becoming and the people who can help them along the way. For example, the "buzz boxes" that begin each chapter with questions that students, faculty, and staff have about the community college experience show the variety of reactions by different people. Also, within the chapter, more buzz boxes appear that provide additional information about being successful. Think of this new feature as a way for people to help students achieve their goals in college and in life.

In addition to the questions and advice provided throughout the chapters, another new feature helps students *relate* to other people more effectively. Emotional intelligence, or the ability to recognize and manage emotions productively, plays an important part in student success. Part of what makes emotional intelligence an important aspect of student success is its focus on self-awareness and self-management (Goleman, 1995). With this in mind, the Emotional Intelligence Check-Up was developed and included in each chapter to allow students to explore a real-life scenario and work through three important steps to self-awareness and self-management: feeling, thinking, and acting. The more self-aware a student becomes, the more likely she can manage herself in tough situations and take a positive action to resolve the situation.

"Get to know the librarians at your college. They can provide lots of help when you have a research project."
—Will, 24, student

These new features have reinforced, rather than shifted, the original focus of *The Community College Experience* books. The first and second editions were written from a burning need to find a practical, easy-to-use text for my students, and that fundamental purpose has not changed in the third edition. In fact, new and revised material has been included to make sure that students are getting precisely the information they need for "just in time" learning. Community college students are busy with college, work, and family, and they deserve to get the essential information they need to help them as they achieve their dreams of graduating from college. This book provides them with only what they need to make that successful transition into college and (back) into the workforce.

To that end, each chapter contains the following features with the focus on basic information or the "what, when, and where" for being successful in college:

"WHAT" will support students

Emotional Intelligence Check-Up. This new feature introduces the emotional intelligence concept to students by providing a real-life student scenario and asking the reader to answer three questions that range from recognizing emotional reactions to creating a positive action plan. The Emotional Intelligence Check-Up focuses on four of the emotional intelligences that make the most difference in student success: optimism, self-regard, problem solving, and impulse control.

Buzz Boxes. New students are often "abuzz" with questions and concerns as they start college. To meet those students where they are, each chapter begins with dialogue (buzz) boxes containing student, faculty, and staff questions that relate directly to the chapter objectives. Within the chapter, these questions are answered in additional dialogue boxes—advice by other students, faculty, and staff. Want to know what the "buzz" is? Read the opening boxes and then look for answers within the text.

Your Terms of Success. Because many community college students are unfamiliar with the terms that are unique to the college setting, this new feature provides a handy overview of common vocabulary they will encounter as well as their definitions.

Integrity Matters. In this updated feature in each chapter, students have the opportunity to explore how integrity—both academic and personal—relates to their own lives and to reflect on how they can act with integrity in all aspects of the college experience.

Tech Tactics. This new feature provides information about the immediate technological support that colleges offer as well as current technology that can assist students in their educational goals; it then goes a step further to provide recommended websites for students.

"WHEN" will students relate to the material

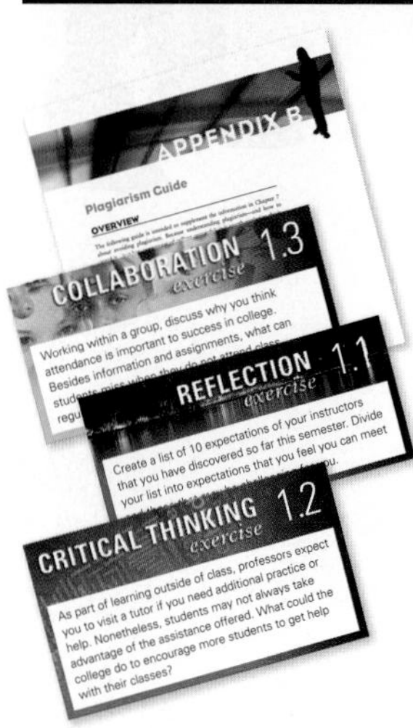

Avoiding Plagiarism. Appendix B provides much-needed information explaining plagiarism and how to avoid it in a variety of college settings. This is an essential read for students who are unfamiliar with college writing and research expectations.

Collaboration Exercises. The collaboration exercises enable students to see the connection between relating to their classmates through the exercises and relating to others in general.

Reflection and Critical Thinking Exercises. These two exercises remain the same throughout this edition.

"WHERE" can students apply what is being learned

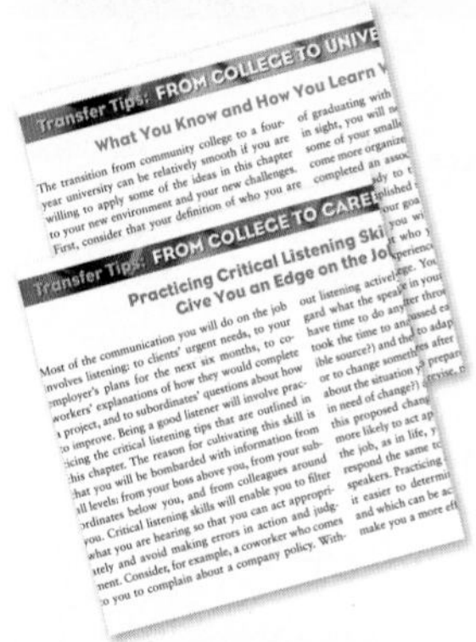

Transfer Tips: From College to University and From College to Career. With the increasing number of students who are transferring between colleges or to work environments, it is becoming more important to help them make transitions smoothly. Each chapter ends with two sections called "From College to University" and "From College to Career," in which the chapter's topic is applied to the world beyond the community college. Students will be able to see how the essential keys to college success are building blocks for life fulfillment.

NEW! CourseSmart eTextbook Available

CourseSmart is an exciting new choice for students looking to save money. As an alternative to purchasing the printed textbook, students can purchase an electronic version of the same content. With a CourseSmart eTextbook, students can search the text, make notes online, print out reading assignments that incorporate lecture notes, and bookmark important passages for later review. For more information, or to purchase access to the CourseSmart eTextbook, visit www.coursesmart.com.

ACKNOWLEDGMENTS

People make a difference, and without the people in my life who support and challenge me, this book would not have been possible. Thank you to Kyle, Emily, and Will. Thank you to my Prentice Hall family as well. And always, thank you to my students who have allowed me to be a part of their families. I also want to thank the following people who reviewed the text and offered invaluable feedback: Gary Corona, Florida State College at Jacksonville; Rebecca Ingrahm, St. Charles Community College; Emily Lasek, St. Louis Community College; James Mendoza, Tacoma Community College; Yolanda Reyna, Palo Alto College; David Rodriguez, San Antonio College; Ethel Schuster, Northern Essex Community College; Peggy Valdez-Fergason, Southwest Early College; and Robert Vela, Austin Community College.

REFERENCE

Goleman, D. (1995). *Emotional intelligence.* New York: Bantam Books.

For Students!

Why is this course important?

This course will help you transition to college, introduce you to campus resources, and prepare you for success in all aspects of college, career, and life. You will:

- Develop Skills to Excel in Other Classes
- Apply Concepts from College to Your Career and Life
- Learn to Use Media Resources

How can you get the most out of the book and online resources required in this class?

Purchase your book and online resources before the First Day of Class. Register and log in to the online resources using your access code.

Develop Skills to Excel in Other Classes

- Helps you with your homework
- Prepares you for exams

Apply Concepts from College to Your Career and Life

- Provides learning techniques
- Helps you achieve your goals

Learn to Use Media Resources

- www.mystudentsuccesslab.com helps you build skills you need to succeed through peer-led videos, interactive exercises and projects, journaling and goal setting activities.
- Connect with real students, practice skill development, and personalize what is learned.

Want to get involved with Pearson like other students have?

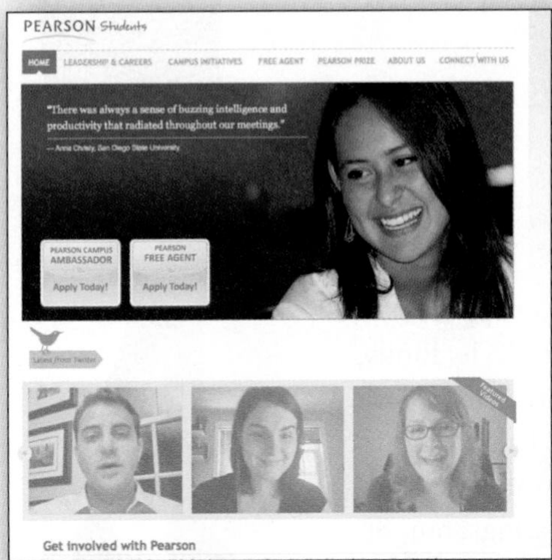

Join www.PearsonStudents.com
It is a place where our student customers can incorporate their views and ideas into their learning experience. They come to find out about our programs such as the **Pearson Student Advisory Board, Pearson Campus Ambassador**, and the **Pearson Prize** (student scholarship!).

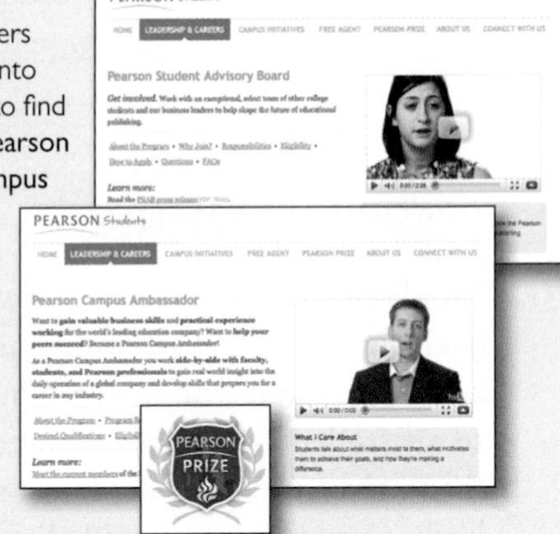

Here's how you can get involved:

- Tell your instructors, friends, and family members about **PearsonStudents**.
- To get daily updates on how students can boost their resumes, study tips, get involved with Pearson, and earn rewards:

  Become a fan of **Pearson Students on Facebook**

  Follow **@Pearson_Student on Twitter**

- Explore **Pearson Free Agent**. It allows you get involved in the publishing process, by giving student feedback.

See you on **PearsonStudents** where our student customers live.
When students succeed, we succeed!

Succeed in college and beyond!
Connect, practice, and personalize with MyStudentSuccessLab.

www.mystudentsuccesslab.com

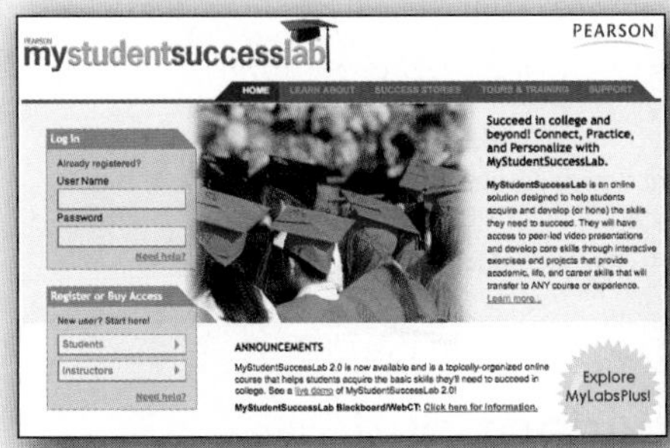

MyStudentSuccessLab is an online solution designed to help students acquire the skills they need to succeed. They will have access to peer-led video presentations and develop core skills through interactive exercises and projects that provide academic, life, and career skills that will transfer to ANY course.

It can accompany any Student Success text, or be sold as a stand-alone course offering. To become successful learners, students must consistently apply techniques to daily activities.

How will MyStudentSuccessLab make a difference?

Is motivation a challenge, and if so, how do you deal with it?
Video Presentation – Experience peer led video 'by students, for students' of all ages and stages.

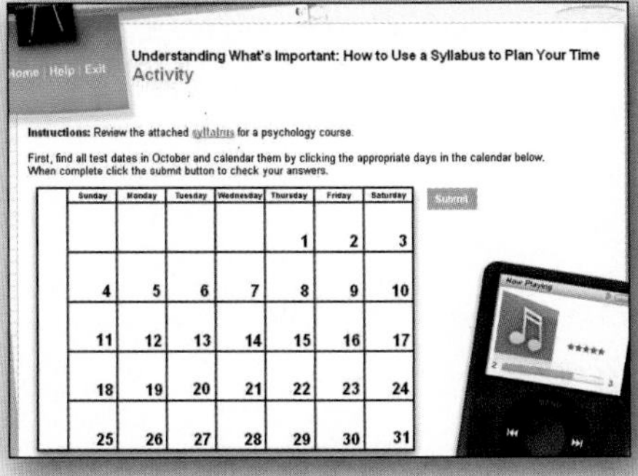

How would better class preparation improve the learning experience?
Practice activities – Practice skills for each topic - beginning, intermediate, and advanced - leveled by Bloom's taxonomy.

What could you gain by building critical thinking and problem-solving skills in this class?
Apply (final project) – Complete a final project using these skills to create 'personally relevant' resources.

MyStudentSuccessLab Feature set:

Topic Overview: Module objectives.
Video Presentation - Connect: Real student video interviews on key issues.
Practice: Three skill-building exercises per topic provide interactive experience and practice.
Apply - Personalize: Apply what is learned by creating a personally relevant project and journal.
Resources: Plagiarism Guide, Dictionary, Calculators, and Assessments (Career, Learning Styles, and Personality Styles).
Additional Assignments: Extra suggested activities to use with each topic.
Text-Specific Study Plan (available with select books): Chapter Objectives, Practice Tests, Enrichment activities, and Flashcards.

MyStudentSuccessLab Topic List -

1. Time Management/Planning
2. Values/Goal Setting
3. Learning How You Learn
4. Listening and Taking Class Notes
5. Reading and Annotating
6. Memory and Studying
7. Critical Thinking
8. Problem-Solving
9. Information Literacy
10. Communication
11. Test Prep and Test Taking
12. Stress Management
13. Financial Literacy
14. Majors and Careers

"I like the videos and the pre-chapter self-assessment because the video helps me visually and the self-assessment tests my knowledge."

—Trey Smith,
Pulaski Technical College

MyStudentSuccessLab Support:

- **Demos, Registration, Log-in** - www.mystudentsuccesslab.com under "Tours and Training" and "Support."
- **Email support** - Send an inquiry to MyStudentSuccessLab@pearson.com
- **Online Training** - Join one of our weekly WebEx training sessions.
- **Peer Training** - Faculty Advocate connection for qualified adoptions.
- **Technical support** - 24 hours a day, seven days a week, at http://247pearsoned.custhelp.com

The Community College EXPERIENCE

Brief

Getting a jump start on college means that you already have a leg up on your classmates who are just settling into their student routines. One of the best ways to do this is to find out what your learning preferences are. Students who understand how and when they *like* to learn are more likely to feel in control of their own success in college. Although you cannot control everything—your instructors, what you study, and how much work you have to do—you can have a say in how you work within those parameters. For example, if you are a social learner, as you may discover in the surveys provided, you will learn to form study groups for classes that are demanding of your time.

YOUR LEARNING STYLE PREFERENCES

Taking control of your learning preferences will enable you to lay a firm foundation on which to build your college success. Knowing your learning styles also helps you understand yourself in other aspects of your life. Information about what you like and dislike, how you relate to others, and how you work most productively will provide direction for achieving your goals and, as Gordon Lawrence (1995) states in his book *People Types and Tiger Stripes,* lead you to make "dramatic improvements in the effectiveness of [your] work" (p. 5). Appendix A offers Neil Fleming's VARK learning styles inventory, which focuses on four learning style preferences: Visual, Aural, Read/Write, and Kinesthetic. In the next few pages, you will complete a personality preference inventory, which can help you see an aspect of who you are. Looking at your values, dreams, mission statement, and goals in light of your learning style can work to create a more complete picture of who you are and how to get where you want to go.

Although learning preferences are not necessarily directly linked to college majors or careers, you can easily see that your learning style preference will come into play when you choose your major and your career. Kinesthetic learners, for example, may be drawn to majors or careers that allow them to move about or use their bodies to complete tasks. Landscape design, auto body repair, culinary arts, and nursing are just a few community college degree programs that would appeal to kinesthetic learners. Review Table 1, which lists possible majors and careers for some learning style preferences, but note that it is not considered an exhaustive list. Also, some majors and careers may speak to more than one learning style preference; for example, an advertising executive who writes, edits, and directs commercials may rely on almost all the learning style preferences on a daily basis as she creates commercials and ads for clients. For sure, she will need to work individually, with peers, and with her boss on different aspects of a project, and she may find that she is needed to complete tasks at different times of the day, even late at night when filming continues long after the typical workday ends.

Harvard psychologist Howard Gardner is well known for his theory of multiple intelligences, which is another term for "what we know, understand, and learn about our world" (Lazear, 1991, p. xiv). Gardner has created eight categories of how we can know and learn.

Verbal/linguistic intelligence is evident in people who can use language with ease; they enjoy reading and writing and may be journalists, novelists, playwrights, or comedians. The logical/mathematical intelligence is demonstrated by an ease and enjoyment with numbers and logic problems. People who have a strong leaning this intelligence like to solve problems, find patterns, discover relationships between objects, and follow steps. Career choices for logical/mathematical thinkers include science, computer technology, math, and engineering.

The visual/spatial intelligence is characterized by anything visual—paintings, photographs, maps, and architecture. People who have a strong visual/spatial sense are usually good at design, architecture, painting and sculpture, and map making. The bodily/kinesthetic intelligence focuses on body movement. It is found in people who enjoy using their bodies to express themselves. Obvious career choices for this intelligence include dancing, sports, and dramatic arts. Musical/rhythmic intelligence encompasses mental proficiency with the rhythms of music and hearing tones and beats. People who have strong musical/rhythmic intelligence may use musical instruments or the human voice to express themselves. Career choices for this intelligence include all types of musical performance.

TABLE 1 Learning Style Preferences, Majors, and Careers

Learning Style Preference	College Majors	Careers
Visual	Art, graphic design, drafting, architecture, interior design	Art teacher, artist, graphic designer, architect, interior designer, stylist
Aural	Music, communications, counseling	Musician, music educator, marketing director, public relations director, counselor
Kinesthetic	Sciences, sociology, computer technology, culinary arts, massage therapy	Nurse, doctor, therapist, networking specialist, computer technician, chef, massage therapist

How you relate to others and yourself is part of the interpersonal and intrapersonal intelligences. People with strong interpersonal intelligence relate strongly with others. They read others' feelings well and act with others in mind. Intrapersonal intelligence centers around the ability to understand oneself. People who possess intrapersonal intelligence know how and why they do what they do. Naturalistic, the eighth intelligence, refers to people who enjoy and work well in an outdoor environment. Naturalistic people find peace in nature and enjoy having natural elements around them.

Learning Preference Inventory

There are numerous ways to see yourself and understand your behavior in certain situations, and many education specialists and psychologists have provided theories on how we take in and process information. They have developed different inventories and personality profiles to enhance your understanding of yourself. As you will discover in Chapter 6, the learning process is somewhat complex; it involves more than just our preferences in how we create knowledge, because there are many factors that influence our ability to take in and process information.

Theories about the two hemispheres of our brain, known as the left brain and the right brain, have given us insight into how people think, learn, and see the world. People who have strong left-brain tendencies are more likely to be logical, to see parts rather than the whole, and to prefer to do activities step by step. They are also more analytical, realistic, and verbal than their right-brained companions. The right-brain tendency shows up in a preference to see the whole picture rather than details, to work out of sequence, and to bring ideas together. Surveys available online can indicate which hemisphere is dominant in your brain.

The Myers-Briggs Type Indicator (MBTI), on the other hand, is a personality assessment that provides you with information about how you prefer to think and act. For example, one dimension of the personality test asks you how outgoing or extroverted you are in certain situations or how reserved, or introverted, you are in social settings. These questions indicate whether you are extroverted (E) or introverted (I). Like brain hemisphere inventories, the MBTI can be found in books or online sources. Samples of the complete inventories are also available.

Other inventories, such as both the Dunn and Dunn Learning Styles Assessment and the PEPS Learning Styles Inventory, focus not only on how a person prefers to take in information, but also on social and environmental learning preferences. These types of inventories provide a thorough view of how you like to learn, whether it is the temperature of the room, the amount of light and sound, or an inclination for moving about as you learn.

Regardless of which learning theory leads you to greater personal insight, as stand-alone models they are somewhat insignificant unless you *use* the information to benefit actual learning. The purpose of the learning plan inventory

FIGURE 1 Learning Plan Categories

Time of Day Preferences: morning, afternoon, night

Intake Preferences: visual, auditory, kinesthetic

Social Preferences: individual, peer(s), mentor (professor, expert, leader, etc.)

Task Management Preferences: logical/analytical, spontaneous/creative

is to provide you with a basic understanding of the factors that influence your learning preferences, which you can use to create an individualized and flexible learning plan for the various tasks and assignments that you will experience in college. Ultimately, greater personal understanding and self-knowledge leads to action, and this learning plan inventory provides you with not only information about how you prefer to learn but also a roadmap for completing tasks and goals successfully by applying your preferences.

The inventory is adapted from the models just discussed, and the statements will help you discover your learning style preference in four areas: task management, time of day, intake, and social learning (see Figure 1).

To complete the inventory in Figure 2, read the statements in each category and circle the number that corresponds most closely to your degree of identification with the statement. The number 1 means the statement is least like you whereas the number 5 means that the statement is most like you. You will calculate your answers after the inventory.

FIGURE 2 Learning Plan Inventory

Time of Day Preference

Read each statement and circle the number on the scale that best represents you (1: Least like me—5: Most like me)					
1. I feel most energized in the morning.	1	2	3	4	5
2. My energy level soars late at night.	1	2	3	4	5
3. I get more accomplished in the afternoon.	1	2	3	4	5
4. I concentrate best before noon.	1	2	3	4	5
5. Late at night is my most productive time.	1	2	3	4	5
6. Afternoon is the best time for me to complete important tasks.	1	2	3	4	5
7. I wait to do projects until I have had a full night's sleep.	1	2	3	4	5
8. I prefer to start and complete projects after I have completed everything else I need to do for the day.	1	2	3	4	5
9. I feel best about working on a project if it occurs between getting started for the day and ending the day.	1	2	3	4	5

continued

FIGURE 2 continued

Intake Preference

Read each statement and circle the number on the scale that best represents you (1: Least like me—5: Most like me)					
1. When I am trying something new, I like to "see" it in my head before doing it.	1	2	3	4	5
2. I can understand a concept best when I hear it explained.	1	2	3	4	5
3. I don't really understand something unless I do it or experience it myself.	1	2	3	4	5
4. I explain my ideas best by talking through them.	1	2	3	4	5
5. I figure out what I think about a topic by experiencing it firsthand.	1	2	3	4	5
6. I like to draw what I'm thinking so others will understand.	1	2	3	4	5
7. When trying to get from one place to another, I am most confident when I have already traveled there.	1	2	3	4	5
8. When trying to get from one place to another, I am most confident if I can see the route I need to take.	1	2	3	4	5
9. When trying to get from one place to another, I am most confident when I am told the directions by someone who has been there before.	1	2	3	4	5

Social Learning Preference

Read each statement and circle the number on the scale that best represents you (1: Least like me—5: Most like me)					
1. I work best alone.	1	2	3	4	5
2. I feel comfortable asking my boss or professor questions when I'm not sure what to do.	1	2	3	4	5
3. I rely on friends or coworkers to help me complete work or figure out what to do when I am stuck on a task.	1	2	3	4	5
4. I need little interaction with others to complete a task.	1	2	3	4	5
5. I'm most comfortable working in groups on a project.	1	2	3	4	5
6. I'm most at ease working on a task that my supervisor monitors closely.	1	2	3	4	5
7. I can get group projects completed faster than when I work alone.	1	2	3	4	5
8. I am more confident when my boss or professor gives me constant feedback as I complete a project.	1	2	3	4	5
9. When others interfere with a project I am working on, I get little done.	1	2	3	4	5

Task Management Preference

Read each statement and circle the number on the scale that best represents you (1: Least like me—5: Most like me)					
1. I enjoy thinking up and starting new projects.	1	2	3	4	5
2. It is easy for me to complete important tasks.	1	2	3	4	5
3. I like to be spontaneous when I work on a project; I go wherever the mood takes me.	1	2	3	4	5
4. I like to have a detailed schedule before I begin a project.	1	2	3	4	5
5. I like to have a general idea of the main goal and then discover what needs to be done as I work toward the goal.	1	2	3	4	5
6. I like to consider the steps to a project first before thinking about the overall picture.	1	2	3	4	5
7. I need to know what the end goal is before I begin a project.	1	2	3	4	5
8. I am considered creative.	1	2	3	4	5

FIGURE 3 Calculation Tables

Time of Day Preference

Morning	Night	Afternoon
1.	2.	3.
4.	5.	6.
7.	8.	9.
Total	Total	Total

Intake Preference

Visual	Auditory	Kinesthetic
1.	2.	3.
6.	4.	5.
8.	9.	7.
Total	Total	Total

Social Learning Preference

Individual	Mentor	Peer
1.	2.	3.
4.	5.	6.
9.	8.	7.
Total	Total	Total

Task Management Preference

Spontaneous/Creative	Logical/Analytical
1.	2.
3.	4.
5.	6.
8.	7.
Total	Total

Calculating Your Score

For each learning preference category, write the number you circled for each statement in Figure 3. Then add up the numbers for each type of question. The higher numbers will indicate your strongest preferences. Afterward, complete Figure 4, labeled "My Learning Preferences." You will use this information to complete your own learning plans.

FIGURE 4 My Learning Preferences

Time of Day	
Intake	
Social	
Task Management	

LEARNING PLAN IN ACTION

Table 2 shows a learning plan in action for a student who works best at night, is both a strong visual and auditory learner, performs best with peers, and prefers to break down assignments into manageable parts.

There are many ways of viewing yourself and creating a plan of action for your work in college, but no single inventory, assessment, or work plan will reflect the exceptional person you are or your unique circumstances; in other words, no matter which inventory you take or what you learn about how you prefer to learn, the results are not the final verdict on your abilities and potential.

The goal then of this learning plan is to provide you with an adaptable, flexible model for putting your learning style preferences into action. It also gives you a roadmap for accomplishing the many goals that you will set for yourself.

TABLE 2 Learning Plan Example

Learning Task: Study for biology midterm	
Time of Day	Night—after dinner
Intake	Visual and auditory—review notes and talk through them with study group
Social	Peers—biology study group
Task Management	Logical/analytical—go in order of the chapters and work with classmate who can help me arrange the material in an order that makes sense and is easy to remember.

Additionally, it can serve as a place to start when faced with situations that require you to work outside your learning preference comfort zone. For example, what will you do, as a morning learner, when faced with completing an important project late at night? Or how will you, as an individual learner, fare when required to collaborate with classmates on an assignment? One way to move outside your learning preference comfort zone is to take time to reflect on how you would act in the same situation and consider how you will meet the challenges discussed in this book. Reflecting on who you are and how you will get where you want to go will help you create your own story of success.

Learning Styles and Career Choices

Discovering your learning style preference and personality type will definitely help you set realistic short-term and long-term goals. For example, discovering that you have a read/write learning preference and work well with deadlines and staying organized may confirm that your long-term goal of being a writer will work well with who you are and how you learn and work. However, identifying your style and type should not limit your choices or keep you from working on areas of your learning style and personality that may be weaker or get less attention. If you are a strong visual learner but are taking a class that relies on listening effectively and critically, you should use that opportunity to become a better listener, to improve your aural learning style preference by following listening tips like the ones found in Chapter 5. Likewise, if you work better alone and have a strong kinesthetic learning style preference, choosing a career as a computer technician may play to your strengths. However, you may also find yourself working with others collaboratively and communicating frequently in writing and verbally.

Therefore, whatever your learning style strengths and personality preferences may be, consider how other styles and types will factor into your short-term and long-term educational goals. Then look for opportunities to strengthen those less-developed sides of your learning and personality so that you can become a more well-rounded person comfortable in a variety of situations.

REFERENCES

Fleming, N. (2009). VARK Learning Style Preferences. Retrieved October 19, 2009, from www.vark-learn.com

Lawrence, G. (1995). *People types and tiger stripes* (3rd ed.). Gainesville, FL: CAPT.

Lazear, D. (1991). *Seven ways of teaching: The artistry of teaching with multiple intelligences*. Palatine, IL: Skylight Publishing.

Myers-Briggs Type Indicator. (2008). Retrieved May 15, 2008, from www.myersbriggstypeindicator.co.uk

CHAPTER one

UNDERSTANDING College Culture and Your Campus

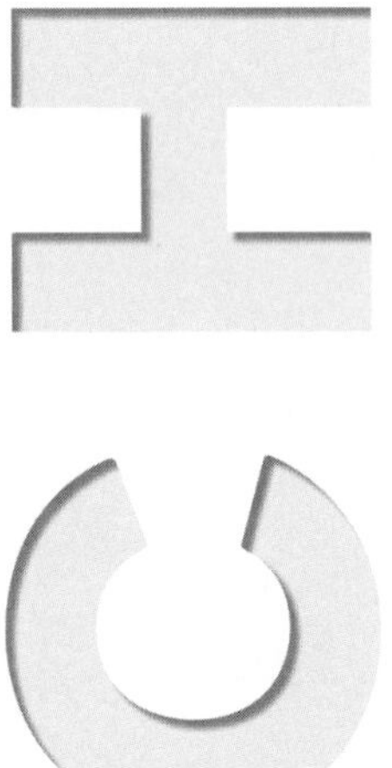

IN THIS chapter

Welcome to college! This will be a time of change for you, but be assured that many people are there to support you along the way. Knowing what to expect will be the first step in transitioning from your "other" life, whether high school, family, or the workforce, into a life of classes, readings, assignments, and growth. The purpose of this chapter is to introduce you to this new culture, to reveal the truths about higher education, to debunk the myths, and to prepare you for meeting the challenges that you will inevitably face. This chapter also provides you with information about what this

"This is my first time in college and I am not sure what to expect. How will this be different than working a job? Or will it?"
—Jerry, 42, student
"My professor keeps talking about a syllabus. What is it?"
—Kamesha, 21, student
"I haven't been outside of my hometown, so college is a big step for me. What can I do to prepare to encounter new people, new ideas, and new challenges?"
—Kandace, 33, student
"I know college is supposed to be different than high school, but how? Will I be totally lost?"
—Sari, 18, student
"I don't get how college works yet. The schedules, the classes, the times, the requirements all confuse me. Can I get help?"
—Willis, 25, student
"What do I need to know about doing well enough to keep my scholarships?"
—Taleeb, 23, student

new environment will look like and what you can expect in terms of communication between the college and you.

More specifically, after completing this chapter you will be able to do the following:

- Identify the transitional issues of going to college.
- Describe the expectations of college.
- Explain the processes of college.
- List and define the resources on campus.

TRANSITION and Transformation

This is an exciting time as you transition into college life. The definition of *transition* means a change, a modification, and you will find that going to college creates a change in you—and not just in your schedule and your workload. You will find that your concept of yourself will change, your relationships will change, and your outlook on your future will change. Each of these changes will require reflection and an investment of your time to make it happen. At the end of your college experience, you will find yourself *transformed* into a new person. You will most likely be more thoughtful and more confident about your abilities; most certainly, you will be more aware of what it takes to earn a degree. However, this change or transformation won't be easy; the following section on transitioning from where you are now to where you want to be will give you a better understanding of what you need to do to make change happen.

For some students, the move from high school to college seems fairly simple—both require reading, writing, testing, and attending class. Students who are taking the step from work to school may also see some similarities between their jobs and classroom work—both require working hard, keeping motivated, and following the rules. If the differences between high school or work and college are that similar, then why do so many college students have difficulty making a successful transition?

"If you treat college like a job, you are more likely to spend enough time on it. If you think it is just an 'add on' to your life, you will find it hard to spend the time you need to be successful."

—Helen, 28, student

The answer to that question can be given by the instructors who see smart, competent students have trouble adjusting to the climate and culture of college because they do not understand what is expected of them. In other words, in order to be successful, students must know how they should be preparing beyond the questions on the next test; they need to know how college works and how to navigate through not only their courses, but also the common challenges that they will face as they work toward a degree or certificate.

Table 1.1 illustrates some of the differences and similarities between high school, a full-time job, and college. Notice that the greatest differences occur between high school and college. There are some similarities between a full-time job and college, although there are also distinct differences.

HIGHER EDUCATION, Higher Expectations

The degree programs at community colleges are shorter than at universities, usually requiring one or two years, but the reality is that you may need to take more time to complete a degree program if you plan to enroll as a part-time student. Also, if you need developmental or remedial classes before you can start on the required curriculum, completion of the program will be delayed.

Community college classes and degree programs are as demanding as their equivalents at four-year universities. Because of technical and industrial standards and career licensing, many courses and programs are, in fact, very challenging. Instructors who teach in the technical, industrial, and business fields are expected to graduate students who can pass licensing exams, which means the standards in the class must be high. If the courses were "easy," then the graduates would be unemployable. Likewise, students who intend to transfer to four-year universities after they complete their general education requirements would not be successful if the courses they took at the community college were not challenging. Community colleges want well-prepared and successful graduates; thus, it is in their best interest to provide courses that require the best work from their students.

TABLE 1.1 Differences between High School, Full-Time Work, and College

High School	Full-Time Work	College
Attendance mandatory in order to meet requirements; at least 6 continuous hours spent in class each day	Attendance mandatory in order to stay employed; at least 8 continuous hours spent at work each day	Attendance possibly not mandatory; different amounts of time spent in class and between classes each day
Very little choice in what classes you take and when you take them	May have little choice in work assignments and when the work is to be completed	More flexibility in when you work on assignments and how soon you complete them before the due date
Moderate to no outside work necessary to be successful	Moderate to no overtime work necessary to complete job duties	Substantial amount of outside work to complete assignments and to be successful
Teachers to check homework and keep you up to date on progress; will inform you if you are not completing assignments and progressing well	Supervisors to check completion and quality of work at regular intervals; will inform you if you are not meeting the standards for the position	Professors to choose whether to check all homework or provide feedback on progress at regular intervals; may not inform you if you are not meeting the standards of the course
Teachers to review material and expect that you remember facts and information	Employers to provide basic information and expectation that you use it to complete the job effectively	Professors to present concepts and theories and expect that you evaluate the ideas, synthesize the ideas with other concepts you have learned, and develop new theories
Frequent tests over small amounts of material with opportunities for grades to be raised if needed	Employee improvement plans to allow you to improve your ratings if needed	Professors' standards and grading criteria, often allowing only a few chances (through infrequent testing/assignments) to meet them

GO FOR THE GOLD BY REMEMBERING SILVER

Making a successful transition will not only include comparing where you have just come from (home, work, or another institution of learning) to college life, but it will also involve breaking down the experience into parts that you can master. To remember what you need to start and end well, remember this simple acronym: SILVER. This stands for Supplies, Instructors' Expectations, Learning, Vocabulary, Effort, and Responsibility.

Supplies, or "The Right Stuff"

Making sure you are adequately prepared for the journey you are about to take is the first step in being successful. You wouldn't head out on a trip to unknown lands without a map, proper gear, and plenty of food and water! Think of your college supplies as part of your survival gear, too. The most important items that you will need at the beginning of the semester are required textbooks and course materials. You can find out what books and materials you will need either through the bookstore or through your professors. Usually an exact list of course materials is included in your syllabus. In high school, books and course materials are provided for each student, but in college, you will be responsible for obtaining and purchasing your own materials—and you will need to do that before or at the very beginning of the semester. Trying to get by without the textbook or required calculator or software can seriously hurt your chances of success and is not recommended. If you find yourself unable to acquire or buy needed materials, then you will need to talk to your instructor immediately to ask about alternative arrangements.

In addition to books and materials, you may also need access to a computer. Your professors will expect that you have a working knowledge of how to use one. If you do not have the skills needed, then seek help from computer lab technicians, special computer classes, and classmates. Having the necessary computer skills as well as regular access to a computer will be integral to your success. Most colleges provide computer labs, email accounts, and printers for student use, but the hours may be limited, they may be crowded at busy times during the semester, and you may have to pay for the pages that you print.

Other "right stuff" items include paper (for both note-taking and printing purposes), pens, a dictionary, a writing handbook, and a thesaurus. As you take more classes, you may need specialized reference books and supplies, such as a graphing calculator, to help you study and complete assignments. A good, sturdy backpack that allows you to carry all your books and notebooks will also be essential. Because you will not have a locker or place to store your things between classes, you will have to find a bag that holds up to the task of carrying heavy materials over a period of weeks. One other item that new students need, which is becoming more essential each year, is a portable storage device that will hold your computer files and allow you to access them at any computer. Thumb drives, also known as flash drives and pin drives, are increasingly popular because they hold a large amount of data and are easy to carry.

Instructors' Expectations

In addition to your supplies, knowing and meeting your instructors' expectations will make a great foundation for success. One essential expectation that instructors have is preparation—yours. You should be ready *before* you get to class by reading the assigned pages or completing the homework. Instructors who prescribe these tasks expect students to prepare—they may even administer quizzes to ensure that students have prepared—and to ask questions about anything they do not understand. Instructors may assume that if you don't ask questions or participate in a discussion, you understand the assignment. They may also hold you accountable on exams for assigned reading that has not been discussed in class.

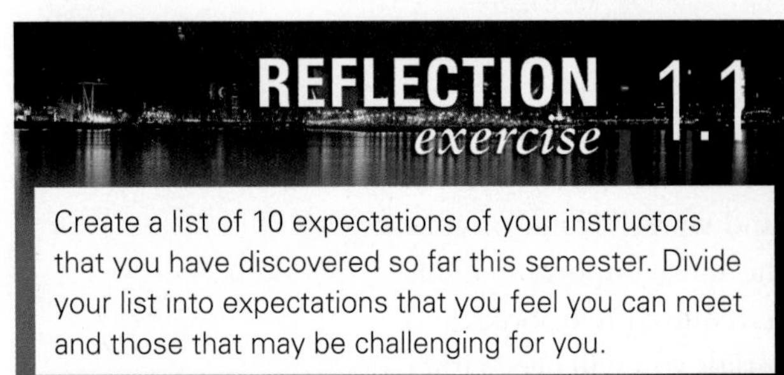

Create a list of 10 expectations of your instructors that you have discovered so far this semester. Divide your list into expectations that you feel you can meet and those that may be challenging for you.

Another expectation is that out-of-class assignments must be typed; in fact, unless otherwise stated, assume that all outside assignments should be word-processed, because they are easier to read and look more professional. If you don't know how to use a word processor, now is the time to learn; relying on others to word-process your work could put you at a disadvantage. You may not be able to control when the person will complete the work, which can make you miss assignment due dates.

Instructors also expect college students to be able to access technology regularly and use it competently. What this means is that your professor will expect that you have consistent access to a computer and the Internet. She will also assume that you have an email account and can send emails—even messages with attachments—successfully. If you lack these skills and equipment, you will need to find out where you can access a computer on campus or off campus and make sure that you have the ability to use it properly.

One last expectation—but not the only one left—is that instructors expect you to use their office hours, the time they are scheduled to be in their offices, to meet with them if you have any questions or need anything. This is a time not only to address any concerns you may have about your progress, but it is also a wonderful chance to get to know your professors better.

Learning

Taking responsibility for your learning is the cornerstone for college success, and in college you will be actively involved in the learning process. Being an *active* learner means that you are no longer a passive participant in your education, listening to a lecture or reading recreationally. Instead, college classes require that you participate in your own learning by reading actively and critically, by completing assignments, by working with other students, and by making connections between the courses you are taking and your life. Active learners also seek out more information about topics and look for ways to improve their understanding of concepts by finding help when needed. In essence, active learners make their education a top priority.

One of the most important shifts in thinking about your learning experience in college is realizing the various ways and places that learning and student support can take place outside the classroom. Professors routinely direct students to learning labs, tutors, or supplemental instruction to help bolster the learning that takes place in the classroom. Consider, then, that classroom learning is only a fraction of the time and activity making up your college experience. In fact, if you follow the standard model for using the number of hours you are in class to determine how many hours a week you should spend studying, class time is only one-fourth of the time you should be devoting to learning. The rest of that time, of course, will be spent preparing for class, but it can also be used working one-on-one with a tutor or reviewing notes and studying with a group. That means that 75% of your college time should be for activities that contribute to your learning when you are in class.

Vocabulary

With a new environment comes a new language. It won't be too long before you are talking about an AA, GPA, and FERPA all at one time. Knowing what terms mean when they are used will make communication clearer. For example, do you know what a credit hour is? It is the unit of measurement that colleges use that usually equals the amount of time you are in class each week during a 16-week semester. What about FERPA? This acronym stands for Family Educational Rights and Privacy Act, and it is important to know because it determines who can access and discuss your grades or other official records. In college, if you are age 18 or over, only you can discuss your grades with a professor. If others, such as a spouse, parent, or employer, want to know how you are doing, then you can allow them access to that information by letting a college official know. The feature titled Your Terms of Success in the accompanying box, as well as in each of the following chapters, provides some of the critical vocabulary you will need in college.

Effort

The comedian and writer Woody Allen once said, "Eighty percent of success is showing up." Definitely, in college classes, you can't be successful unless you attend regularly. College professors may not take attendance or make an issue of students who are not present; however, it is still your responsibility to attend. If you are receiving financial aid through grants or loans, your attendance may be important to continued funding in the future. Some colleges even require students to pay back funds received if they fail to attend classes regularly.

Irregular attendance will not only mean missed lectures and jeopardized financial aid, but also result in missed information about assignments, tests, and grading. Especially in courses that build on concepts (such as math, foreign languages, and writing), your lack of attendance can lead to problems with successfully doing assignments and performing on tests later in the semester.

If you miss a class or intend to miss a class, you should mention this to your professor. Although you may not need a doctor's excuse, you should be prepared to justify your absence, especially if you have missed an exam. Most professors, though, may not care why you were absent or may not distinguish between excused or unexcused absences. Instead, they will simply insist that you find a way to come to class and keep up with the work.

Attending class is just part of the effort you will put forth; you will also need to produce quality work. Writing a paper and turning it in is only part of the requirement. You also have to adhere to the standards of the course. If your professor asks for a 10-page paper that argues a contemporary topic and uses five sources, you must follow those guidelines. In some instances, you may receive no credit for completing an assignment if you have not followed the requirements.

Spending more time to complete an assignment *usually* translates to better quality, but this is not always the case. For example, someone who types 30 words a minute will need less time to produce error-free assignments than someone who "hunts and pecks" at the keyboard. The quality of your work is what you will be graded on, not the number of hours you spend doing it.

Responsibility

No doubt you already juggle numerous responsibilities, and going to class and studying are just more tasks that you must complete each week. Handling your responsibilities skillfully will take a positive attitude, respect for yourself, and

Your Terms of **SUCCESS**

WHEN YOU SEE . . .	IT MEANS . . .
AA	Associate of Arts; a degree program offered by community colleges, consisting of about 60 credit hours; usually transfers to a four-year institution as part of the core curriculum.
AAS	Associate of Applied Science; a degree program offered by community colleges, consisting of about 60 credit hours; usually does not contain as many core courses as an AA and is not designed for transfer, but is intended for students who will enter the workforce after graduation.
Academic integrity	Doing honest work on all assignments and tests.
AS	Associate of Science; a degree program offered by community colleges, consisting of about 60 credit hours; usually transfers to a four-year institution as part of the core curriculum; emphasizes science courses.
Core curriculum	Also called general education requirements or basic courses; the common courses that almost all students who earn a bachelor's degree complete.
Corequisite	A course that must be taken at the same time as another course.
Course content	The material that will be covered in a course.
Course objectives	The goals of a course.
Credit hour	The unit of measurement colleges use that usually equals the amount of time you are in class each week during a 16-week semester.
Degree plan	A list of classes that you must complete successfully in order to be awarded a degree.
Disability accommodation policy	A policy that states how accommodations for documented disabilities will be handled.
FAFSA	Free Application for Federal Student Aid; a form that is completed each year to determine financial aid eligibility.
FERPA	Family Educational Rights and Privacy Act; federal law that regulates the communication and dissemination of your educational records.
GPA	Grade Point Average; each earned grade is awarded grade points that are multiplied by the number of credit hours taken; dividing total grade points (quality points) by total credit hours results in the grade point average.
Grading criteria	The standards by which an assignment is graded.
Prerequisite	A course that must be taken *before* one can take another course.
Quality points	The points determined by a grade point multiplied by the credit hours for a course; for example, an A (4 grade points) in a writing class (3 credit hours) will equal 12 quality points; used to calculate grade point average.
Syllabus	The contract between an instructor and a student; provides information about the course content, course objectives, grading criteria, and course schedule.

maturity. Take, for instance, a student named Laura. She knows how important being responsible for herself and her son is. She has spent many years relying on herself and a few family members to meet her responsibilities. Obviously, as a student she has the responsibility to take notes, study for tests, and attend classes regularly. But she also has the responsibility to ask questions when she doesn't understand or to resolve any conflict that may occur.

"One of the biggest differences between college and high school is that professors expect you to be totally responsible for *everything*—your work, your progress, your degree plan, and your job search."
—Cornelius, 20, student

With responsibility also comes maturity, which is the foundation for many of the other components of college culture. Without a mature attitude and outlook, the other parts are unattainable. Even simple, seemingly obvious actions can help you present yourself as a dedicated, mature student—for example, paying attention during lectures, presentations, talks by guest speakers, and videos. Although this sounds self-evident, it is sometimes forgotten after the first few weeks of the semester. Work on looking at the front of the room and avoiding distractions. A common barrier to paying attention, besides staring out the window, is doing homework in class. Instructors frown on students who use class time to study for other classes or complete assignments that were due at the beginning of class. Just remember that the instructor sees what you are doing—that you are not paying attention—and will make note of it.

INTEGRITY MATTERS

Your college transcript, which includes your grade point average, can reveal more than just the grades you earned in courses. It can also disclose academic integrity issues, should you have them. For example, some colleges make notations on students' transcripts if they have failed a class because of plagiarism or cheating. Sometimes referred to as "FX" grades, these marks can be evidence that a student did not follow academic integrity policies.

In some cases, these marks can be deleted from transcripts if the student successfully completes an academic integrity workshop or successfully completes a certain number of semesters without any other violations.

YOUR TURN What is your college's academic integrity policy? ■ How does the registrar's office designate failing grades that are due to academic integrity violations? ■ Are there any programs at your college to help students understand and follow the academic integrity policy?

____

____

____

____

____

EMOTIONAL INTELLIGENCE *Check-Up*

Optimism

Emotionally intelligent people acknowledge their feelings in a situation, stop and think about what is involved, and then choose an act that will best help resolve any problems. Read the following common situation and work through the three steps in the boxes.

What emotions do you have in this situation?
FEEL

What is the optimal outcome of the situation for you?
THINK

What attitude and positive action will help you achieve the outcome you want?
ACT

SITUATION

Your dream is to get a college degree. You have waited a while to finally be in a place where you can afford tuition and have the time to devote to taking classes, studying, and completing assignments. After attending orientation, you are even more excited about achieving your dream because you met some other students—many just like you—as well as college employees who really want you to succeed. However, when you get back home, you have a phone call from your boss about your new schedule, the one you negotiated so that you can go to college and not have to quit earning money. You also get a message from your significant other, concerned that you won't be able to spend time with her because you will be busy all the time for the next two years. You are afraid that both have bad news for you because of your decision to earn a degree. What do you do?

Small but important actions that convey maturity and readiness to meet college expectations include staying for the duration of the class, limiting off-topic conversations with classmates, refraining from eating or participating in distracting activities, and getting ready to exit class only after the instructor has dismissed everyone. One everyday activity that causes big problems in class is the use of cell phones, headsets, and other electronic communication devices. In some classes, such as a chemistry lab, the distraction can be dangerous. Some colleges have strict policies forbidding the use of cell phones and pagers in class. There may be exceptions, however. For example, if you work in a field that requires your immediate attention in the event of an emergency or if you have a gravely ill family member, ask whether you may leave these electronic devices turned on. If your college does not have a policy, turn off your cell phone and pager in class anyway. Students who answer social calls in class appear immature and unconcerned about their education.

A more important way to demonstrate maturity in college is to understand and appreciate constructive criticism from your instructor. When you receive advice or comments about your work or progress in the course, look at it as an opportunity to learn more about yourself and the expectations of college. The instructor's job is to educate you and help you learn more about the world; it is not the instructor's job to undermine those efforts by cutting you down.

Although it is a great confidence builder, positive feedback does not necessarily challenge you to do better or indicate where you can improve. Be open to the challenge of receiving constructive criticism about the quality of your work. It takes a mature person to value constructive criticism and learn from it and to remember that your professors, counselors, and advisors want to help you be successful, so they will often set high standards that they know you can achieve.

Chapter 4 discusses diversity and relationships in depth, but it is worth mentioning here that dealing with diversity, conflict, and controversy takes a certain level of maturity. Effectively meeting any challenge to your belief system or values will demand that you act with integrity and openness. Because the purpose of getting an education is to stretch your mind and expand your ideas, you will need maturity to help you put all that new information into perspective.

CONTROVERSIAL CONTENT

For the most part, college will be a straightforward experience—you will learn the expectations and when you meet them, you will be successful. There are, though, other aspects of college culture that may be uncomfortable or even shocking to you. All colleges value diversity, whether in the student body population or in the backgrounds of its faculty. Most definitely, you will find diversity in ideas and theories among the subjects that are offered, which may challenge your beliefs and values. Still other subjects may contain material that you find disrespectful, offensive, distasteful, or disturbing. Besides the reading and discussing of controversial issues, your college may produce student and faculty work that contains language, images, or situations that you find offensive.

"You have to be prepared to be challenged in college—if not, what is the point? I feel I have grown more since I have encountered subjects and performances that I would have never seen outside of college."

—Louis, 39, student

What should you do if you encounter college "culture shock"? First, remember that the purpose of college is to provide you with a wider worldview and understanding of diversity—even if that diversity involves different ideas and theories. Second, remember that you have the right to an opinion and a feeling about what you encounter in college. There is no reason you should hide your feelings or attitudes about what you are learning and experiencing. With this said, the third point to remember is that with your right to an opinion, you also have an obligation as a college student to examine your previously held beliefs and evaluate how they are being challenged in your courses or as you participate in college activities. You also have the responsibility to appreciate that there is more than one way to view an "offensive" idea or image. Figure 1.1 provides a list of possible subjects that could be controversial to you or other students.

CRITICAL THINKING *exercise* 1.2

As part of learning outside of class, professors expect you to visit a tutor if you need additional practice or help. Nonetheless, students may not always take advantage of the assistance offered. What could the college do to encourage more students to get help with their classes?

FIGURE 1.1 A Sample of Possible Controversial Subjects

- The existence of God, higher being
- Conservatism and liberalism
- Nudity in art, photography
- Sexuality, including homosexuality and adultery
- The creation of the universe
- The theory of extraterrestrial life
- Evolution
- The beginning of life
- Scientific investigation and experimentation (stem cells, cloning)
- Socioeconomic theory

HOW College Works

Now you know what to expect and what is expected of you in college, but knowing a few other customary practices will help you go from being a "tourist" to a "native." The following information will provide you with a better understanding of how college works beyond what happens in the classroom.

SCHEDULES

First, it is helpful to note that colleges organize class time around semesters or terms, which can be as short as 4 weeks, usually during the summer, or as long as 16 weeks. Many colleges have at least four semesters: fall, spring, first summer term, and second summer term; the summer terms are shorter than the fall and spring terms. Other colleges organize the academic calendar around 10- or 11-week terms. If you are unsure how many weeks the semester is, count the number of weeks from the first day of class until the last day of finals. You can find the information in the college catalog or in the course outline of your syllabus.

College classes are scheduled on different days during the week. This arrangement may differ significantly from your high school schedule. In college, you may take classes once a week, as is the case for evening or night classes, or you may take them on Mondays, Wednesdays, and Fridays or just Tuesdays and Thursdays. Usually, colleges do not offer classes on Friday nights, so if you take classes in the evening, you will take them either once or twice a week, Mondays through Thursdays.

Exceptions to this schedule occur during shortened terms such as summer semesters or intersessions

Making the transition to college is an important first step, but you don't have to do it alone.

Workbook/Jupiter/Getty Images

in which you may go every day during the week. Also, you may have a lab or special class that meets only once a week but is tied to another class such as biology or chemistry. The best advice for new students is to read the schedule of classes carefully before registering, and as always, ask an advisor, counselor, instructor, or fellow student if you have trouble reading your schedule.

"Students who understand how to schedule their classes—not only what to take but when to take it—are more likely to be successful in all of their classes. Use shorter terms to catch up or focus on a hard class."

—Pierre, 38, advisor

Colleges award credit hours (remember this term from earlier in the chapter?) based on how many hours a week you are in class during a regular semester (summer or intersession terms will double or quadruple the number of hours a week as compared to a regular semester). Thus, a three-credit-hour class will require that you spend about 3 hours in class per week—some classes may last only 50 minutes three times a week. Exceptions do exist: Labs are often worth one credit hour, but they may meet for more than one hour one day a week.

Figure 1.2 shows a typical schedule of a full-time student. Notice the "TR" under the "Days" column; "T" stands for Tuesday and "R" for Thursday. Thus, the biology class meets both Tuesday and Thursday whereas the lab meets on Thursday only. As noted, labs and other special classes may meet for more than one hour a week, but they are usually worth only one credit hour. Although the classes in this schedule meet two-and-a-half hours each week, they are given three credit hours. Three hours is often an approximation of the time spent in class.

If the schedule in Figure 1.2 reflects a 16-week semester, this student will spend over 40 hours in class for the semester. During summer or intersession terms, you will spend about the same number of hours in class but will attend class more often and for a longer period of time.

Because Figure 1.3 is a schedule for a 4-week term, the classes meet for more than three hours a week. In this case, students meet for 10 hours a week for 4 weeks, which will equal 40 hours or the equivalent of the total number of hours a three-credit-hour class will meet during a 16-week term.

FIGURE 1.2 16-Week Class Schedule

Fall 2012 (16-Week) Schedule

Course ID	Course Name	Days	Time	Credit Hours
ENGL 030	Composition Fundamentals	MWF	8:00–8:50 A.M.	3.0
BIOL 110	Biology	TR	8:00–9:15 A.M.	3.0
BIOL 112	Biology Lab	R	9:25–11:25 A.M.	1.0
MATH 034	Intermediate Algebra	MWF	10:00–10:50 A.M.	3.0
COLL 101	Freshman Seminar	TR	12:15–1:30 P.M.	3.0
Total Hours				13.0

FIGURE 1.3 4-Week Class Schedule

Summer 2012 (4-Week) Class Schedule

Course ID	Course Name	Days	Time	Credit Hours
MATH 101	College Algebra	MTWRF	8:00–10:00 A.M.	3.0
ENGL 101	Composition I	MTWRF	10:10–12:10 P.M.	3.0
Total				6.0

GRADES

What is a discussion about college expectations without mentioning grades? For sure, grades are an important part of your education, and at the same time they are unimportant. How can something be both important and unimportant? Grades are important because they often reflect your level of achievement on an assignment or in a course; they are also important for obtaining and maintaining scholarships and financial aid. Additionally, grades are important to family, friends, and employers who may be supporting you financially and emotionally. Many people view grades as a reflection of a level of success. For instance, most of the people you ask would view a student who has straight A's as someone who is smart and successful. Earning good grades can motivate you to do your best and give you more confidence as you earn them.

Although good grades feel great when you earn them, grades are not always an indication of your success or lack of success in mastering a subject. James M. Banner, Jr., and Harold C. Cannon (1999), in their book *The Elements of Learning*, define grades as follows: "Grades are evaluations of your work, not of your character or intelligence. You may be a wonderful person but a failure as a biologist. You may find it impossible to do satisfactory work in history but may excel in all other subjects" (p. 160). Banner and Cannon assert, therefore, that grades have limitations. They are a necessary part of evaluation, much as you are evaluated on your job. However, as Banner and Cannon point out, grades do not show the whole picture of who you are. Grades, then, are only part of the story of your education.

If grades only sometimes indicate a level of success in a course and sometimes not, what are you to do? How will you know when to worry about your grades and when to concentrate on learning the material? The purpose of this chapter is to help you answer these questions for yourself by explaining how professors grade and how you can make good grades in college. The chapter also discusses what you can do to deemphasize making a good grade and increase your attention to mastering the material of the course. This is not to say, however, that grades are never important. They are significant because they are a way to describe the work you have done in a class. However, grades alone are not the magic carpet to success in college; they are only part of

"Be sure you are aware of what kind of grades you need to make to keep your financial aid. Know what you need to make *before* the semester begins."

—Enola, 26, counselor

the story of your achievements. Your goal should be to strike a balance between caring about your grades and caring about improving your skills and increasing your knowledge.

As stated earlier, college professors grade a student on his or her ability to meet the standards of the course or of a particular assignment. Effort is definitely a necessary part of earning good grades—and you will earn the respect of your professor and fellow students by demonstrating an intense effort to master the concepts of a class—but it is only one part of achieving success in a course. College professors expect you also to meet the standards, sometimes called *grading criteria,* of the course. Figure 1.4 shows a potential set of criteria for a college-level paper. In this case, the criteria are for an A paper.

Knowing how your college assesses student performance is a start to improving your overall outlook on grading. The following is a typical grading scale in college:

100–90	A
89–80	B
79–70	C
69–60	D
59–0	F

Some colleges may use a plus or minus next to a letter grade such as A– or C+. Usually, colleges that allow for pluses and minuses will also alter the grading scale to designate the different grades. Here is an example of a grading scale that includes plus and minus grades:

100–94	A
93–90	A–
89–87	B+
86–84	B
83–80	B–

Each semester, the registrar will calculate your grade point average, or GPA, and post it to your transcript. Because the calculation of your GPA requires a little

FIGURE 1.4 **Grading Criteria for an A Paper**

- An excellent introduction with engaging hooks, setup, plan for essay, and/or main idea
- An original, significant thesis that offers insightful interpretation or thought
- An inventive and logical organizational plan
- Smooth and varied transitional expressions, phrases, and sentences that provide unity and coherence
- Strong conclusion that ends the essay effectively
- Expressive, clear style with sophisticated sentence structure and word choice
- No more than three major grammatical errors

mathematical skill, it is important to know how your registrar figures it. Hours are the number of hours you are in class each week. As discussed previously, classes are usually worth three credit hours. Science or specialized classes that have labs usually carry four credit hours. Depending on the course and the program, credit hours can be as many as six or as few as one. To know how many hours a course carries, check the description in the college catalog, because some classes meet for more hours a week than they are worth in terms of credit. Letter grades carry a point value called *quality points*. Table 1.2 shows how many quality points each letter grade is worth.

Courses that are designated developmental or remedial usually do not figure into your grade point average, so they do not carry any quality points. If you audit a course or receive AP or CLEP credit for a course, you will not receive quality points either. In other words, although you receive credit on your transcript for taking the course or taking an equivalent of the course, the class will not factor into your grade point average. Before you figure your GPA, you will need to figure your grade points for each class (see Table 1.2). You arrive at your grade points by multiplying the quality points for the grade you received by the number of hours the class is worth. For instance, if you took a four-hour class and you made a B, then you will multiply 4 (hours) by 3 (quality points for a B).

Evan is taking 15 hours (five 3-hour courses) this semester; if he receives an A, B, and three C's, then his grade would be calculated as shown in Table 1.3.

Finally, divide the grade points total by the hours total (39/15). Evan's GPA would be 2.6.

TABLE 1.2 Grades and Quality Points

Letter Grade	Quality Points
A	4
B	3
C	2
D	1
F	0

TABLE 1.3 GPA Calculation Table

Hours	Grade (Quality Points)	Grade Points Hours × Quality Points)
3	A (4)	3 × 4 = 12
3	B (3)	3 × 3 = 9
3	C (2)	3 × 2 = 6
3	C (2)	3 × 2 = 6
3	C (2)	3 × 2 = 6
15 Hours		39 Grade Points

COLLABORATION *exercise* 1.3

Working within a group, discuss why you think attendance is important to success in college. Besides information and assignments, what can students miss when they do not attend class regularly?

COLLEGE Resources

Now that you have a better understanding of college culture and what is expected of you, it is time to examine how your college looks. Getting to know the layout of the campus and the people who work there is important to understanding the culture. For example, knowing where to go when you need to use a computer will make your ability to complete an assignment a little easier. Finding your professor's office may save you time and stress when you need to talk to him about an upcoming test. Of course, the more you are on campus, the better able you will be to find people and places that will help you no matter what you need.

Knowing where to go to find services and people is only part of learning about your college. Another important aspect is finding and using the information that the college produces for students. College publications are a great place to find information about courses, programs, scholarships, activities, and policy changes. It is important that you regularly read these publications in order to stay up to date with what is going on.

THE CAMPUS

Find a map of your campus and study it for a few minutes. How many buildings does it have? How much parking space? How much "green" space or landscaping? Are there any unique features to your campus that make it an inviting and exciting place? Familiarizing yourself with your campus is probably the first activity you did when you enrolled in classes. If you have not taken a tour or simply walked around the campus, do so within the first few weeks of the semester. Locate the library, the student center, student parking, the bookstore, the business office, and the registrar's office—just to name a few destinations.

The more you know about your campus's layout, the easier it will be to find what you are looking for when you need it most. Using your map of the campus or your memory, check off in Figure 1.5 the types of buildings or departments within buildings that you know are present at your college.

If your college has more than one campus, familiarize yourself with the layout of other college property. You may have to travel to a satellite campus to take a test or to pick up materials for a class. If you have the time and the other campus is not too far away, ask for a tour. At the very least, familiarize yourself with any of the items you marked "not sure" in Figure 1.5.

COLLEGE CATALOG

The college catalog is an essential document during your academic career. All the information that you need to apply for financial aid, to choose courses, and to graduate is contained in the catalog. You will also find out what you are required to do to complete a degree. The academic calendar is usually placed at the beginning of the catalog. There you will find the dates for registering, dropping courses, and taking final exams.

It is important to read and keep your college catalog because if the college changes any requirements of your degree program, you will be able to follow the guidelines that were published the year you began the program. For instance, if you are working on an office management degree and you have taken three semesters of courses so far, you will not necessarily have to adhere to new requirements that are made at a later date.

FIGURE 1.5 Campus Layout Checklist

Building or Area	At My College	Not Sure
Student center or union		
Library		
Bookstore		
Administration building		
Theater or auditorium		
Snack bar or food court		
Athletic training facilities (indoor or outdoor)		
Science labs		
Technical and industrial training facilities		
Computer labs		
Separate divisions (such as technical and industrial, computer information systems, allied health, business, and general education)		
Individual departments (such as accounting, drafting, welding, and natural sciences)		
Student parking		
Benches and tables for meeting outside		
Quiet study space inside		

STUDENT HANDBOOK

The student handbook, which provides you with specific information about student conduct, academic standards, and services, is another valuable publication. Usually, the handbook contains descriptions of career services, the bookstore, computer labs, and financial aid offices. Academic information including probation and suspension for misconduct and qualifications for making the dean's list can also be found in the student handbook. Most schools view the student handbook as a legal document that outlines what students can do in certain situations, so be sure to read it closely and keep a copy at home or in your book bag.

COLLEGE NEWSPAPER

College newspapers differ from the college catalog and student handbook in that students are usually the ones who are responsible for the content. Within a college newspaper, you will find articles about upcoming events; reports on changes on the college campus; editorials on important student issues; profiles of programs; and advertisements for used books, performances by musical groups, and anything else that students want to announce. The college newspaper is also a forum to explore controversial topics and to discuss sensitive issues.

Newspapers always need students to interview, write, edit, and publish. If you are interested in working for the newspaper, contact the editor or visit a journalism or composition professor.

BULLETIN BOARDS

Even with the increased use of the Internet, the bulletin board is still an important way to get a message to students. Found all over campus, bulletin boards usually advertise used books, needs for roommates and part-time jobs, and upcoming campus events. Bulletin boards within academic buildings often announce four-year university programs, summer workshops, and other types of academic activities.

IT'S IN THE SYLLABUS

Anything that professors hand out in class is a communication tool. The syllabus is one of the most important documents that you will receive in class, so be sure to read it carefully. In the syllabus you will usually find the following information:

- Instructor's name; office location, phone number, and hours open to students; and email address
- Prerequisites for the course
- Course description from the catalog
- Textbook information
- Course objectives, or what you will accomplish by the time you finish the class
- Course content, or what topics will be covered throughout the semester
- Assignments and due dates
- Grading criteria
- Attendance and late work policies
- Academic integrity statement (which also appears in the student handbook)
- Disability accommodations policy
- General policies for classroom conduct

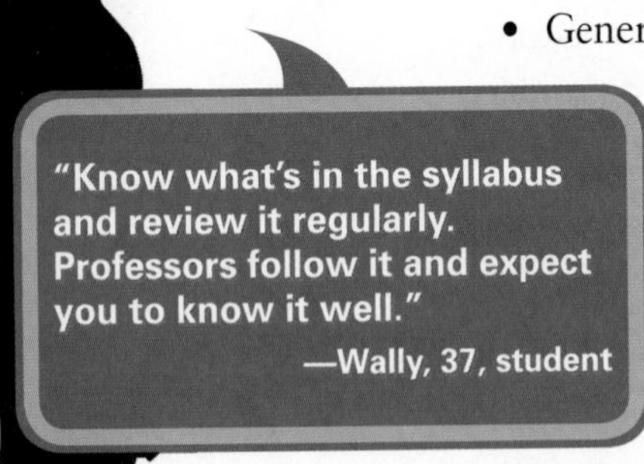

"Know what's in the syllabus and review it regularly. Professors follow it and expect you to know it well."
—Wally, 37, student

The syllabus is considered a contract between the student and the instructor. This means that not only will the syllabus describe what is expected of you during class, but it will also discuss what you can expect from the instructor. Both of you—student and instructor—will be bound by what is stated in the document. Reading the syllabus closely and following it regularly will keep you on top of class policies, expectations, and assignments.

Other essential information that is handed out in class includes directions to assignments, photocopied readings, study questions, and notes. Regard anything that is given to you by the instructor as important, even if you are told, "This won't be on the test."

You should also consider the grades and written comments you receive as communication from your instructors. Be sure to read any comments or suggestions that are written on papers and exams, ask questions if you don't understand them or they are illegible, and save all feedback until the semester is over.

PUT IT ONLINE

The college's website is where you can find the most current information about classes, academic programs, and contact information for professors. It is easier to update information on a website because it doesn't involve printing and distribution, so it is more likely to provide the most accurate information. College websites usually list phone numbers and email addresses of professors and deans, which makes contacting them easier.

In addition to general information about degrees and departments, your college's website may give you access to professors' syllabi and assignments. This provides a good opportunity to investigate what courses you want to take based on the course objectives and assignments.

TECH TACTICS

Using Technology to Get Ahead

Numerous websites provide information about succeeding in college. The College Board has many tips for new-to-college students that can help them navigate financial aid and studying. There are even websites devoted to specific groups such as first-generation and Latino college students. There are GPA calculators, too, that can help you calculate your grades. All of these resources are at your fingertips and can greatly enhance your education.

RECOMMENDED SITES

- www.collegeboard.com/student/csearch/where-to-start/150494.html The College Board debunks the myths of community colleges.
- www.unt.edu/pais/howtochoose/glossary.htm University of North Texas provides an exhaustive list of common terms you may encounter in college. Terms like *audit* and *work-study program* are defined so that you can be more knowledgeable about the college experience.
- www.back2college.com/gpa.htm Back to College's website provides a handy grade point average calculator that allows you to put in your grades and determine your GPA. The site also provides information and links for raising your GPA.

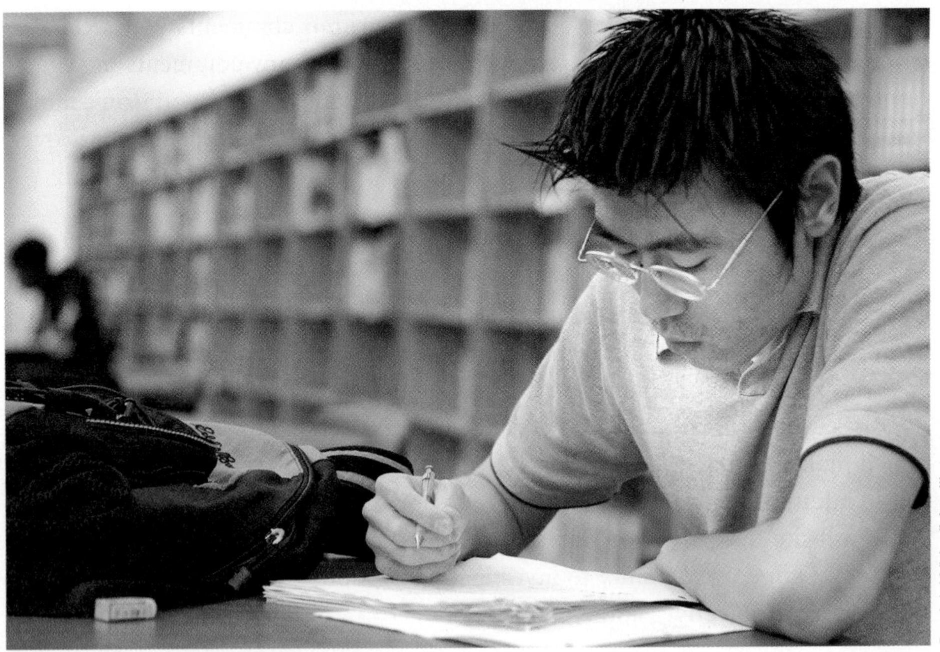

Students who have "the right stuff" such as access to a computer, textbooks, and other materials and equipment that are required for classes are much more likely to be successful.

Patrick White/Merrill

CAMPUS ORGANIZATIONS

Campus organizations or student groups are another part of college life you will want to learn more about. Depending on how large your college is and how involved the students are, you may find a variety of student organizations and clubs in which to participate. Even if your time is limited, consider getting involved in some way. You may be able to get on an email list or a social networking site to keep up with events and meetings—if you cannot make those same events and meetings every time. Campus organizations include, but are not limited to, student government, student leadership programs, and clubs focused on certain interests (e.g., gay, lesbian, bisexual, and transgendered issues; political action; community service; academic honors and distinctions; religious or spiritual development; and career exploration). Getting involved will help you transition to the college and provide immediate connections with students, faculty, and staff.

REFLECTION *exercise* 1.4

The information you have already received will help you navigate college more smoothly. Organize the different sources of information by type and answer the following questions: What information have you received by email or the Internet? What information have you received from an advisor? Finally, which kinds of information are most useful to you and why?

Transfer Tips: FROM COLLEGE TO UNIVERSITY

The Changes in Culture and College Services

If you are moving from your community college to a larger, more diverse university, you may experience a slight culture shock despite the semesters you already have under your belt. In addition to a bigger campus with more buildings to find and more students to meet, you may find that a university seems more impersonal. Many students who transfer from a smaller community college complain that professors do not seem to care about them personally and that they lack the support and guidance they received at their previous school. Transfer students also note that expectations increase—and their grades decrease—especially as they move into their majors and begin working toward a career.

Culturally, you should expect that your new university will offer more activities and groups than your smaller community college. You also should expect some kind of adjustment period as you get used to your new professors' expectations of you. Statistically, transfer students do experience a slight drop in GPA. This drop, however, is not necessarily an indication that they were not properly prepared for transfer by their community college.

All in all, the culture shock you experience when transferring to a four-year university will depend on how much bigger and how much more different the school is from your community college. Just remember that whatever differences you notice, there are people at the four-year school who can help you deal with the adjustment. Seek out counselors, advisors, faculty, and students to help make your transition smoother. Your campus map and list of faculty and administrators will point you in the right direction.

Transfer Tips: FROM COLLEGE TO CAREER

How the Culture Will Change Again

Just as you had to adjust to college culture, you will have to make a new adjustment to the workforce if you have never held a full-time job. When starting your first job out of college, you will experience a period of getting used to the way the office or business works. You will encounter new terms, new methods of doing things, and new people. In addition, you will experience working in groups or teams to accomplish tasks, and you will be expected to communicate orally and in a written format. You may also rely more heavily on electronic mail and computers to do your work. Certainly, integrity will be an important part of your working experience. There will be less supervision and more expectation that you do the work you say you will do.

Paying attention to how others act on the job can alleviate any anxiety that you may feel. Just as you made friends and found mentors in college, you should look for others who can offer guidance and help as you learn the ropes of a new career. Also, think about how you adjusted to college and use the same strategies to make your new working environment seem less foreign and more comfortable.

References and Recommended Readings

Banner, J. M., Jr., & Cannon, H. C. (1999). *The elements of learning*. New Haven, CT: Yale University Press.

The College Board. (2008). *Succeeding in college: What it means and how to make it happen*. Plano, TX: College Board.

Dabbah, M. (2009). *Latinos in college: Your guide to success*. Scarborough, NY: Consultare.

Newport, C. (2005). *How to win at college: Surprising secrets for success from the country's top students*. New York: Broadway.

Nist-Olejnik, S., & Patrick Holschuh, J. (2007). *College rules!: How to study, survive, and succeed in college*. Berkeley, CA: Ten Speed Press.

Watkins, B. D. (2004). *Everything you ever wanted to know about college: A guide for minority students*. Camillus, NY: Blue Boy Publishing.

CHAPTER two

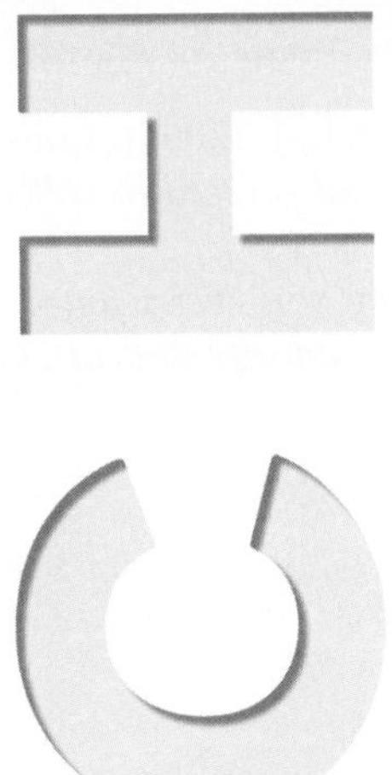

SETTING Goals and Staying Motivated

IN THIS chapter

Now that you have explored what college is like in Chapter 1, this chapter is all about you, because knowing who you are will help you lay a solid foundation on which to build success. Starting with understanding yourself seems like the easiest of subjects, but getting to the point of really knowing yourself will take time. You are now a college student and your journey will be an exciting one, but it will also be one in which you will find yourself changing, growing, and defining or redefining who you are and who you want to be.

More specifically, after completing this chapter you will be able to do the following:

- Discover your story.
- Set your goals and create a mission statement.
- Determine the motivators for you.
- Develop your support system.

YOUR Story

The question "Who are you?" sounds easy to answer. You may start by listing a variety of characteristics. For example, you are a male, age 25, married, father of a son, an electrician, and a Native American. Or you are a single female, age 19, part-time sales assistant, full-time student, and mountain climber. But what are you beyond those labels? Where have you been? What are you doing now? Where are you going and where do you want to be? Now the questions get a little more difficult and take more time and thought to answer. The point is that you need to have some idea of who you are, or at least an idea of where you want to be, when you begin college.

Maybe you can say that you don't know who you are yet, but you hope that enrolling in classes and pursuing a degree will help you come to a better understanding of who you are. Don't worry, though, if you cannot immediately articulate the essence of you. This question—"Who are you?"—and the possible answers have been intriguing human beings for thousands of years. In his book *Who Are You? 101 Ways of Seeing Yourself* (2000), Malcolm Godwin explores the ways that we have tried to answer this question. From body types to ancient Indian mysticism to workplace dynamics, there are numerous ways you can learn more about what and how you think. The ultimate goal is to know yourself and your environment well enough to reach your goals.

Of course, who you are will change, maybe dramatically, as you take classes, encounter new subjects, and research interesting topics. But taking the time now to think and reflect about yourself will help you map your course throughout the community college experience and beyond—returning to work, raising a family, attending another college, having a fulfilling career. This chapter assists you in understanding who you are by helping you identify what you know and how you learn. This chapter also aids in your decisions about who and what you want to be while helping you make the transition into college.

YOUR BACKGROUND

To discover your story—and to write your future—you will need to consider where you began. Your background, which includes your family, your culture, and your experiences, will serve as a foundation for creating a life. Think about your personal history and how it has shaped who you are. Also, consider how your family has influenced you as well—what beliefs have they instilled in you? What is their attitude toward your college aspirations? Who you are and how you have developed will be part of your value system as well as part of the foundation for setting goals for future achievements. If you have had great support and good educational experiences, you may find envisioning your future degree rather easy. However, if you have had substantial challenges in your life, you may need more support and resources to see that you can indeed be successful. No matter what your background, you are now a college student with a unique life story and a wonderful opportunity to be successful. Your college will give you the chance to write a life story that includes a college education.

"I realized that when I thought about my goals they seemed to match perfectly with my values. Now anytime I want to accomplish something, I ask myself, 'Do I value that activity?'"

—Sue Li, 21, student

YOUR VALUES

Part of your life story will include your value system. Values can be inherited from your parents, or they can come from what your culture, religion, or ethnicity regard as important. Values can also be formed from both positive and negative experiences. For example, a value of yours may be honesty, which means that you try to be truthful and straightforward in most situations and that you expect others to be honest with you. If you value hard work, then you strive to do your best in your life. If a friend has treated you with compassion, you may value sensitivity to others. On the other hand, if you have been discriminated against in the past, you may now value open-mindedness in others.

The importance of knowing and understanding your values is that this knowledge can help you set realistic goals. If you value a satisfying career, for instance, you will set goals supporting that value. Therefore, you will probably investigate careers and fields that are challenging and interesting. If you value a stable financial future, you will set goals that enable you to earn enough money to provide for your needs and wants. If you value your family, you will make spending time with them a priority. Your values should be a true reflection of who *you* are and what *you* believe.

Think about a typical student named Juanita. Her mother wants Juanita to consider electrical engineering, perhaps because she values financial stability and success or career prestige. What if one reason Juanita hesitates at choosing a major and career path is that she values a career that helps the human condition? What if she also wants to learn more about how we recover from illness? If she decides to adopt her mother's values and ignore her own, what kind of future can you envision for her? Although her mother's intentions may be well meaning, Juanita will have to compromise herself in order to meet her parents' goals for her, and she will probably suffer some regret in the future.

INTEGRITY MATTERS

Staying true to your values is part of integrity. If you try to please others or adopt their values when you do not completely agree with them, you will lack integrity. This may not be an issue for you until you are tested on those values.

For example, you may have been raised with the value of staying true to your ethnic or cultural heritage, even at the expense of meeting someone new or experiencing a new culture. Now that you are in college, you may find that you are exposed to a variety of ethnicities and cultures and that you enjoy and appreciate learning more about other perspectives and lifestyles.

YOUR TURN Have you ever taken on someone else's values that were not truly a reflection of your own? ■ Why did you? ■ What was the outcome? ■ What did you learn about yourself?

____

____

____

____

____

Does this example mean that you should ignore others who have helped you figure out what you want to be? Certainly not. But you should pay attention to what you want when you do get help with your educational and career goals. Be open to others' suggestions, but make sure you feel comfortable with your final decision. Those who truly want you to succeed will be proud of you when they know you have achieved your heart's desire, not theirs.

YOUR DREAMS

As you consider your goals, you will also want to think about your dreams. What do you want to do that you have not written down because you feel it is too far-fetched? There are many stories of people who denied their dreams and took jobs that provided them with financial security and prestige, only to discover that their lives were not fulfilled because those were not their values.

"The best advice I ever got was to follow my passion, which is fixing cars. Once I let myself do that, my goals were there in front of me and I was able to work with my advisor to help me create a plan to achieve them. I had wasted too much time before then trying to create goals that pleased other people."

—Jeremy, 26, student

Why don't more people follow their dreams? First, they may not know what they are. Second, these same people may be scared. Following what one's heart wants often contradicts what one's head is saying. Third, some people need to make the "safe" choice first before they feel confident that they can fulfill their dreams. In other words, they may need to take a job that pays well so that they can save money to fulfill their dreams at a later date.

Although you may not be able to drop everything right now and follow your heart, you should at least start thinking about what you really want to do with your life as you plan your college degree.

Your Terms of **SUCCESS**

WHEN YOU SEE . . .	IT MEANS . . .
Background	The experiences you have had that make up who you are.
External motivator	Something that comes from outside of you and drives you to achieve a goal.
Internal motivator	Something that comes from inside you and drives you to achieve a goal.
Long-term goal	A goal that will take a month, a semester, a year, or several years to complete.
Mission statement	A statement in which you describe how your values and goals will create your life's mission.
Motivation	What keeps you moving toward your goal.
Priority	Something that is important at a particular moment.
Short-term goal	A goal that takes an hour, a day, or a week to complete.
Value	What you believe in.

YOUR GOALS and Mission Statement

To fulfill your mission in life, you will need to have a plan. Setting goals and achieving them will put you on the path to fulfilling that mission. If you are not used to writing down tasks for the day or voicing your plans for the future, you will need to start working on making lists and talking about what you want to be and do.

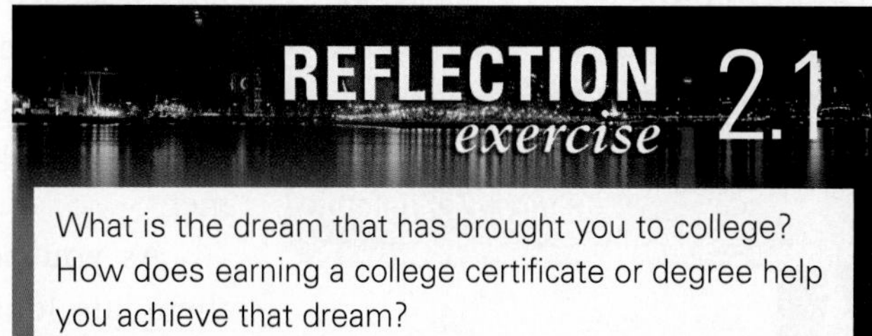

What is the dream that has brought you to college? How does earning a college certificate or degree help you achieve that dream?

From your list of values and your mission statement, you will be able to formulate goals that support both what you believe in and what you want for yourself. The fact that you are reading this book is evidence that you are someone who has set a goal and is working toward achieving it. Also, the fact that you are in college says that you value education as a means of improving your life. You may have overcome many obstacles to get where you are today. You may have faced pressure from your family and friends to join the workforce on graduating from high school rather than go to college, or you may have gotten negative feedback from others when you decided to stop working, or stop working as much, to get a degree.

Nonetheless, realize that setting and achieving goals is not as easy as writing them down and crossing them off. You will encounter obstacles, some of which may threaten to knock you off course. Flexibility and determination are the keys to achieving your goals despite setbacks.

YOUR MISSION STATEMENT

Mission statements are declarations of what people or institutions believe in and what they hope to accomplish. Mission statements, then, are usually broad strokes of the overall picture of what you want to accomplish. Values are the foundation of a mission statement. If you are unsure of your values, then your mission statement will not be easy to understand and follow. Thus, you need to know what you value before you can write a mission statement.

As you meet your goals and learn new things, your mission will likely change and your mission statement will need to be revised. The following is an example of a mission statement that you can use as a model for writing your own.

Sample Personal Mission Statement

My mission is to have a fulfilling personal and professional life that allows me to meet new people, take on new challenges, and have flexibility in my schedule. As a mother and wife, I want to have a close relationship with my family, acting both as a caregiver and as a role model. As a teacher, I will be dedicated to providing students with the best possible education to prepare them for a four-year university curriculum as well as for the demands of the world of work.

SETTING GOALS

To build on your mission statement—and to fulfill that mission in the process—you will need to set goals that you can achieve. A goal is something that you work toward—it may be to learn how to cook macaroni and cheese, to quit a bad habit, or to write a novel. Whatever your goals, they should be reasonable and attainable in the time frame that you have assigned. For instance, if you want to lose 10 pounds in one week, you may need to rethink the time in which you would like to achieve your goal. A more reasonable goal would be to lose 10 pounds in four months. Reasonable goals are more likely to be met.

"Be realistic about what you want to achieve and when you want to achieve it. I know I cannot take 16 hours a semester—it is not a realistic goal for me to take on more classes than I can handle."
—Camry, 21, student

As you begin to think about your goals, consider dividing them into long-term goals and short-term goals. Certainly, one of your long-term goals is to earn a degree. This goal may take one year or more, depending on how many degree requirements you need to complete or how many other responsibilities you may have. Short-term goals that contribute to the long-term goal of earning a degree include completing your classes successfully, studying for exams, or working on research papers.

TECH TACTICS

Using Technology to Get Ahead

Goal setting is much easier when you have techniques or processes for deciding what to achieve and for creating a pathway to success. There are numerous websites available to help you do just that and stay motivated in the process. Find what works best for you and then stick to it.

RECOMMENDED SITES

- www.motivateus.com Motivate Us is a site that provides numerous quotes and stories that can inspire you when you feel you cannot take another step forward.
- www.goal-setting-guide.com/goal-setting-tutorials/smart-goal-setting The Goal Setting Guide reminds us that goals must be specific, measurable, attainable, realistic, and timely (SMART).
- www.maryannsmialek.com/resources/articles/roadblocks.html Dr. Mary Ann Smialek offers another perspective as to why we encounter roadblocks on the way to achieving our goals. Whether it is fear of failure or emotional issues, she offers direct advice for getting around obstacles that stand in your way.

When you make your list of goals, consider the following guidelines:

- Make your goals attainable and reasonable.
- Break larger goals into smaller goals that will lead to fulfillment.
- Think of setting goals in these time frames: 1 week, 1 month, 1 semester, 1 year, 5 years, 10 years.
- Regularly review your goals and make changes as necessary.

Because it is difficult to plan 10 years into the future, make a list of goals that are tied to the near future. For instance, if you want to own your own business in the next 10 years, think about how to structure your short-term and long-term goals by looking at examples like the following:

Long-Term Goal (10 Years)

- Run a successful landscape design firm.
- Provide landscaping for low-income properties.

Long-Term Goal (5 Years)

- Work for a landscape design firm.
- Continue community service and encourage coworkers to participate.

Long-Term Goal (3 Years)

- Complete my associate's degree in landscape design and management.
- Continue community service work.

Short-Term Goal (9 Months)

- Complete two semesters of landscape design classes.
- Continue working at the garden center.
- Plant and maintain my own flower and vegetable garden.
- Participate in a community service project that landscapes low-income properties.

Short-Term Goal (1 Semester)

- Complete the classes that will count toward my degree.
- Look for a community service project that landscapes low-income properties.

Short-Term Goal (1 Month)

- Help a friend plant new trees.
- Attend a local lecture on seasonal planting.
- Begin research for a final paper on plant diseases.

Short-Term Goal (1 Week)

- Study for my classes.
- Apply for a job at a garden center.
- Weed and fertilize the backyard.
- Take a hike in the park.

No matter what you want to achieve, be sure that you write down all your goals and review them every few months to assess your progress. Henriette Anne Klauser has made a career of helping people write down their dreams and goals so they can finally realize them. In *Write It Down, Make It Happen: Knowing What*

You Want and Getting It! (2001), Klauser states, "Writing down your dreams and aspirations is like hanging up a sign that says 'Open for Business.' . . . Putting it on paper alerts the part in your brain known as the reticular activating system to join you in the play" (p. 33). In other words, the process of writing down your goals tells your brain to start paying attention to your ambitions and makes you aware of opportunities to achieve them.

MANAGING YOUR GOALS

You will see this suggestion throughout this book: To accomplish anything, set goals by writing them down. Even something as simple as spending two hours preparing for class should be written down as a goal for the day or week. Goals must be manageable, however. Too many goals and you could become overwhelmed at the thought of meeting them all, or you may feel like a failure for not accomplishing everything. Avoid the temptation to overschedule and be realistic about how long it will take to complete your goals for the day or week. Too few goals and you will likely feel like a rudderless ship, easily veering off course.

Once you have written down your goals, communicate them to your coworkers, family, and friends. Enlist them to help you meet your goals, especially if you need to schedule time to study and complete assignments. For example, tell them that you must have the evenings free of distractions, or make arrangements with them to have a weekend or weekday to yourself to study. Don't assume that because they know you are in school they will also know you need extra time and personal space to get your work finished. Managing your time will be much easier if your priorities and goals are concrete, realistic, and communicated to those around you.

STAYING ON TRACK

As you work toward your goals, make an effort to eliminate anything that keeps you from focusing on them. If you think you don't have time to accomplish two short-term goals during the week, examine where you have been spending your time and eliminate the activities that do not contribute to your goals.

If you watch seven hours of television a week and aren't achieving your short-term goal, whether to become more informed, to relax, or any other sought-after result, then spend that TV time doing something that does contribute to your goal. In addition to meaningless activities, anything that distracts you and is unnecessary in your life should be eliminated, including a habit that is destructive or dangerous, such as taking drugs. In fact, making a goal of staying healthy (e.g., eating right, exercising, de-stressing your life) is not only a good goal in itself, achieving it will help you achieve your other goals.

If you are unsure whether your activities contribute to your goals, take a few minutes to list what you have done this week and determine how each activity has supported or not supported one of your goals. Table 2.1 gives some examples.

MANAGING YOUR PRIORITIES

A discussion of values and goals cannot be complete without also talking about priorities. Simply stated, a priority is something that is important at the moment.

TABLE 2.1 Activities That Contribute to or Distract from Your Goals

Activities That Contribute to Your Goals	Activities That May Distract You from Your Goals
Practicing correct car maintenance allows you to get to school and work safely.	Socializing excessively depletes the time and energy you have to focus on your goals.
Exercising allows you to remain healthy and reduce stress.	Mindlessly watching TV may not contribute to learning.
Proper eating and sleeping will keep you healthy and reduce stress regularly.	Using drugs and alcohol is dangerous and keeps you from focusing on goals.
Reading the newspaper keeps you informed, helps improve reading skills, and contributes to learning.	Sleeping and eating irregularly creates stress, which inhibits the ability to reach goals.

Today your top priority could be studying for an exam, but later in the day, it could be taking care of a sick child, which means that studying will have to come second if at all. Priorities, by their very nature, can change weekly, if not daily or even hourly.

Your actions also reflect your priorities. If you say that your first priority is to pass your classes this semester but you spend all your spare time playing basketball with friends, then your social life as well as a little exercise is really your top priority. You must make sure you know what your priorities are and take action to satisfy them. You may also need to express your priorities to others so that they can help you stick to them.

"My coursework has to be in my top three priorities each day. Of course, each day it changes which is my first priority, but if my education doesn't make the top three, I know that my goal to earn a degree will not be fulfilled."
—Lee, 23, student

STAYING Motivated

One of the hardest parts of setting goals is maintaining the momentum to achieve them. There will be times in your academic career when you will feel overwhelmed by the responsibilities you have, and you will feel unsure of your ability to handle it all. When you feel weighed down by all that you have to accomplish for a particular week or day, try to calm down first. If you can, talk with a friend, an instructor, or a counselor and explain your frustration and stress. Sometimes an instructor who knows you are feeling overwhelmed by expectations in a course will help you find resources to keep on track. A friend may also volunteer to help by studying with you.

IDENTIFYING MOTIVATORS

To keep yourself motivated, it is worth understanding what motivates you and how you can use that information to meet your goals. Most studies of motivation identify two types: internal and external. Usually, internal motivators are preferred for long-term success, because the direction comes from inside. For example, you may have a desire to learn more about autism in your psychology class because your nephew has been diagnosed and you want to have a better understanding of what he is going through. If you are in college to become a better person rather than to earn $120,000 a year, you are more likely to stay true to your goal in the long run.

On the other hand, external motivators are incentives from outside yourself. Your employer may be offering a bonus, for example, to all employees who maintain a 3.5 GPA while in college. External motivators are not completely bad, although they are considered less powerful over time by experts on motivation. You can improve your likelihood of achieving your goals if you examine what motivates you and, if you are primarily motivated externally, what kind of intrinsic motivators can be added to encourage accomplishing your goals. In Activity 2.1, write down several current goals as they relate to earning your degree. For each goal, determine any external motivators for achieving the desired results. Then be sure to record an internal motivator for each goal. Finding that internal motivator, even if strong external incentives exist as well, can be the difference between giving up and achieving success.

"The students who maintain a positive attitude whenever they hit a speed bump are more likely to achieve their goals than the ones who start thinking negatively."
—Barbara, 49, advisor

OVERCOMING OBSTACLES

Even if you identify clear motivators for achieving your goals, there will be times of doubt, and sometimes it will seem as though there are too many obstacles blocking your path to making your dreams a reality. For example, you may register for a class only to find out you need to complete a 30-hour internship in addition to all the coursework. Or you may do well for the first half of the semester, only to lose focus when your child is sick and needs your time, energy, and attention. Your professors know that you will probably experience some sort of challenge during the semester, but they will also expect you to have the ability to move around those obstacles while still striving to complete your classes successfully. In extreme cases, you may want to talk with your professors or your advisor if your challenges seem insurmountable. They may be able to offer strategies to keep you on track while dealing with issues outside of class.

ACTIVITY 2.1 Goals and Motivators

Goal	External Motivator	Internal Motivator
Example **Complete my degree in early childhood education**	My supervisor will promote me to daycare manager and I will get a raise.	I will feel more comfortable talking to parents about their children's progress. I will be able to provide the best educational experience for the children in my pre-K class.

EMOTIONAL INTELLIGENCE *Check-Up*

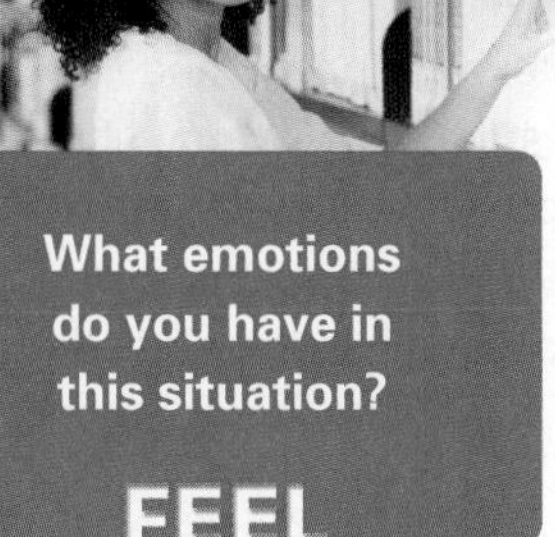

Self-Regard

What emotions do you have in this situation?

FEEL

What is the optimal outcome of the situation for you?

THINK

What attitude and positive action will help you achieve the outcome you want?

ACT

Emotionally intelligent people acknowledge their feelings in a situation, stop and think about what is involved, and then choose an act that will best help resolve any problems. Read the following common situation and work through the three steps in the boxes.

SITUATION

Your goal is to be a nurse and work with hospice patients. However, you have taken an anatomy and physiology class twice and have still not been able to pass. Your advisor has warned you that if you fail the class a third time, you will not be able to graduate from the program at your college. Since you enrolled in the program, he has questioned you about your academic goals and has tried to steer you toward a degree in art education. Although you know you have had difficulty in science classes because of your learning disability, you don't want to give up on your dream. You also feel as though you would be letting down your family, who thinks that being a nurse is more prestigious than being a teacher or an artist because the pay is better for nurses.

Whatever obstacles you face while you are in college—or anytime in life—you can and should examine what is blocking your progress and what would happen if you just decided to give up. Sometimes, seeing the consequences of not achieving your goal can motivate you to continue striving. In Activity 2.2, you have the opportunity to think through potential—or even real—obstacles you may face while working toward your goal. When you identify an obstacle, include the result if you decided to give up and also if you decided to persevere. Finally, create a short action plan, which is another method for staying motivated to achieve your goals, to make sure that you take whatever obstacle, roadblock, or challenge you may encounter and turn it into motivation to continue on your path.

Although we are often aware of the big reasons that derail us from our goals, we often forget about the day-to-day activities and issues that can sidetrack us, if only for a short time. Even small obstacles, taken collectively, can have a major effect on whether or not our long-term goals are accomplished. To work around minor obstacles and stay motivated to complete your goals, learn how to structure your activities so you have the opportunity to succeed. Chip and Dan Heath, in *Switch: How to Change Things When Change Is Hard* (2010), focus on how to motivate people to change. They describe "action triggers," methods for getting someone to do something, as having a "profound power to motivate people to *do*

ACTIVITY 2.2 From Obstacle to Action

Goal	Obstacle	Result of Giving Up	Result of Reaching Goal	Action Plan to Succeed
Example				
Earning a nursing degree	Failing chemistry	Never realize my dream job; stuck working in a job I don't like	Feel good about myself that I can do things that are challenging	Retake chemistry and create a study group; find chemistry tutor; keep specific weekly goals for succeeding in the class

ACTIVITY 2.3 Goals and Action Triggers

Goal	Action Triggers
Example	
Study 2 hours for statistics test	Put book and notes on nightstand so that when I wake up, I will have it ready to study for 30 minutes that morning.
	Take book and notes with me to soccer practice so that I can study 1.5 hours.

the things they know they need to do" (p. 210). Activity 2.3 is designed around the principle of "preloading a decision" by creating action triggers that help motivate you to complete a task.

COLLABORATION exercise 2.2

Working within a small group, exchange mission statements with each other. Using a classmate's mission statement, write down two long-term goals and four short-term goals that would be appropriate for the classmate, based on his or her mission statement. Share your predictions with the group and discuss how well they matched your classmate's actual goals.

REMAINING RESILIENT

Resiliency is the ability to remain flexible and "bounce back" after experiencing setbacks or challenges. Learning to be resilient will be a key to achieving your goals. To stay motivated and resist the temptation to give up because of the stress of obstacles in your way, first review your short- and long-term goals. Is there anything you can change to make your goals more reasonable or attainable? Have you allowed enough time to achieve them? Revising your goals or your time line may be necessary to keep yourself on track. Second, think positively about yourself and your progress. Many students before you have successfully juggled a job, classes, and a family. That is not to say that they did not doubt themselves along the way or suffer any setbacks. The difference between these students and those who were not successful is that they persevered because they believed in themselves more often than not. Tell yourself that you can get through stressful times. Finally, consider your commitment to your goals. Are you willing and able to do whatever it takes to reach them? You may be motivated, but are you committed? Commitment takes a devotion to a goal that is unrelenting even in the face of adversity. Be sure you are committed to both the ups and downs of earning a degree.

When setting your goals, remember to include personal goals as well as academic goals.

Shutterstock

YOUR Support System

Even the most dedicated student cannot do it all alone. In fact, behind every successful college graduate is a good support system, usually comprising family, friends, and community members. It is no secret that succeeding in college will take more than just studying hard—you will need to surround yourself with people who encourage you to do your best. There will be times when you need others for academic, emotional, and even financial support. Recognizing who in your circle of friends, family, and contacts will be your best resources is part of the process of creating a support system that will inevitably be part of your college success.

YOUR FAMILY

Whether you live with your parents, you are a parent, or you are somewhere in between, your family is an important part of who you are and what you will become. Your family has influenced your values and beliefs, and your family members may be a part of the reason you have enrolled in college. For many students, staying in college and being successful depends on the support of family. If your family will be an important part of your life as you pursue a degree, then you will need to consider how they will support you and what you need to communicate with them about the time commitments of studying and taking classes that may reduce your time with them. As you begin your first semester in college, you need to ask yourself several important questions:

- Who in my family will support my decision to attend college?
- What types of financial support can I expect?
- What kinds of emotional support can I expect?
- How may my relationships change with my family?
- What can I do to communicate my needs while I am in college?

Answering these questions early and communicating your feelings at the beginning of the semester will make it easier for you to keep the lines of communication open in the long run. If you don't feel comfortable talking face to face with your loved ones, you could write a letter. At the very least, getting your thoughts down on paper first can help you polish what you want to say before you say it. Figure 2.1 provides a sample letter you can use for ideas to write your own family.

FIGURE 2.1 Sample Letter to Family

Dear Family,

I want to first thank you for encouraging me to attend college. I am very excited and a little nervous, but because you have been so supportive of my decision, I know that I have a good support system to be successful. I do, though, want to let you know what you can expect as I take college classes. First, I will have to spend time at the college going to classes, meeting with my professors, and studying. I may not be able to participate in all the family activities and responsibilities that I used to because of tests, papers, and lab assignments. I may also not be available to help you in the ways that I did in the past because I will be devoting most of my time to school. However, when I do get breaks between semesters, I will do my best to use that time to reconnect with you. Remember that this won't be forever—I will be graduating before we know it.

I also hope that I can count on you if I need someone to talk to. Encouraging me to continue during the times I get a little stressed will help me feel as though I can do it. Your understanding that I am doing something valuable and good for my future is important to me.

Sincerely,

You

YOUR FRIENDS

Another important part of your support system is friends. You may not be able to choose your family members, but you have more choice as to which friends will be positive influences on your college experience. If you have friends who have also attended or are attending college, you will have a great opportunity to connect with each other on this common pursuit. Even if you do not attend the same college, you can develop a support system with them based on your similar experiences. You can share advice and study strategies as well as a shoulder to lean on when you feel stressed. Knowing that a friend is also pursuing college success can often give you the motivation to continue working hard.

"My biggest supporters have been my friends who are also in college. I learned early on to make more friends who have the same goals as I do and ignore anyone who says that I can't achieve my goals."
—Edgar, 29, student

Although friends, especially those who are in college too, can provide a solid support system, not all friends, just as not all family members, will be a positive influence as you work toward your certificate or degree. Those who are not supportive may be very open about their anger, jealousy, or disappointment that you are pursuing a different path than theirs; others will be more subtle. Some friends may fear loss of time together or even replacement by new friends. In some cases, you may discover that your values no longer match your friends' ideas, which may signal a time to lessen your contact with them.

For sure, you will be busier than previously, and keeping in touch will be more difficult. Letting friends know that you may not be able to give them as much time as in the past can help you create some necessary distance. Of course, there is always the option of being upfront and honest about any lack of support. Telling certain friends that you need positive relationships while you are in college may be the message they need to hear to change their attitudes toward your exciting endeavor. If they still don't get the message, it may be time to eliminate them from daily contact.

YOUR COMMUNITY

There are a variety of places you can look for support as you make your way through college. Your community may offer support to college students such as you. Check out your local community center to see whether they offer workshops on time management or study skills; the local library may sponsor book clubs or study groups. Area churches, temples, and synagogues may provide financial support for students in need. Most communities support residents' goals to go to college and earn degrees because of a feeling that as more residents achieve college degrees, the greater will be the likelihood that the community improves. A gesture as simple as offering a discount for college students at a local store is a sign that the area businesses recognize and value students' hard

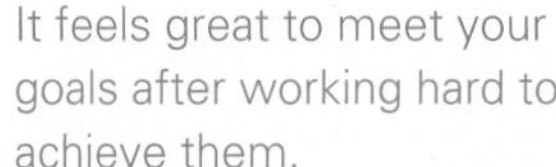

It feels great to meet your goals after working hard to achieve them.

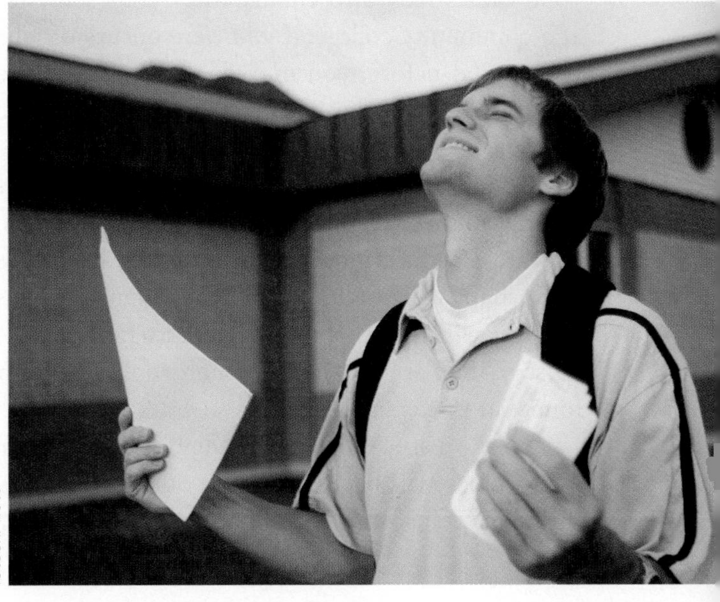

iStockPhoto

work in college. Local community leaders may also be willing to provide internships or mentoring sessions for students who could use extra advice and guidance throughout college. See what your community has to offer, or start your own community support group.

CRITICAL THINKING *exercise* 2.3

Who is part of your support system so far? Are they mostly family or friends? Make a list of people and describe what kind of support they provide. Is it financial? Emotional? Academic? Spiritual?

REFLECTION *exercise* 2.4

What have you learned so far about yourself? What information in this chapter has been most helpful to you in discovering how who you are will help you succeed in college?

Transfer Tips: FROM COLLEGE TO UNIVERSITY

What You Know and How You Learn Will Change

The transition from community college to a four-year university can be relatively smooth if you are willing to apply some of the ideas in this chapter to your new environment and your new challenges. First, consider that your definition of who you are will change by the time you transfer, perhaps dramatically. You will likely be more confident in your abilities and you will be better able to handle the stress of juggling numerous responsibilities. Second, your values may also change after your semesters at a community college; if you were unsure of what you valued before, you may finally have a clearer picture of your belief system. On the other hand, you may be more confused than ever about what you believe after studying different religions, psychological theories, and social ideas. Because higher education values inquiry and research, no matter what shape your values are in by the time you transfer, you will find support as you struggle to make sense of it all at both the community college and the four-year university.

Third, just as your knowledge of yourself and your values will have changed, your goals will go through a transformation. Although your main goal of graduating with a four-year degree will still be in sight, you will notice that you have already met some of your smaller goals. You have probably become more organized. Perhaps you have successfully completed an associate's degree. Just the fact that you are ready to transfer credits means that you have accomplished some necessary steps to fulfilling the rest of your goals.

Finally, you will be able to revise your statements about who you are because of the changes you have experienced after taking classes at a community college. You may even be able to include a career choice in your statement. Also, you may know yourself better through understanding your motivators, as discussed earlier. However, you will need to be prepared to adapt to different teaching styles and new pressures after you transfer.

Now, to prepare yourself for the next step, you will need to revise, preferably on paper, your mission and values statements. You will also need to realize that you may have to adapt the learning styles that you have felt most comfortable with—or to explore and use new styles—at your four-year school.

Transfer Tips: FROM COLLEGE TO CAREER

Goals and a Mission Will Help You Succeed

Many businesses rely on creating mission statements, strategic plans (long-term goals), and operational plans (short-term goals) to chart a course for their success. Because you have experience writing your own mission and goals, you will be able to contribute to your company's planning because you understand how the company's values underlie its mission and how its goals create its road map to success. Your experience in goal setting will also help you to write departmental or personal goals. If you understand how values, mission, and goals fit together, you will be better able to create goals that are explicitly linked to the focus of your workplace.

References and Recommended Readings

Beals, M. P. (1994). *Warriors don't cry.* New York: Pocket Books.

Dickerson, D. J. (2000). *An American story.* New York: Anchor Books.

Glass, L. (1997). *Toxic people: 10 ways of dealing with people who make your life miserable.* New York: St. Martin's.

Godwin, M. (2000). *Who are you? 101 ways of seeing yourself.* New York: Penguin.

Heath, C., & Heath, D. (2010). *Switch: How to change things when change is hard.* New York: Broadway Business.

Klauser, H. A. (2001). *Write it down, make it happen: Knowing what you want and getting it!* New York: Simon & Schuster.

Lawrence, G. (1995). *People types and tiger stripes* (3rd ed.). Gainesville, FL: CAPT.

Rodriguez, R. (1982). *Hunger of memory: The education of Richard Rodriguez.* New York: The Dial Press.

Smiley, T. (2006). *What I know for sure: My story of growing up in America.* New York: Anchor Books.

three CHAPTER

MANAGING Your Time and Energy

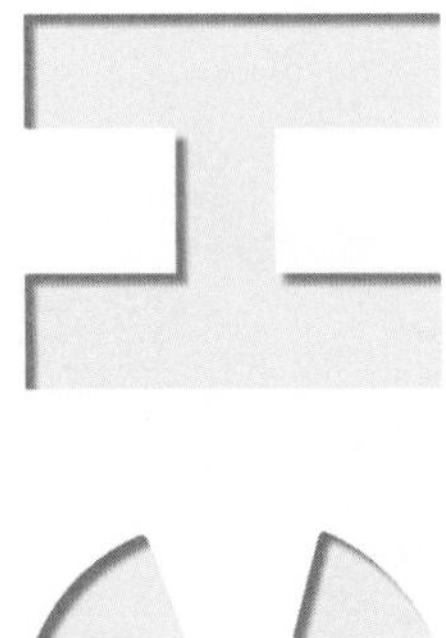

IN THIS chapter This chapter focuses on different time management options that can help you stay on task and handle tough situations throughout your college career. It also spends time explaining how maintaining your energy is part of your time management strategy. Your goal in reading this chapter will be to find the most appropriate method for you to keep time and energy in balance with one another.

"What all will I be expected to do in college? If I know the answer to that, I may be able to structure my time efficiently."
—Kiki, 18, student
"When I have the time, I don't have the energy. What can I do to have both at the same time?"
—Rita, 40, student
"I am pretty good at managing my time at home. How will being at college be different?"
—Mason, 39, student
"How can I help my students see that procrastination may be the difference between a passing and a failing grade?"
—Natasha, 33, instructor
"If it weren't for the last minute, I would never get anything done. Any tips for managing my time more effectively?"
—Lindsey, 27, student
"I have never really had to manage my time before—my parents and teachers always told me when to do things. Where do I even start?"
—Leonard, 17, student

More specifically, after completing this chapter, you will be able to do the following:

- List college-related activities that will need to be considered when you create a time management plan.
- Describe different time management strategies that you can use to build your time management plan.
- Explain the connection between time management and energy management.
- Identify reasons for procrastination and create a plan for eliminating it.

IS TIME on Your Side?

Is it surprising that the number one biggest challenge reported by college students is time management? Why do so many students identify time management as an area they need more help with? One answer may be that many of them are adding another responsibility to their busy lives. Another answer could be that they are now expected to do things they haven't done before or haven't done for a long time. Being a student demands more than just showing up for class. There is plenty of work to do outside of class—at home, in the library, on the computer,

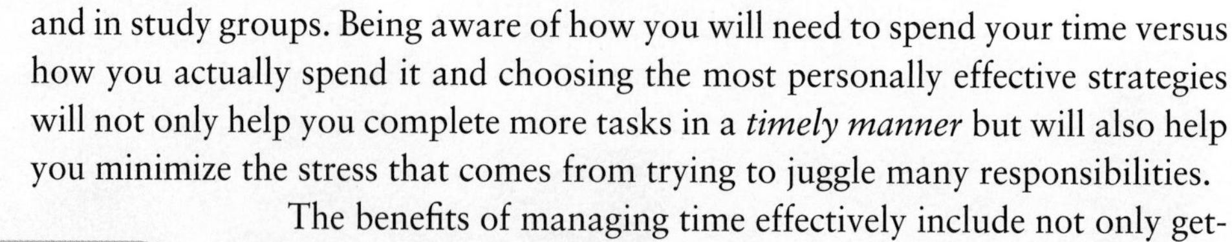

and in study groups. Being aware of how you will need to spend your time versus how you actually spend it and choosing the most personally effective strategies will not only help you complete more tasks in a *timely manner* but will also help you minimize the stress that comes from trying to juggle many responsibilities.

> "The most successful students take control of their time instead of the other way around. They know what they need to do and how long it will take them."
>
> —Susan, 61, instructor

The benefits of managing time effectively include not only getting tasks completed, but also experiencing the success of accomplishment. Darwin B. Nelson and Gary R. Low (2003), in their book *Emotional Intelligence: Achieving Academic and Career Excellence,* state that "[a]n important by-product of good Time Management is a feeling of self-control—we are managing our responsibilities, not being managed by them" (pp. 100–101). In other words, managing your time effectively will help empower you to take control of your life and what happens in it. You will certainly feel more in control of your time after you complete this chapter!

GETTING ORGANIZED

The first aspect to consider when it comes to managing time and stress is getting organized. Seems like a simple idea, but think about how much time you have wasted before when you couldn't find something or how you missed an important event because you didn't write it down. Nothing is more stressful than knowing you could have done better if you had been organized! Getting organized for success, however, doesn't have to take a lot of money and time. If you use a few simple strategies, you can save yourself both time and energy in the long run. To help get organized, think of the three *S*'s (supplies, space, and same time): getting the right *supplies* (including a calendar), keeping your *space* clean and organized, and checking your "to do list" or calendar at the *same time* each day.

SUPPLIES FOR SUCCESS

Pens, pencils, calculators, paper, notebooks, and thumb drives, oh my! In addition to books, lab manuals, and computer supplies, there are many other items you will need in college to get organized and complete assignments. What you *need* will depend on what you are taking and your instructors' expectations. What you *want* to get in addition will depend on your preferences and budget. At the very least, a good, sturdy backpack that can accommodate all your books and notebooks—and that doesn't break your back—should be high on your supply list.

Many a good student has fallen victim to "assignment amnesia." This occurs when otherwise smart students believe they can remember all of their assignments and appointments without writing them down or consulting their syllabi and course outlines. Fortunately, there are measures you can take to prevent an attack of assignment amnesia, such as using a calendar or device like a cell phone that keeps track of your assignments and to which you can also add all the other tasks you need to complete from your personal, professional, and college life.

For a paper calendar, you have many different types from which to choose. Once you determine the type that works best for you—a monthly, weekly, or daily calendar—make a habit of writing down your tasks, no matter how big or small. The following example shows one possible list for a student's daily activities.

Thursday

- Make appointment to have oil changed
- Pick up medicine for Terry
- Take Phillip to baseball
- Study for history quiz on Friday
- Read 30 pages for English
- Get book from library

A typical monthly calendar, as shown in Figure 3.1, allows you to see several weeks at once so that you can remain aware of upcoming events, but often there is little space on a monthly calendar to write down detailed information such as the daily activity list just shown.

FIGURE 3.1 Monthly Calendar

Sunday	Monday	Tuesday	Wednesday	Thursday	Friday	Saturday
					1	2
3	4	5	6	7	8	9 picnic—noon
10	11 work late	12	13	14	15 pay bills	16
17	18	19	20	21 play rehearsal 7:00	22	23
24	25 nutrition exam 10:00	26	27	28	29	30 birthday party 2:00

FIGURE 3.2 Weekly Calendar

Sunday	Monday	Tuesday	Wednesday	Thursday	Friday	Saturday
3–8 Work on paper	8:30 Work 2:00 Geology 3:00 Trig 5:00 Pick up dinner 7:00 Study for Accounting	9:00 English 11:00 Acct. 6:00 Help sister with painting	8:30 Work 2:00 Geology 3:00 Trig	9:00 English 11:00 Acct.	8:30 Work 2:00 Geology 3:00 Trig 7:00 Movie with friend	8–10 Clean house 3-4 Exercise 6–11 Study

A weekly calendar such as Figure 3.2 allows you to see an entire week at a glance. A weekly calendar provides room to write out details of each activity; however, it is often difficult to anticipate what you must do the next week.

Daily calendars usually provide the most space to write your day-to-day tasks and appointments, as in Figure 3.3. However, this kind of calendar may be the most difficult to work with if you need to plan ahead. Because you have no visual cue for the rest of the week or month, you may overlook important events or be surprised by them. A daily calendar works best if you are extremely organized and can plan ahead effectively; alternatively, use it in addition to a monthly calendar.

SPACE CONSIDERATIONS

The right stuff and the ideal calendar are just the first steps to managing your time well; there is more you must consider. To manage your time most effectively and efficiently, create a clutter-free space where you can study and complete assignments. If you don't have a place in your house or apartment that you can call your own, a comfortable chair or seat at the kitchen table may be all that you can spare. Make sure it is comfortable and quiet and has adequate space for books, notebooks, and other supplies. It has to be a place where you *want* to be or it will be difficult to go there to stay on task.

"Want to save time? Get organized. Have all your papers and books in the same place. Don't waste time looking for things."

—Neyo, 22, student

SAME TIME, SAME PLACE

A good system for writing down your daily tasks and establishing a place to complete your assignments are a good foundation to managing your time well

FIGURE 3.3 Daily Calendar

MONDAY March 12, 2012	
7:00	Wake up, shower, get ready for school
8:00	Drive to school, arrive early and study in the library
9:00	College Algebra
10:00	English 2
11:00	Study for Biology exam
12:00	Eat lunch and review notes for College Algebra
1:00	Biology—EXAM!!
2:00	Drive to work
3:00	Work
4:00	
5:00	

and reducing the negative effects of stress. However, there is one last tip: Create a routine. In other words, every evening write down your goals for the next day and every morning review what you need to do for the day. Knowing what to expect for the day will make surprises less likely. As you complete each task, scratch it off the list. You will get the satisfaction of a completed job and can focus on the next task.

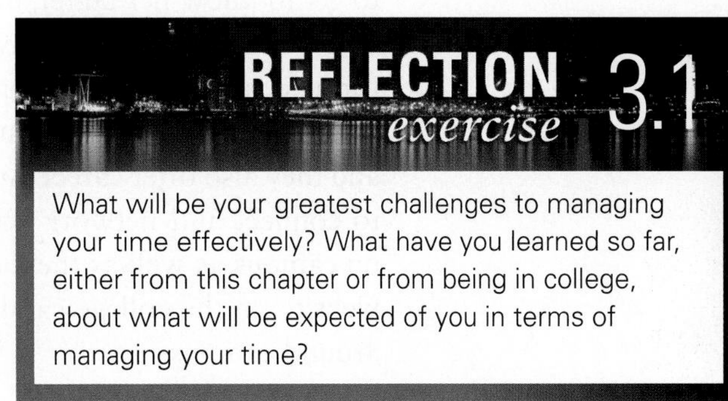

What will be your greatest challenges to managing your time effectively? What have you learned so far, either from this chapter or from being in college, about what will be expected of you in terms of managing your time?

IT'S TIME for College

As you have already discovered, going to college is about learning new ways of doing things and adjusting to different expectations and experiences. It is worth knowing, too, that your college is a time-conscious place. The classes are set on semesters or terms; classes meet at specific times and days during the week; there are certain dates that you can enroll in classes and talk to the people who work there; and there are other special dates such as financial aid deadlines and tuition payment due dates that help keep your college running smoothly. Without the college's effective time management strategies, you would not be able to get the classes you need and the degree you want!

It is important, then, to be aware of how the college manages its own time, and the best place to start is the academic calendar. You will be able to find this on your college's website or in the college catalog. The academic calendar will provide many important dates including, but not limited to, the following:

- Deadlines for registering and filing financial aid forms
- Date for the beginning of classes (or instruction)
- Drop/add dates for changing your schedule
- Due dates for tuition payment
- Withdrawal dates for leaving college before the semester is over
- Registration dates for the next semester
- Holidays or breaks within the semester and between semesters
- Last day of classes (or instruction) and finals week

As with other activities throughout the semester, being aware of the dates on the academic calendar will help you have a smooth semester and guide you to prepare for the next one.

In addition to the academic calendar, there are other out-of-class activities that you will need to be aware of as you plan your time during the semester. Your instructors will have office hours, or days and times they will be available in their offices, that are listed in the syllabus. These hours are for you to make an appointment to see your instructor if you need help on an assignment, want to get to know her better, or would like to talk about your progress in the class. You will also want to be aware of the hours of such services as the library, tutoring center, and computer labs. Last but not least, most colleges have student life activities that provide entertainment or additional educational opportunities, and they also offer career and community activities that give you the opportunity to connect and network with others. The business hours of different services on campus as well as the dates for special events may be found on your college website, in the college catalog, in the student newspaper, or on bulletin boards around campus.

MAKING TIME FOR CLASSES

How much time should you devote to classes? Some first-time students seriously underestimate the amount of time needed to prepare for a class, study for tests, and complete assignments. Unfortunately, they often realize their error only when an assignment is due or a test is given. A common formula for calculating the amount of study time is to multiply the number of credit hours for the course by three. For example, a demanding class that carries three credit hours and meets three times per week for 1 hour each time will require 9 hours per week of out-of-class work. These 9 hours plus the 3 hours in class means you will spend a total of 12 hours studying and attending that one class each week. Multiply 12 hours by four classes and you will have a 48-hour college work week. Add 40 hours of work on the job and you will be spending 88 hours per week working on your job and your classes!

Other classes may take a little less time, and you may be able to spend only 2 hours for every 1 hour you are in class, which would mean that you will spend 6 hours plus the 3 hours you are in class for a total of 9 hours each week. Either way, you will be spending anywhere from 36 to 40 hours a week if you are taking 12 credit hours a semester. This, of course, is assuming you are taking a 16-week course. For shorter terms, such as 4 weeks, you will be spending much more time in and out of class.

"I thought I could go to classes and that would be it for the time I spent on college. Boy, was I wrong. I know now that I have to factor in time to study and work on assignments as part of my time in college."
—Juan, 25, student

Looking at Figure 3.4 can be overwhelming for students, especially if they work more than 25 hours and take more than 12 credit hours per semester. A full-time student who also works full time can expect to spend half the hours in every week working on classes or her job (and that doesn't include time to sleep)! Studies have shown that the reality of how much time students spend outside of class is much lower than the recommended number of hours, but students often find that how much time they spend varies from semester to semester, depending on what kinds of classes they take.

To see how the recommended study hours look when they are scheduled throughout the week, check out one student's calendar. This student works a full-time job 40 hours a week and is in class 12 hours each week.

Given the student's schedule shown in Figure 3.5, will she be able to find the 48 hours she needs to attend and study for college classes? If she were to add 2 hours a night after class—assuming that she felt like studying after a long day—she would study an additional 10 hours during the work week, leaving 22 hours and 15 minutes of studying to be completed in her "spare time."

Look at the calendar again. In order to reach 48 hours of studying and class, where will Laura include additional study time? Will she need to study every

FIGURE 3.4 Student's College and Work Schedule

Responsibility	Contact Hours per Week	Outside Hours per Week	Total Hours per Week
College Algebra	3	6–9	9–12
Composition 101	3	6–9	9–12
US History	3	6–9	9–12
Reading	3	6–9	9–12
Work	25		25
			TOTAL: 61–73

FIGURE 3.5 Laura's Monthly Calendar

Sunday	Monday	Tuesday	Wednesday	Thursday	Friday	Saturday
7:00–10:00 Study	6:30–7:30 Get ready for school	6:30–7:30 Get ready for school	6:30–7:30 Get ready for school	6:30–7:30 Get ready for school	6:30–7:30 Get ready for school	7:00–10:00 Clean house, shop
10:00–11:00 Go to church	7:30–7:45 Travel to work	7:30–7:45 Travel to work	7:30–7:45 Travel to work	7:30–7:45 Travel to work	7:30–7:45 Travel to work	10:00–11:30 Soccer
11:15–12:30 Lunch with parents	8:00–12:30 Work	8:00–12:30 Work	8:00–12:30 Work	8:00–12:30 Work	8:00–12:30 Work	11:30–12:15 Lunch with team
12:45–3:45 Study	12:30–1:15 Eat lunch and run errands	12:30–1:15 Go to doctor's appointment	12:30–1:15 Eat lunch with friend	12:30–1:15 Eat lunch and walk 1 mile	12:30–1:15 Eat lunch and study	12:15–2:00 Run errands
3:45–5:45 Do yard work	1:15–4:45 Work	1:15–4:45 Work	1:15–4:45 Work	1:15–4:45 Work	1:15–4:45 Work	2:00–6:00 Go to library and do research
6:00–7:00 Eat dinner	4:45–5:00 Travel	4:45–5:00 Travel	4:45–5:00 Travel	4:45–5:00 Travel	4:45–5:00 Travel	6:00–7:00 Fix and eat dinner
7:00–8:00 Walk 3 miles	5:00–5:45 Eat dinner and study	5:00–5:45 Eat dinner and study	5:00–5:45 Eat dinner and study	5:00–5:45 Eat dinner and study	5:00–7:00 Eat dinner with friends	7:00–9:00 Study
8:00–10:00 Do laundry, get ready for next week	6:00–9:30 Classes	6:00–9:30 Classes	6:00–9:30 Classes	6:00–9:30 Classes	7:00–9:30 See movie	9:00–10:00 Answer email and watch TV
10:00 Go to bed	10:00 Go to bed	10:00 Go to bed	10:00 Go to bed	10:00 Go to bed	10:00 Go to bed	10:00 Go to bed

INTEGRITY MATTERS

Sometimes doing what is easiest, even if it is not the right thing to do, seems like the best way to manage time effectively. For example, a student who does not have enough time to finish a paper may be tempted to download one from the Internet, use someone else's previous work, or ask someone else to write it. Such an action certainly allows the student to turn in a paper on time, but it is not the way to act with integrity. In fact, such a short cut actually *shortchanges* the educational process. A student who "saves time" by not doing her own work for a class risks more than not learning from the assignment; she may find herself in serious academic jeopardy when the professor confronts her with the evidence she did not do her own work.

YOUR TURN In what ways have you saved time by not doing something or not doing it right? ■ How did you feel about not completing the task or by not completing it to the best of your ability? ■ What have you learned about acting with integrity and managing your time?

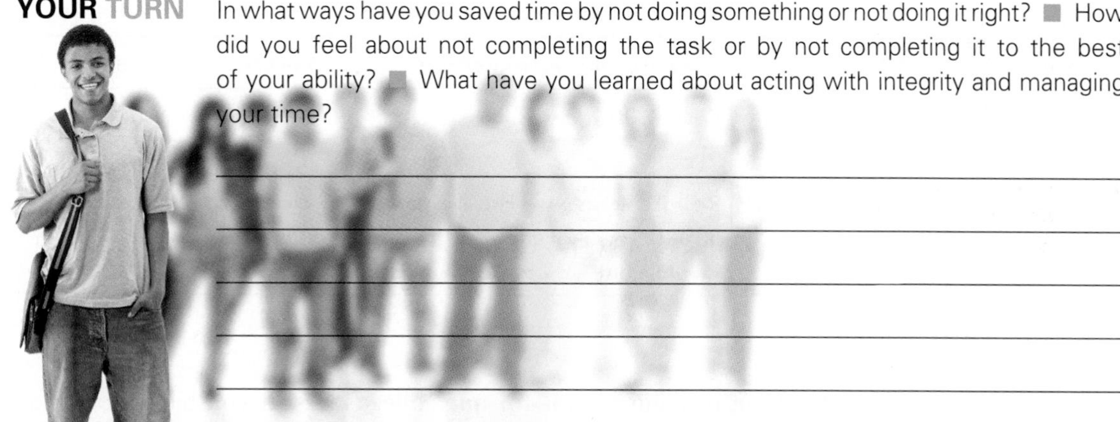

waking moment that she is not at work, in class, or taking care of herself and her other responsibilities? If she cannot devote that much time to her college classes, would Laura need to take fewer classes, ask for help with home responsibilities, or cut back on her hours at work? Despite what some may think, Laura doesn't have to give up her dream to be in college, but she will need to rearrange her schedule. Without doing so, she will not be able to meet the demands of her classes. However, she can feel some comfort in knowing that getting up a little earlier, multitasking, and using her weekends for studying at longer intervals can be short-term changes to her schedule.

BUT WHAT DO I DO?

The question sometimes arises as to what you should be doing for those 6 to 9 hours for each class every week. First, you will need to read any assigned material *before* class. Another activity that will need to be part of your outside study time is reviewing your notes from class and filling in any information gaps that you were not able to get by working with a classmate. Rewriting your notes after the discussion of the chapter or topic is another very important way you can spend an hour for the week. Of course, you will need to budget time to complete assignments, such as review questions at the end of a chapter or a research project.

FIGURE 3.6 One-Hour-a-Day Time Management Plan

Day of the Week	Time	Assignment	Completed	
Sunday	3:30–4:30 P.M.	Read Chapter 5 and take notes while reading. Review notes after reading the chapter once.	Yes	No
Monday	7:00–8:00 P.M.	Review reading notes as well as class notes. Define all vocabulary terms that are key to the chapter and that are unfamiliar.	Yes	No
Tuesday	11:15–12:15 P.M.	Answer study questions that accompany the chapter.	Yes	No
Wednesday	8:00–9:00 P.M.	Create sample test questions on flash cards and write the answers on the back.	Yes	No
Thursday	7:00–8:00 P.M.	Complete homework questions for the chapter.	Yes	No
Friday	5:30–6:00 A.M. 3:30–4:00 P.M.	Review flash cards.	Yes	No
Saturday	3:30–4:30 P.M.	Rewrite notes from the entire week of class. Include any material that was assigned in the reading but not covered in class.	Yes	No

The plan in Figure 3.6 is for *one* college class. If you have more than one, you will need to add an hour each day of the week for each three-credit-hour class that you are taking.

Even with the best intentions, many students, however, opt to cut back on studying because other activities, such as running errands and participating in their children's activities, are necessary parts of their lives and cannot be eliminated or rearranged. Realistically, you may be able to cut back on studying in some classes at slower times; however, you should not eliminate study hours for all classes throughout each semester. Your best bet is to recognize that taking college classes is a tremendous time commitment and to work your other responsibilities (except maintaining your health) around them as best you can. You won't always be able to put college as your first priority, but you will need to make a conscious effort to put studying near the top of your list most of the time.

"When I realized that I was spending 23 hours a week hanging out with friends, I made some quick changes. I never knew until I tracked my time each day that two or three hours here and there could add up to the equivalent of a part-time job."

—James, 22, student

ANALYZING YOUR TIME

Recognizing that we all have the same number of hours, analyzing your time is another step to effective time management. Tim Hindle (1998), in his book *Manage Your Time,* suggests keeping a time log of your day that is divided into 30-minute increments (p. 9). Separate from your calendar, the purpose of a 30-minute time log is to help raise your awareness of what you are doing throughout the day. You can make your own time log like the one in Figure 3.7 to keep up with one day's worth of activities, but be sure to give yourself time to write down your activities either every few hours or at the end of the day. Keeping an eye on how you spend your time will help you make realistic time management goals and will keep you from wasting too much time or miscalculating how long it takes you to complete tasks.

FIGURE 3.7 Time Log Example

Time	Wednesday's Activities
7:00 A.M.	Get ready for classes; eat breakfast
7:30 A.M.	Review notes for business class
8:00 A.M.	En route to school
8:30 A.M.	Business Communications
9:00 A.M.	Class, continued
9:30 A.M.	Class, continued
10:00 A.M.	See advisor to plan next semester's classes

Asking "Where did the time go?" and "What do I do with my time?" is a start to analyzing your time. You will also need to analyze your time management skills—or how well you use your time wisely to meet your goals and stay healthy in the process, such as with the assessment in Activity 3.1 that asks 10 questions about your time management abilities.

CRITICAL THINKING exercise 3.2

What do you see as your greatest time management strengths? What are your time management weaknesses? What will you do to build on your strengths while also addressing your weaknesses?

BACK-DATING TIME MANAGEMENT PLAN

If there is one piece of advice that experienced students want to pass along to new students to help them manage their time better, it is that even though they sound the same when spoken aloud, the words *due* and *do* don't mean the same thing. Starting the night before a project is due may create more stress than is necessary. Therefore, the method of creating "do" dates before your assignment is "due," or back-dating assignments, is essential if you are going to create habits of completing work successfully. For example, let's say you have a career exploration paper due on the 24th of this month (see Figure 3.8). In order to build enough time into your schedule, you can use a calendar to divide the possible steps to completing your paper and fill in the calendar according to the time you have to work on the paper. When back-dating assignment tasks, remember to provide adequate time between tasks so that you can reflect on the work that you have done and approach the assignment with "fresh eyes" each time.

Figure out where you can squeeze in a little time to accomplish important tasks.

Jakob Heibig/Digital Vision/Getty Images

ACTIVITY 3.1 Personal Time Assessment

Circle the number (1–Never, 2–Sometimes, 3–Usually, 4–Always) that best describes your experience.

Statement	Never	Sometimes	Usually	Always
1. I arrive to class prepared.	1	2	3	4
2. I review my notes within 24 hours of class.	1	2	3	4
3. I spend my time on campus talking with professors, studying, or doing research.	1	2	3	4
4. I have study goals, and I achieve them each week.	1	2	3	4
5. I feel prepared for tests.	1	2	3	4
6. I spend enough time on assignments.	1	2	3	4
7. I get enough sleep each night.	1	2	3	4
8. I spend some time each week doing something I enjoy.	1	2	3	4
9. I have enough time to take care of most of my personal needs.	1	2	3	4
10. I get support from others to help me meet my educational goals.	1	2	3	4
Score each column.	______	______	______	______
Total:				______

Score Range	Meaning
40–32	You do a good job of managing your time. For the most part, you are satisfied with how you manage your time and what you accomplish each week.
31–26	You are doing a good job managing your time for most activities. Identify your weaker areas and create a plan to improve time management in those areas.
25–19	You may be dissatisfied with your time management and find only a few goals are met each week. Review what you are doing right with some of your time and make a plan that will draw on your time management strengths.
18 or less	You may feel as though you are not meeting the majority of your goals during the week. An honest look at your goals, your necessary activities, and your priorities is needed.

FIGURE 3.8 Back-Dating Time Management

Sunday	Monday	Tuesday	Wednesday	Thursday	Friday	Saturday
		1	2	3	4	5
6	7	8 1:00 P.M. Receive paper assignment	9 6–7:30 P.M. Choose paper topic; brainstorm or freewrite on topic	10	11 9–10:30 P.M. Reread brainstorming list; create a draft outline	12
13 3–5:00 P.M. Write first draft of paper	14	15 11–12:00 noon Visit writing lab for assistance with paper	16	17	18 8:30–10:30 P.M. Write second draft of paper, incorporating tutor's advice	19
20 3–4:30 P.M. Write final draft of paper	21	22	23 8–9:00 P.M. Edit and finalize paper; print out on quality paper; place in backpack	24 2:00 P.M. Turn in paper	25	26
27	28	29	30			

MANAGING Your Energy

Just as important as managing your time is managing your energy. Think about this scenario: You have all weekend off from work and your spouse has taken the kids to visit the grandparents. Therefore, you have 48 hours of complete solitude to write a research paper that is due on Monday. Sounds ideal, doesn't it? But what if you have the flu for those two days? Does the time mean anything when you don't have the energy to do any work? What if, instead of having the flu, you pulled two double shifts and haven't slept more than 5 hours in two days? Will you be able to use your free 48 hours productively or will you need to take care of yourself?

Time, in other words, is only valuable if you have the energy to use it well. Thus, you need to be aware of how you feel, how energetic you are, and how willing you are to use your time wisely. To determine when during the day you feel the most energetic, place an X in the appropriate column for each time of day in Activity 3.2. If you work nights and sleep during most of the day, create your own box with the times you are awake.

In addition to the time of day, your energy levels rise and fall during the week. Do you find yourself tired on Monday mornings, but full of energy on Fridays? Or do you feel worn out by Thursday evenings, but rejuvenated on Sundays? Depending on your work, school, and personal schedules, you will find that you have regular bursts of energy at certain times of the week. To determine which days of the week you feel most energetic, write an X in the appropriate columns in Activity 3.3.

IDENTIFYING TIME AND ENERGY ZAPPERS

Despite your best efforts in managing your time and energy, there will be times when you find your best laid plans are interrupted by needy people and last-minute changes in plans. A few distractions during the day can be a nice break

ACTIVITY 3.2 Time of Day Energy Levels

Time of Day	High Energy	Neutral	Low Energy
6:00 A.M.			
8:00 A.M.			
10:00 A.M.			
12 noon			
2:00 P.M.			
4:00 P.M.			
6:00 P.M.			
8:00 P.M.			
10:00 P.M.			
12 midnight			

ACTIVITY 3.3 Day of Week Energy Levels

Day	High Energy	Neutral	Low Energy
Sunday			
Monday			
Tuesday			
Wednesday			
Thursday			
Friday			
Saturday			

from the mundane tasks of going to school and working or caring for a family. However, if they take so much time away from your studies that you can't seem to keep up with the pace of your classes or they stress you out, you will need to find ways to eliminate or at least lessen the frequency of intrusions like the following.

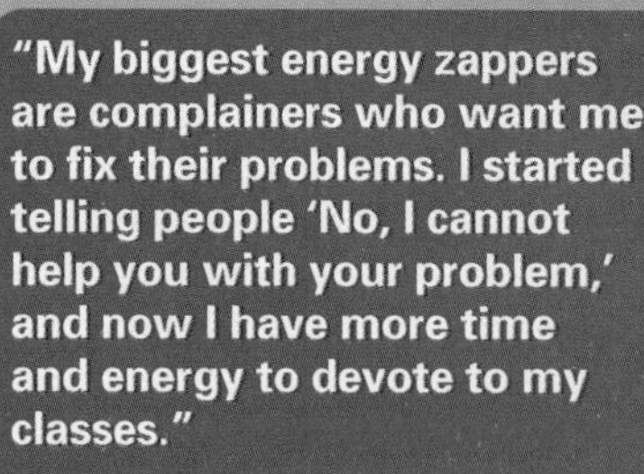

"My biggest energy zappers are complainers who want me to fix their problems. I started telling people 'No, I cannot help you with your problem,' and now I have more time and energy to devote to my classes."
—Myles, 18, student

- People who want your attention and time but don't really need it
- Interruptions such as unnecessary phone calls
- Fatigue and illness
- Personal problems
- Mindless television watching
- Internet surfing that serves no purpose
- Continuous "chatting" online
- Playing video or computer games
- Inability to say no
- Procrastination
- Poor organization
- Inability to concentrate because of learning difficulty, medication, or stress

Now is the time to block out the zappers. You won't be able to afford the time that they waste, and you will need to be proactive in getting rid of them. Some will be easy to reduce or get rid of, such as playing video games or hanging out all day with friends; others will be more difficult, such as learning to say no to people or eliminating procrastination. The key to getting rid of energy and time wasters is to take on the easiest ones and work on the others through goal setting. Of course, one person's time waster is another person's stress reliever. If you find that playing a video game or going to a movie with friends is necessary to refresh yourself before tackling other important tasks, schedule it as part of your weekly routine. When those activities keep you from finishing others, it may be time to reassess how often you do them.

One way to help manage your energy is by becoming aware of activities that relax you when you are stressed or that allow you to refill your energy reserves. In Activity 3.4, place an X in the appropriate column next to each activity—or in both columns if warranted, or neither. Use this chart when planning your time, scheduling activities that rejuvenate you or help you recharge when you need more energy. If an activity helps you wind down, you may want to schedule it after you have completed major tasks.

RUNNING LOW ON TIME AND ENERGY

There will be times when you find that goals for the day or week are still left on your list, but you don't have the time and energy reserves that you hoped to have. Sometimes life throws us a curveball, and our beautiful plans are mangled if not completely destroyed. If you find yourself in such a situation, then you will ben-

EMOTIONAL INTELLIGENCE *Check-Up*

Impulse Control

Emotionally intelligent people acknowledge their feelings in a situation, stop and think about what is involved, and then choose an act that will best help resolve any problems. Read the following common situation and work through the three steps in the boxes.

SITUATION

You have a paper due in two days and you have not started on it at all. In fact, you haven't even picked a topic. However, your best friend is coming into town and has tickets to a concert you have been wanting to go to for over a year. Your friend also wants to stay with you while he is in town, but you know you will be tempted to stay up all night—like when you were younger—having fun and catching up with him. You had made plans with him months ago, before you knew you had a paper due the same week he was coming into town, but you also didn't plan ahead and start working on it early. You don't want to cancel your plans and you don't want to fail the paper. What should you do?

What emotions do you have in this situation?

FEEL

What is the optimal outcome of the situation for you?

THINK

What attitude and positive action will help you achieve the outcome you want?

ACT

ACTIVITY 3.4 Time and Energy Relaxers and Reenergizers

Activity	Relaxer	Reenergizer
Watching television		
Spending time with family or friends		
Pleasure reading		
Doing housework		
Exercising (light to moderate)		
Gardening		
Talking on the phone		
Writing		
Cooking		
Shopping		
Napping		
Participating in a hobby		
Surfing the Internet		
Organizing closets, drawers, files		
Enjoying a nice meal		

efit from changing goals and priorities quickly and eliminating unnecessary items from your "to do" list. For example, perhaps you had planned to bake a friend a birthday cake from scratch, but you don't have two hours to do it. What can you do? How about buying a cake on the way to your friend's house? The outcome is still the same: Your friend has a cake for his birthday. Or you hoped to get all the bills paid by the end of the day, but you don't have the time and energy left. Pay the bills that are due the soonest and complete the task the next day.

There will be some days when you just can't do it all. You may find that you cannot read the assigned chapter in your sociology class the night before. If this happens to you—and it will at some point in your college career—then create a back-up plan as you did with the birthday cake. Avoid giving up completely if you run out of time or energy; do something, even if it is just a little bit. Can't get to the library to start looking for sources for your research paper? Create an outline or a task list instead, and go to the library the next day. Do something that keeps you moving forward, but don't give up. You will have more energy and time the next day to complete new tasks.

Working within a group or with another classmate, describe the types of activities that can zap students' time and energy; then create solutions for managing them. Present your ideas to the class.

Your Terms of SUCCESS

WHEN YOU SEE . . .	IT MEANS . . .
Academic calendar	The college's calendar that provides important dates throughout the semester. May include due dates for tuition payments and dropping classes.
Add/drop dates	The dates on your academic calendar when you can add or drop a class from your schedule. Usually occurs within the first week of classes.
Class schedule	Your schedule of classes for the semester.
Course calendar/course outline	Your instructor's calendar that provides important dates throughout the semester; may include due dates for projects and tests.
Daily calendar	A calendar that shows one day at a time.
Due date	The day that an assignment must be completed and turned in.
Energy zapper	An activity or person that lowers your energy levels.
Finals week	The week scheduled in the academic calendar in which final exams will be held. Your class meeting time may change during this week.
Last day of instruction	The date on the academic calendar that shows when the last day of the regular class meetings will occur. Usually comes before finals week.
Monthly calendar	A calendar that shows one month at a time.
Office hours	The hours your instructor is in her office and available to meet with students. Your instructor's office hours can be found in the syllabus.
Procrastination	The act of delaying an activity.
Reenergizer	An activity or person that increases your energy levels.
Student study day	A date on the academic calendar in which no classes or final exams are held. It is intended for students to have a day of studying before the week of finals begins.
Time management	A strategy for controlling how you use your time.
Weekly calendar	A calendar that shows one week at a time.
Withdrawal date	The date on the academic calendar showing the final day that you can withdraw from all of your classes. When you withdraw from classes, a "W" will be added to your transcript next to the classes from which you withdrew.

WHY WAIT until Tomorrow?

What if the student in the Emotional Intelligence Check-up feature had started her assignment early and all she had to do was print it out before heading to bed at a reasonable hour? Certainly, her stress levels would be much lower and her work would most likely be her best. Not all students manage their time wisely all the time, but procrastination does not have to be a necessary part of going to college.

PROCRASTINATION PITFALLS

Postponing an activity or task, whether because you think it will not take too long to finish or you find more interesting activities to do, can have serious consequences. For example, if you put off researching your legal terminology paper until the night before, you might find that the library has closed early or that access to online databases is down. You may even discover that your computer is not working or your printer is out of ink. Underestimating the amount of time needed is another serious consequence of procrastination. Writing a paper may have taken you a few hours in high school, but in college, it may take you days if not weeks to do the research, drafting, and revising that is expected of college-level work. At the very least, you will not be able to get any help you may need if you wait until the last minute. Professors won't be available, classmates may be completing their own work, and tutors may be booked up with appointments.

> "I learned that procrastination can be bad the hard way—when I failed a test because I waited until the night before to study. Fortunately, I changed my time management habits because of it."
>
> —Lawalia, 21, student

Procrastination then can be a barrier between you and success; for sure, it can cause you unnecessary stress. Managing your time and planning ahead will, however, minimize the likelihood that you will procrastinate.

PROCRASTINATOR TYPES

To break the cycle of procrastination, it may be helpful to consider why you procrastinate and what that says about who you are. Nike's slogan "Just do it!" sounds simple, but it doesn't work for everyone. Determining your procrastinator type will help you find the solution that works best for you. For example, do you procrastinate in certain classes? Do you procrastinate when faced with certain types of assignments? What reward do you get for not doing the work ahead of time? Some students crave the rush of doing an assignment at the last minute. They believe that the only way to motivate themselves is to hear a clock ticking down the hours or minutes left. Others are afraid of failing or not doing well on an assignment. This fear makes starting an assignment overwhelming. Still others just have too much to do every day, and they cannot find time because they have set up their lives so that there is no time left for college work. Finally, there is the person who feels that anything worth doing is worth doing perfectly. The trouble comes when they cannot complete an assignment perfectly, so they choose not to do it at all. Table 3.1 provides more details for the four types of procrastinators just described. Think about what type you are and which strategies you would use to break the procrastination cycle.

ELIMINATING PROCRASTINATION

A few quick and fast tips can help you eliminate the urge to procrastinate. Remember, these are habits that must be used every day you have something to do.

TABLE 3.1 Procrastinator Types

Adrenaline addict	The adrenaline addict craves the rush he feels when he waits until the last minute. Without the faster heartbeat, he can't seem to get motivated to complete any assignment. He finds doing assignments in small chunks well before they are due bores him to tears. If he's not completely exhausted after the process, he gets no satisfaction in the work he has done.
Fearful loafer	The fearful loafer worries what will happen when she completes the assignment. Will she pass? Will she fail? Will she have forgotten something important to include? Will her professor like her work so much that she will be expected to perform at that level all the time? It does not matter what scenario the fearful loafer dreams up, it will make her worry too much to get started on time, and she will wait until the last minute when she has to face her fears.
Stretched-thin slacker	The stretched-thin slacker wants to complete assignments on time, but he has too many assignments, too many activities, and too many responsibilities to get it all done. Instead of focusing on completing one task, the stretched-thin slacker takes on more to avoid handling what he has.
Paralyzed perfectionist	The paralyzed perfectionist always wants to do her best, but when she doesn't think she can do her best, she doesn't want to do anything at all. The paralyzed perfectionist won't even start unless she knows the end product will be her best work ever.

Practice one or more of them any time you feel the need to put off until tomorrow something that has to be done today.

- *Write down what you must do.* Use your back-dating time management strategy to make a time line for your project. Break the task apart into smaller chunks that each take 30 minutes to an hour to complete.
- *Just do it, no matter how you feel.* Start right here, right now, and don't think about finding a better time to begin.
- *Reward yourself.* When you complete a particularly difficult project, give yourself a special treat—an extra hour of sleep, a favorite television show, or some time with friends.
- *Keep the end in mind.* Remind yourself of the reason that you are in college and think about how this project supports that goal. For example, that research paper will make you a better communicator at your future job.

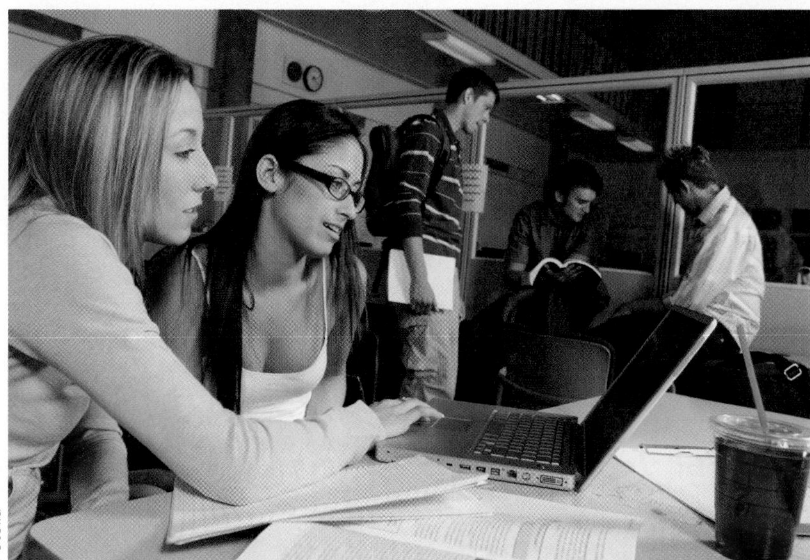

Fotolia

Schedule your study time just like you would schedule an appointment each week.

TECH TACTICS

Using Technology to Get Ahead

Technology such as cell phones, video games, and the Internet can provide opportunities to avoid doing your college work. Instead of limiting access to them, use them instead to help you manage your time. Cell phones have timers, alarms, and calendars that can keep you on track. The Internet can connect you to friends through social networking sites to provide a support group for your classes. Video games (or other fun activities) can be your reward for completing assignments on time.

RECOMMENDED SITES

- www.studygs.net/timman.htm Study Guides and Strategies provide excellent tips for students who are working to improve their time management strategies.
- www.psychologytoday.com/articles/200308/procrastination-ten-things-know *Psychology Today*'s Procrastination: Ten Things You Need to Know provides a list of reasons people procrastinate and what you can do to minimize its negative effects.
- www.dartmouth.edu/~acskills/success/time.html Dartmouth's Academic Skills Center provides links to additional resources for college students who need to manage their time more effectively.

REFLECTION exercise 3.4

Do you procrastinate? If so, which type of procrastinator are you? What can you do differently to eliminate procrastination while in college?

- *Leave it to the pros.* Write a list of pros and cons for doing the project on time and then for *not* doing it on time or at all. Decide which list you can live with.
- *Look in the mirror.* Review Table 3.1 on procrastinator types. Once you determine why you procrastinate, you will become better able to make changes in your habits.

Transfer Tips: FROM COLLEGE TO UNIVERSITY

How to Handle the New Pressures on Your Time

A good time management strategy that works for you will serve you well when you transfer to a university. Yes, there will be more work and more expected of you when you get closer to completing a bachelor's degree, but there may also be less direction from professors. They will assume you have solid time management skills. The more you practice now, the better you will be able to handle even more restrictions on your time. Additionally, there will be more for you to do as you work toward completing a four-year degree. You may find yourself participating in a career-related club, interning to get experience for your résumé, talking to professors about graduating, and putting together applications for jobs.

Try out a few strategies and find what works, but also talk to students who have already transferred to find out what new expectations you will encounter.

Transfer Tips: FROM COLLEGE TO CAREER

Improving Time Management on the Job

If you decide to go directly from college to work, or back to work, your time and stress management skills can be the difference between a dreaded job and a life-fulfilling career. Time management will be even more important on the job because your actions will affect more people. Just as in moving from college to university, the more you practice good time management skills, the more likely you will be able to complete assignments on time. Beware, though, that on the job, the stakes will be much higher than they were in college. Using a calendar and writing down daily tasks will help you keep on top of your "to do" list. There may be times when you won't be able to manage your time as effectively as you wish, but if you can be honest and speak up quickly, you may be able to save others' time as well.

References and Recommended Readings

Dodd, P., & Sundheim, D. (2005). *The 25 best time management tools and techniques: How to get more done without driving yourself crazy.* Chelsea, MI: Peak Performance Press.

Hindle, T. (1998). *Manage your time.* New York: DK Publishing.

Leland, K., & Bailey, K. (2008). *Time management in an instant: 60 ways to make the most of your day.* Franklin Lakes, NJ: The Career Press.

Nelson, D. B., & Low, G. R. (2003). *Emotional intelligence: Achieving academic and career excellence.* Upper Saddle River, NJ: Pearson.

Sibler, L. (1998). *Time management for the creative person: Right-brain strategies for stopping procrastination, getting control of the clock and calendar, and freeing up your time and your life.* New York: Three Rivers Press.

CHAPTER four

CULTIVATING Relationships and Appreciating Diversity

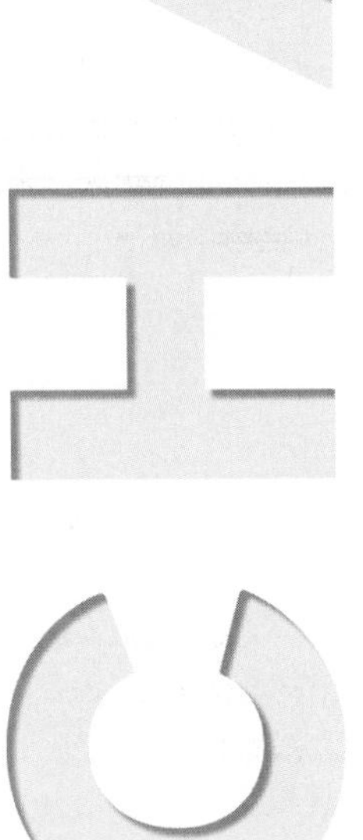

IN THIS chapter One of the easiest parts of college can be the hardest for busy college students. The easy part to making friends and forging relationships is that people are everywhere—in class, computer labs, and the library—and everyone shares at least one thing—college—in common. As you will discover, getting to know those around you is essential to your well-being and happiness while you are working on your degree. The hard part, however, is making the time to cultivate relationships. As a community college student, you

"Besides getting to know my professors and classmates, who else will I need to get to know in college?"
—Farida, 22, student

"I wish more students would take advantage of talking to me during my office hours. What should they know about taking advantage of the time?"
—Curtis, 35, instructor

"My family encouraged me to go to college even though neither of my parents have a degree. What do I need to know to keep my relationship with them strong?"
—Mario, 18, student

"I spend a lot of time listening to students talk about conflicts they have in the classroom—they don't know how to address challenges they have effectively. What advice can I give them?"
—Andre, 27, advisor

"I think I am pretty open and accepting of all people. Why do I need to study diversity in college? Isn't everyone like me?"
—Kari, 23, student

"I have been stereotyped as an older female returning to college after a long time away. What can I do to learn how *I* may also be stereotyping others?"
—Quincy, 53, student

most likely have other activities that fill your schedule outside of class: work, family, hobbies, church, and friends. Part of this chapter's purpose is to show you the benefits of starting and maintaining strong relationships with people on campus.

In addition to making friends and connections with people in college, this chapter also discusses diversity as an issue to be explored and appreciated. You will certainly notice that the people you encounter in college are from a variety of backgrounds and you will most likely meet numerous people who have differing values, goals, opinions about politics and religion, and ways of leading their lives. An important component of being an educated individual is understanding that college is, in part, about learning to listen to others, understanding their points of view, and appreciating them in the larger context of humanity. This chapter, then, presents you with several categories of diversity—to be sure, there are as many categories as there are people—to explore and discuss with your instructors, classmates, and others. There is also discussion of instances in which a lack of appreciation for others' differences can lead to prejudging them, or worse, discrimination. All of these topics will help you create and maintain mutually respectful relationships with others while broadening your own appreciation of diversity and encouraging others as well.

More specifically, after reading this chapter, you will be able to do the following:

- Describe the different types of people and their roles on your campus and list the benefits of cultivating relationships in college.
- Explain the importance of appreciating diversity.
- Discuss how stereotyping, prejudice, and discrimination are related.
- Understand the process of resolving conflict in relationships.

CULTIVATING Relationships in College

Research has shown that getting to know at least one person, no matter who it is, on your campus will increase the likelihood that you will stay in college and complete your degree (Kuh, Kinzie, Schuh, Witt, et al., 2005). Whether it is the janitor or a career counselor, getting to know someone beyond just her name, title, and face is to your advantage while you are in college.

You have probably noticed already that there are many people who work at a college—and most of them are there to support and guide you through your college experience. Equally important to understanding where buildings and services are located is knowing who does what on your campus. It will save you time to know, for example, that getting copies of your transcript involves speaking with someone in the registrar's office or that checking on loan applications will include contact with a financial aid officer. These people and many others are charged with the task of helping you succeed each semester you are in college, and it will make your transition from either high school or the world of work much easier if you are familiar with the various common jobs on campus.

PROFESSORS

There may be no one more important to your college and possible future career success than your professors. They do not just provide you with access to content and support as you think critically about the subject matter; they also can be mentors and resources as you complete your degree and start a career. One way to start out on the right path to a good relationship is to greet each professor with a smile and a "Hello" when you see her in and out of class. College professors see their relationships with students outside of class as part of their advising and mentoring duties. For many instructors, their students are not only people in their classes, but they are also potential graduates from their programs or transfer student success stories. Being friendly in and outside of class is a great way to start on the path to a strong, valuable relationship during your college career (and maybe even after)!

"I meet with all of my instructors at least once every semester. I like them to see that I am interested in the class and my progress. Plus, I get to know them better, which makes going to class more enjoyable."

—Karis, 23, student

Relationships built on acknowledgement of others' boundaries (in this case, professors' expectations and policies) as well as respect and integrity are stronger and more authentic than superficial connections. Because each instructor's expectations in terms of class preparation and policies regarding attendance, late work, and make-up exams will differ, be mindful that rules that apply in one class may be different in another. To cultivate a solid relationship with your professor, make the most of the time that you have to meet with him before or after class and during his office hours. Unlike the brief time you may have before or after class, office hours are best used for questions about material that was previously covered, assignments and policies that were previously explained, and anything else that does not pertain to the day's lecture or in-class activity. Sometimes students only see office hours as a time to discuss a problem; office hours should be used for positive visits as well—stopping by to say "Hello" or to follow up on an idea that sparked your interest in class are great ways to strengthen a relationship.

It would be a perfect world if there were no conflicts in your interactions with instructors. However, there may be a time in your college career when you don't feel as though you have a strong, respectful relationship. If you experience conflict with a professor, be sure to discuss the issue as soon as possible—and in private. Use "I" statements to explain your perspective rather than "you" statements. For example, saying "I am confused about what our exam will cover" is better than saying "You were confusing when you talked about the exam." Using "I" statements also underscores your control over your actions and reactions during the conflict. Look, too, for common ground that can help you manage the conflict maturely and respectfully.

Although a good relationship with your professors is a key to enjoying your education experience, remember that professors are not equals in the relationship and still must challenge you to learn and stretch your concept of yourself and others as well as evaluate you during and at the end of the term. It will be important for you to understand boundaries in relationships, as discussed later in the chapter.

ADVISORS, COUNSELORS, AND LEARNING SUPPORT STAFF

In addition to professors, some of the most important relationships that you will forge during college will be with people whose sole job is to make sure you succeed. Counselors and advisors will be key people in your academic career, so be sure to take the time to get to know these individuals. Tutors, mentors, and other support staff can also play important roles in the success of your college experience.

Advisors

Your advisor may be the first person you encounter at college. An advisor explains to you what courses you should take, how many hours you should schedule per semester, and how to plan ahead. An advisor works for you; it is his or her job to see that you complete your degree as smoothly as possible. You may be lucky enough to have the same advisor throughout your college career. In that case, regular contact will help keep the lines of communication open. If you have a different advisor each semester, you may wish to find one person on whom you can rely to act as a regular advisor. That person may be a former professor or a counselor who has advised you in the past. The goal is to find someone on campus who has an interest in your education beyond one semester.

Counselors

You should take the opportunity to get to know at least one counselor on your campus. Whether it is a career counselor or a disability counselor, make it a point to schedule an appointment while you are in college. Getting to know counselors is a great way to obtain more information about the school and its services. For example, a career counselor may inform you of a career fair or recruiting day. He can also help you prepare a résumé and practice interviewing. Counselors for students with personal issues are another valuable resource for you. Even if you do not need personal counseling, you may benefit from a relationship with someone who does it professionally. This type of counselor can give you tips for managing stress and dealing with difficult people, just to name a few experiences you may have in college.

"One of the best relationships I have with someone on campus is with my disability counselor. She is my biggest cheerleader when I do well in a class. I see her regularly so that I can get the support I need."

—Ashley, 27, student

Tutors, Mentors, and Student Leaders

In addition to the key people already mentioned, a variety of other people work or volunteer their time to help students achieve their academic, career, and personal goals. For example, working one-on-one with a tutor in a learning assistance lab can provide you with a unique relationship, because a tutor can really get to know what your learning needs are and how to help you fulfill them. A tutor can be a great resource for understanding the material for a class because he is often a student himself or has just recently taken the class.

Student or peer mentors are other helpers you can find on your college campus who can be instrumental in keeping you on track to success. Peer mentors are usually current students who have been successful in their classes and are willing to provide support to new students who may need extra encouragement to navigate the choppy waters of the first few semesters. Peer mentors may give you advice for studying, for choosing a degree, or for balancing family, work, and college. And just think—if you are also successful, you may be a great peer mentor for a student who is just like you when you started!

Finally, you may come in contact with student leaders, whether in special clubs, associations, or student government. Unlike peer mentors, whose primary role is to work one on one with learners, student leaders work with both students and the college or organization to provide leadership in certain areas. For example, you may encourage a student government representative to ask college officials for more family-friendly activities that you can attend with your children. If administrators agree, then the Student Government Association may work with you and other students to find out which activities are best and you may even help organize an event to get more students involved.

CLASSMATES

Getting to know your classmates can make the difference between struggling all alone and meeting new challenges with a like-minded support group. Who else can relate to the challenge of studying for a chemistry final exam than the students in the class with you? Think about it: Your classmates may be a majority of the people who populate your college campus. You may get to know well only three or four professors throughout your college career, but you have the potential of meeting and working with hundreds of students.

In addition to sharing experiences with your fellow students, you can also rely on them as study partners or emergency note-takers if you can't be in class. Another benefit to making friends with classmates is that you can learn about other classes, instructors, and degree programs from them. Their firsthand knowledge could help you choose the best classes and the most promising programs.

Getting to know your classmates can be relatively simple, especially because you will be sitting close to them during each class. Here are a few tips for creating lasting relationships with fellow students:

- Introduce yourself to those sitting around you. It may be helpful to arrive early and start conversations with other students.
- Exchange phone numbers or email addresses with classmates who seem reliable and trustworthy. You may need to call someone if you miss class.
- Offer to study with someone. Not only will you help a classmate, but you will also help yourself learn the material.
- Keep in contact with friends even after the semester is over. Although you may not share classes anymore, you still can study and offer support to one another.

"I share with my family all my accomplishments. I put my tests on the refrigerator when I do well. I also share with them when I am stressed out. I have found they really support me when I explain what is going on with me."

—Lakeshia, 27, student

FAMILY AND FRIENDS

Entering college will be a new experience not only for you, but also for your family and friends, especially if they have not gone to college. Communication, then, will be the key to weathering any changes in your relationships. They need to know how you feel about going to college, and they need to be aware that you will be going through changes while you are there. Surely you will be experiencing changes in your outlook on life, your belief in yourself, and your attitude toward the future.

When these changes occur, people around you may react differently. Some will be supportive and excited that you have created personal goals and are achieving them. A few, however, may react negatively, possibly jealous of your success or your new "lease on life" because they either did not have the same

INTEGRITY MATTERS

The underlying factor of integrity in a relationship is trust. If you can trust others, then you will be better able to learn, grow, expand, and improve yourself. If you do not have trust, then you may shut yourself off from others and experiences that are new to you. Trusting others takes time—it isn't an overnight event. Give people reasons to trust you and then deliver on your promises. Likewise, put your trust in others, giving them an opportunity to prove themselves trustworthy.

A specific part of trust in relationships is reliability or, expressed another way, doing what you say you will do. If your classmate asks you to take notes for him on days he cannot be in class and you fail to do so each time, then you lack reliability. Your classmate will not be able to trust you to help him. If you agree to take notes knowing that you may not be able to do it, then you are not being honest—with him or yourself.

YOUR TURN How have you demonstrated that you are trustworthy? ■ What was the effect? ■ In what areas of your life could you trust others—or even yourself—more? ■ What can you do to improve trust?

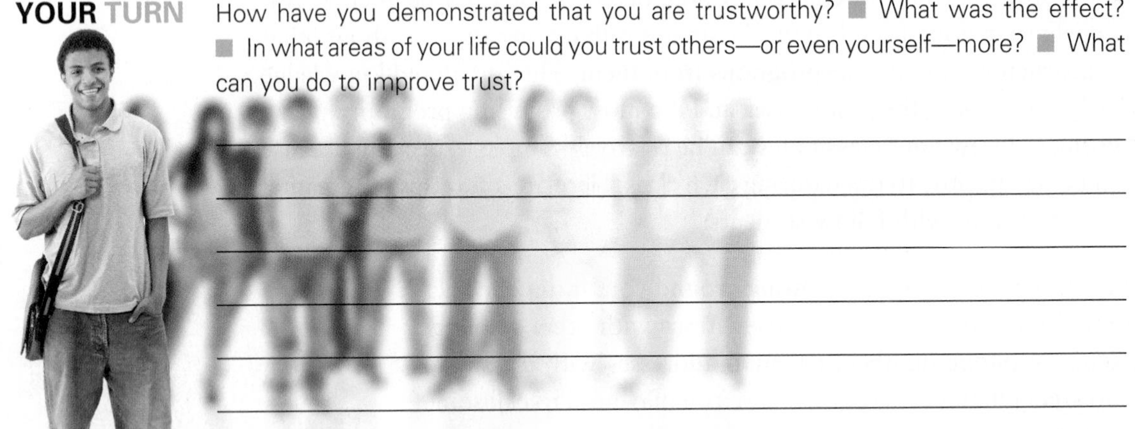

opportunities or squandered the chances that they did have. Others who react negatively may be insecure about themselves and feel "dumb" around a person in college; these same people often fear that once the college student graduates, he or she will leave them for a "better" spouse or friend. Also, there are parents who do not want to acknowledge that their children are grown adults who are and should be making decisions on their own; parents are also often worried that their children will be exposed to value systems and beliefs that are very different from what they taught. Whatever the reasons that the people around you react to the changes you experience, be comforted by the fact that you will survive, and better yet, you will have more of an understanding of the *diversity* of opinions that you will encounter. Learning how to deal with different people in college will allow you to apply what you learn to your personal relationships.

REFLECTION *exercise* 4.1

What relationships on campus have you cultivated so far? What challenges might you have in getting to know tutors, student leaders, and mentors?

Your Terms of SUCCESS

WHEN YOU SEE . . .	IT MEANS . . .
Administrator	A person who manages staff at a college.
Advisor	A person who works with students to provide guidance and planning for a degree.
Ageism	Discrimination toward a person in a certain age group.
Counselor	A person who advises students on personal, academic, or career matters.
Diversity	A state of difference; variety.
Due process	Formal procedures designed to protect a person's rights.
Faculty	A person or persons who teach.
Homophobia	Irrational fear of homosexuals.
Instructor	A person who teaches.
Mentor	A person who provides advice or guidance.
Peer mentor/peer leader	A person of equal status who provides advice or guidance.
Racism	Hatred of a race; discrimination toward a person of a certain race.
Sexism	Hatred of a gender; discrimination toward a certain gender.
Sexual harassment	Unwanted or offensive sexual advances, usually by a person in a superior position.
Tutor	A person who provides academic support.

APPRECIATING Diversity

An exciting part of college is that you will meet and work with people from different age groups and backgrounds. Unlike a traditional university, at your community college you may be part of a study group that includes a grandparent, home-schooled teenager, veteran, administrative assistant to a dean, full-time detective, and minister. Because of this variety, community college students need to be especially sensitive to others' values and perspectives, which is one of the purposes of diversity.

"I thought I was open-minded until I started taking classes and attending events on campus. I am amazed at how many ideas and people who have them are out in the world. I feel like I still have a lot to learn about others."
—Mary-Li, 28, student

A simple definition of *diversity* is "difference" or "variety." Another term heard when diversity is discussed in a college setting is *multiculturalism*. Although the two words have different implications, they often have the same motivation—to expose the community to a variety of ideas, cultures, viewpoints, beliefs, and backgrounds.

When people talk about diversity, they usually mean diversity in race, gender, ethnicity, age, and religion. Colleges that want to promote diversity on their campuses often look for opportunities to hire and enroll people from different backgrounds than the majority of the campus population. They do this with the belief that diversity enriches the educational experience for all because it exposes faculty, staff, and students to new ideas and challenges our preconceived notions of the world around us.

GENDER AND SEXUAL ORIENTATION DIVERSITY

The latest educational statistics show that almost two-thirds of the college student population across the country is female (American Association of Community Colleges, 2010). In the past few decades, women have enrolled in college in record numbers. It may seem strange to think that several decades ago, there were far fewer women in college, especially in law and medical schools. No doubt, you will encounter gender diversity at your college, and what this means for you is that you will have plenty of opportunities to work with both men and women and explore any preconceptions you may have about the differences between the sexes. You may have to pay more attention to society's assumptions about gender and be more attuned to how language, art, and the sciences, among other disciplines, perpetuate gender stereotypes.

Sexual orientation is another type of diversity that you will more than likely encounter in college if you have not already. Homosexuality and bisexuality are just two categories of sexual orientation diversity. Organizations such as the Human Rights Campaign (www.hrc.org) strive to educate others about discrimination that can—and does—occur because of the stereotypes and prejudice that exist regarding sexual orientation. Why should you know more about sexual orientation as a part of diversity? Sexuality is part of the human experience, and one purpose of higher education is to help you better understand and appreciate your own and others' human experience. Recognizing sexual orientation as a category of diversity gives you a more complete picture of humankind.

Sexual Harassment

Colleges and universities as well as many workplaces have been aggressively educating students and employees about recognizing and preventing sexual harassment for decades. Sexual harassment, by legal definition, refers to a superior, or a person in power, sexually harassing a subordinate, or a person with less power than the harasser. College and employee policies often broaden the definition, however, to include any unwanted sexual advances that create an uncomfortable situation or hostile environment. This broader definition means that, in college, a student can sexually harass another student or a student can sexually harass a professor—or any other scenario that involves students, prospective students, and employees and guests of the college. To further round out the definition, women can sexually harass men and people can experience sexual harassment from colleagues of the same sex.

Despite educational programs for new students and required seminars for employees, colleges—like any place where people live and work—are not immune to instances of sexual harassment. According to Katz (2005), the American Psychological Association surveyed female graduate students about their experiences in college. The survey results found that 12.7% of female students experienced sexual harassment and 21% avoided taking certain classes for fear of being sexually harassed. Surveys about sexual harassment in the workplace paint a dimmer picture, with 31% of female employees and 7% of male employees claiming to be sexually harassed at work.

Educating yourself about the seriousness of sexual harassment, your college's policy on the subject, and common behaviors often considered sexual harassment are steps in the right direction to minimizing incidents. For sure, sexual harassment is no laughing matter, and a review of your college's statement on the matter will reveal the college's discipline policy for those who sexually harass others. Some college policies list the following behaviors as sexual harassment:

- Offensive jokes or comments of a sexual nature
- Requests or demands for sexual favors in return for favorable treatment or rewards (e.g., a good grade)
- Unwanted physical contact or assault
- Showing or distributing sexually explicit materials to others
- Posting sexually explicit images or websites in college-owned online course management systems or emailing those images or links to websites from college-owned computers

Although not always considered sexual harassment if material is not distributed to others, accessing sexually explicit websites with college-owned computer hardware and software may be prohibited conduct that will result in disciplinary action on the part of the college and possible criminal charges.

As with all forms of diversity in which possible problems can arise, be sensitive to others; treat everyone you meet on campus with respect; and be honest with others if you feel uncomfortable in a situation or with certain conversational topics.

RACIAL, ETHNIC, AND CULTURAL DIVERSITY

Over the last 20 years, colleges have embraced and developed multicultural studies in response to the past emphasis on "white, male, Western" history, ideas, and culture. Cultural and racial ignorance at its worst has led to the deaths of millions of people all over the world. Understanding and appreciation for the diversity in culture and ethnicity at its best create connections between peoples who have much to learn from each other. Figure 4.1 provides you with tips that can help you better appreciate diversity.

GENERATIONAL DIVERSITY

The idea that our parents' generation is vastly different from our own, which will be greatly different from our children's generation, is considered a fact of

FIGURE 4.1 Tips for Appreciating Racial, Ethnic, and Cultural Diversity

- Work to eliminate all racial, ethnic, or cultural stereotypes or slurs from your thoughts and vocabulary. Stop yourself before you speak and ask, "Is this a stereotype or could it be offensive to some?"
- Racial, ethnic, and cultural jokes, images, and cartoons are insensitive at best, harassment at worst. Avoid making fun of others' heritage. Be sensitive to others' backgrounds.
- Learn more about your heritage and culture.
- Strive to learn more about cultures that are new and different to you.
- Participate in college and community cultural celebrations.
- Attend seminars, guest lectures, and artistic performances about different cultures and countries.
- Do not tolerate others who exhibit racial and cultural insensitivity. If you don't feel comfortable saying something to them, then avoid them and similar situations in the future.

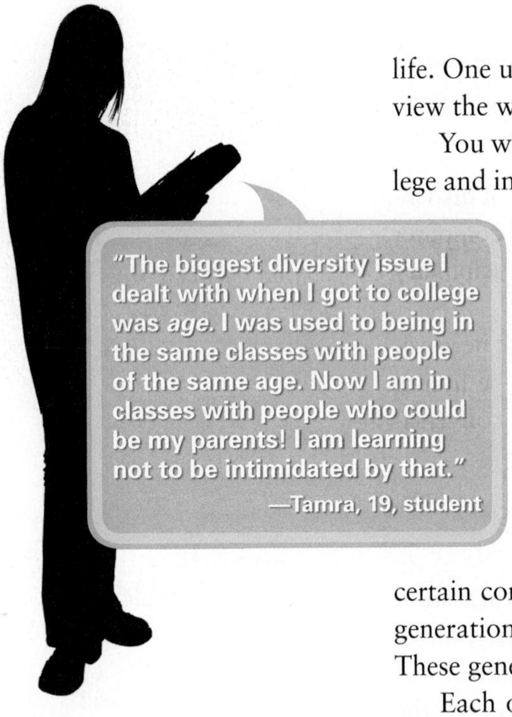

life. One unifying viewpoint among the generations is that different generations view the world differently.

You will, no doubt, encounter generational diversity at your community college and in the world of work—more so than in generations past. The American Association of Community Colleges (2009) cites the following statistics: The average age of a community college student is 29; 42% are between 22 and 39 and 43% are 21 or younger.

> "The biggest diversity issue I dealt with when I got to college was *age.* I was used to being in the same classes with people of the same age. Now I am in classes with people who could be my parents! I am learning not to be intimidated by that."
> —Tamra, 19, student

What is a "generational cohort" and what does it mean for your college and work experience? According to Ron Zemke, Claire Raines, and Bob Filipczak, in their book *Generations at Work: Managing the Clash of Veterans, Boomers, Xers, and Nexters in Your Workplace* (2000), a generational cohort is a group of the population that was born within a certain period of time, that marked as important some of the same world events, and that hold certain common values. In their book, the authors recognize and describe four generations that can be found in the workplace (and college for that matter). These generations are defined and described in Table 4.1.

Each of the generational groups, the authors contend, holds certain values that influence how they work with others and how they achieve personal success. The diverse core values and attitudes can create enriching experiences for generations that work together, or they can be a cause of conflict for those who do not understand and appreciate fellow students and coworkers of a different generation. Misunderstanding generational differences at its worst can become ageism, which is discriminating against someone because of his or her age. The key with generational diversity—as with all types of diversity—is to learn more about yourself and others and appreciate the differences.

TABLE 4.1 Generations, Birth Years, and Core Values

Generation	Birth Years	Core Values
Veterans	1922–1943	Dedication, sacrifice, patience, respect for authority
Baby Boomers	1943–1960	Health and wellness, optimism, personal growth
Generation Xers	1960–1980	Diversity, fun, self-reliance, global thinking
Nexters or Millenials	1980–2000	Civic duty, morality, street smarts

OTHER KINDS OF DIVERSITY

Dealing successfully with diversity includes more than working well with people from different national, religious, or political backgrounds, or with different abilities or disabilities; you will also need to consider the diversity of attitudes and work ethics. For example, not everyone you meet in college or in your career will value the same things you do. What will you do if you work with people whose values conflict with your own? What will you do if the differences between your own and others' work ethics cause conflict?

You will get the opportunity to experience these differences in class when you are assigned a group project or presentation. Even if you all are the same gender, race, religion, and age, you will still find that each of you is different and has different expectations and opinions of the assignment. Being able to work with others, regardless of their learning and work styles, is a skill. The more you are exposed to diversity, the more you will be able to handle and appreciate the differences between you and everyone you meet.

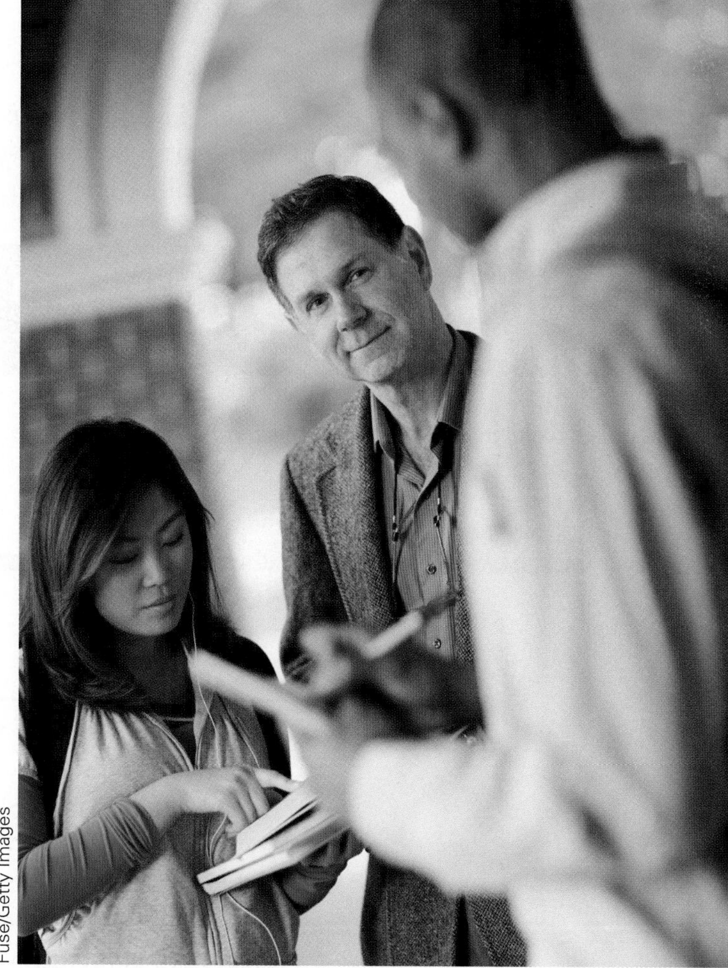

It is important to make the time to develop relationships with professors, advisors, and classmates.

Fuse/Getty Images

TEACHING STYLES DIVERSITY

You will encounter many different teaching styles. It has been said that most professors teach the way they learn best, but there are college instructors who use a variety of teaching methods to encourage student learning. You will be more successful if you can identify each teaching style and understand how to adapt to it. Gone are the days of saying, "I just can't learn in her class. She doesn't teach the way I need

TABLE 4.2 Teaching Styles

Teaching Style	Description	Tips for Success
Lecture	Professor talks for the majority of the class; a brief outline may be included; questions are limited or discouraged; usually very structured	Practice good listening skills; record lectures with permission; take good notes during class and review them frequently
Discussion	Professor poses a question and requires students in the class to answer and build on an idea or theme	Practice good listening skills; record theme or question for the discussion; note repeated ideas; record essence of each person's contribution; participate in discussion
Project	Professor bases class learning on projects; provides instruction for assignment; assigns roles; monitors progress	Make connection between project assignment and course objectives; ask for feedback during project to make sure you are progressing; refer to course materials for extra help
Problem solving	Professor poses or writes a problem on the board; walks through solving the problem	Break process down into steps; identify any step that is unclear; ask for extra practice and feedback if needed

her to." Like the people who must work together in groups with sensitivity to one another's personalities, you, too, will need to identify your learning style and how it will fit into your professor's teaching style. Ideally, your instructor will recognize that his students have different learning style strengths and adapt his material to those learning styles, but not everyone you will encounter in college will vary his teaching style to meet your needs. Your best bet is to be ready to learn no matter what the teaching style.

To help you recognize the different methods of teaching, Table 4.2 contains a description of each and tips for making the most of the different types of classroom instruction.

CRITICAL THINKING *exercise* 4.2

There are some communities and groups around the world that believe a "pure" (no diversity) group, race, or community is ideal. What would be the benefits of being in a group that valued "sameness"? What would be the drawbacks?

FIGHTING Hate

To understand the problem of hate in our world, all you have to do is open a newspaper or click on the latest news story online. Hatred for others because of skin color, religious beliefs, or sexual orientation has fueled violence and discrimination all over the world. Whether it involves millions of people being slaughtered in a third-world country or one person being beaten up for his beliefs, the remedy to begin combating hatred is the same: learning to understand others and appreciate diversity. To do that, we must confront the very ideas and processes that lead people to greater acts of hatred.

STEREOTYPES

Stereotyping is an oversimplified opinion of someone or something. We often use stereotypes to make quick decisions every day. When choosing a checkout line, we may make a quick decision as to which is the fastest based on the people in line and what they have in their carts. When playing outfield on a softball team, we may stereotype the smaller players as weaker hitters, which will cause us to move closer to the infield. Parents also encourage children, who have difficulty making complex decisions, to stereotype strangers in order to protect them. Although these stereotypes are not necessarily harmful, they can create problems

TECH TACTICS

Using Technology to Get Ahead

Online classes provide a rich learning environment and one of the benefits to online learning is that students can participate without being "seen"; this often means that the stereotypes and prejudices we often have about how someone looks cannot be used in cyberspace. However, it may also mean that students must be extra sensitive when they make comments or post in online classes. Because they cannot tell the age, race, gender, socioeconomic status, or much of anything else about fellow students, students should respond to others and address the material in ways that clearly communicate while understanding that others may not agree.

RECOMMENDED SITES

- www.bucks.edu/online/dlresources/etiquette.htm Bucks County Community College provides a brief quiz on "netiquette." How polite are you online? The answers to your responses will help you figure out what areas you need to work on.
- www.kent.edu/dl/Technology/Etiquette.cfm Kent State University provides a focused list of the most useful reminders for acting appropriately online.
- www.netmanners.com This site focuses mostly on business applications to Internet etiquette, but it gives a great foundation for any type of electronic communication.

for us. Our superficial analysis may put us in the slowest checkout line; we may move so close to the infield that the smaller player hits the ball over our heads; we may confuse children about the characteristics of a stranger, making it difficult for them to trust adults.

Stereotypes can serve a purpose in the short run, but as the examples illustrate, stereotypes do not take into consideration all the facts. For the most part, stereotypes keep us from having to think about the complexity of issues, leaving us unable to appreciate the beauty of diversity. In essence, stereotypes are shorthand for evaluating situations and making decisions, but if used repeatedly, they can become prejudice and discrimination.

PREJUDICE

Prejudice is literally "pre-judging" a person or situation without knowing the facts. Prejudice is often based on stereotyping, showing how stereotyping can easily become negative. Let's take a seemingly harmless example of stereotyping that can result in prejudice: If you assume that all smaller softball players are weak hitters, then you may take that stereotype a bit further by disliking playing with smaller players because they don't make the game very challenging.

Like stereotyping, prejudice is a judgment based on little or no information or misinformation about a person or subject. In other words, it is based on ignorance or lack of correct information. That is why education is so important—you can avoid prejudging people or situations by learning about them and making decisions based on *knowledge* rather than ignorance. Although we cannot always avoid stereotyping, we can eliminate prejudice and subsequently eradicate discrimination by making the decision to learn about others.

There are a variety of ways we can categorize and classify ourselves and others. Understood as one way of knowing ourselves better, these types of diversity are helpful tools. If they are used to stereotype and then make judgments about people based on these stereotypes, then the categories become means to discrimination.

Sexist Attitudes

The increased number of women in college has changed the culture to be more sensitive and inclusive to women, but stereotypes and prejudice about females still exist. However, sexism is not limited to prejudice against women. Men, too, can suffer from sexist attitudes that are based on stereotypes.

Homophobia

Sexual orientation prejudice often takes the form of homophobia, or fear of homosexuals. Homophobia is sometimes born out of ignorance of sexual orientation diversity, and sometimes it comes from a person's own background and values.

Racist Attitudes

Racist attitudes can be obvious or subtle. People can hold racist views, like all other prejudices, and not realize that they are being intolerant of others. Asking people of other races what kinds of racism they experience is one way to under-

EMOTIONAL INTELLIGENCE *Check-Up*

Independence

What emotions do you have in this situation?

FEEL

What is the optimal outcome of the situation for you?

THINK

What attitude and positive action will help you achieve the outcome you want?

ACT

Emotionally intelligent people acknowledge their feelings in a situation, stop and think about what is involved, and then choose an act that will best help resolve any problems. Read the following common situation and work through the three steps in the boxes.

SITUATION

Your college has just started an organization for gay, lesbian, bisexual, and transgendered students. Because you grew up in a small community that was not tolerant of sexual orientation diversity, you have some preconceptions of what such an organization will do to the campus community. Although your new friends in college want to join because they want to get involved in an organization that supports gay marriage and AIDS awareness (two annual rallies that the organization sponsors), your classmates who grew up with you in your small community are completely opposed to such a group and have told you they will not be able to be friends with you if you join or even associate with members. What do you do?

stand what they perceive as prejudice. Monitoring your own words, actions, and attitudes is another way to be more sensitive to other races and cultures. You may think you don't mean any harm by what you say or do, but the recipients of your ideas may not always agree.

Ageist Attitudes

As you read earlier in the chapter, different generations have different values and viewpoints. An environment in which people from different generations work closely together can be exciting or tense, depending on how much people are willing to recognize, understand, and appreciate their generational differences. Problems arise, though, when people have prejudicial attitudes about a certain age group. We usually think that ageist attitudes stereotype mainly older people, but younger people can also experience prejudicial views directed at them.

DISCRIMINATION

Discrimination occurs when an action is taken on the basis of a prejudice. If, for instance, you decide that you do not want to play softball against teams with smaller players because you believe they are not as fun as teams with bigger players, then you have discriminated against smaller players and their teams. Because of recent laws and lawsuits, colleges and other places of business are sensitive to discrimination issues and spend substantial time and resources educating employees about the subject. It will be an important part of your education to understand how and why people discriminate so that you can be prepared for similar problems stemming from prejudice, which is why this chapter spends a considerable amount of time on this subject.

Sexism, racism, and ageism are the most common types of discrimination in the workplace. Even though most organizations strive hard to eliminate overt discrimination, other types of prejudice can often appear in everyday situations. For example, a coworker may declare that she won't hire anyone from a certain college because she believes that all its graduates are more interested in partying than working. Your boss may state his disdain for people from a certain part of the country and then refuse to promote an employee who is originally from the same area. Although you may not be able to change everyone's mind, you should be attuned to these more subtle, and sometimes acceptable, forms of discrimination and make an effort to eliminate them.

COLLABORATION *exercise* 4.3

Working in a group, choose one of the groups noted previously who often encounter prejudice and discuss how the college or the community can help people appreciate this type of diversity. What events could help the community learn more about fighting hate or more about celebrating diversity?

RESOLVING Conflict

While you are in college, you may find yourself in a conflict that must be resolved in order for you to be successful and satisfied. The conflict can arise with a family member, a classmate, or even a professor. How you handle the conflict may have long-term consequences that directly tie to your ability to complete a degree. Oftentimes, a minor conflict, such as miscommunication or a misunderstanding, can easily be resolved. Other times, the disagreement may be larger than you can handle with a calm conversation.

CREATING BOUNDARIES

Because you will be surrounded by a diverse group of people, it may be difficult for you to create and maintain the traditional boundaries that exist between students and their counselors, professors, administrators, and learning support staff. It almost seems contradictory, but boundaries may be necessary at the same time that you are getting to know others. Why should you refrain from close relationships with professors and advisors when you need them to get to know you if you are to ask for a referral or recommendation?

For one, some colleges discourage intimately personal relationships between professors and students, just as many companies prohibit the same type of overly friendly relationships between supervisors and employees, because such relationships can be problematic. For example, intimate relationships can result in perceived or actual unfair evaluation or treatment. Because a professor is considered a superior, the college views the professor's role as one of authority and power. Many sexual harassment policies and laws are built on the imbalance of power between a person in authority and a subordinate.

Another possible problem is that other students may see the relationship as favoritism and feel as though they are being treated unfairly. Additionally, sexual relationships between students and college personnel are sometimes strictly prohibited at colleges. If you have not already done so, check your student handbook regarding your college's policy about relationships between students and faculty. Ultimately, you will need to make the decision that is best for you and your situation as to how friendly you should be with faculty or other college officials.

If you get along well with your professor and genuinely enjoy her company, then your best move is to respect the professor–student relationship while you are in class. You can do this by meeting your professor during her office hours on campus and keeping conversations focused on your progress in your classes and your career plans. You can then continue the friendship after you have finished the semester and have no intentions of taking another class with that professor again. Some friendships between professors and students are long-lasting, so consider cultivating them once the class is over.

WHEN A PROBLEM ARISES

A time may arise when you have a problem in one of your classes. If it does, you can be assured that the college's employees will work with you to resolve it. There are, however, rules and procedures regarding how to resolve a problem at a college. Knowing and following these procedures will ensure that any problem is handled appropriately and quickly.

The first step to resolving a conflict in class is to define the problem. Is it a communication problem? Is it a problem with the course material? Is it a problem with the course standards? Once you have defined the problem, your next step is to discuss the problem with the person involved directly. If the problem is with your instructor, make an appointment during her office hours to discuss the issue. If you are emotional—angry, upset, nervous—wait until you have calmed down to meet. Your goal in talking with the instructor is to resolve the conflict.

"I once had a problem with a professor when I misread a comment he wrote on a graded paper. I was angry for two days. When I went to talk to him, I realized I had misread his handwriting and that he actually agreed with a point I had made. Now I know to speak up sooner when I think there is a problem."

—Wayne, 30, student

For the process of conflict resolution to work, you will need to complete the first two steps. Starting at the top will only delay resolution. If you are not satisfied with the result or if you feel the problem has gotten worse, not better, move to the next step: talking to the department chair or dean. You

Spencer Grant/PhotoEdit

Spending time getting involved in campus activities and volunteer opportunities is a great way to get to meet new people.

will no doubt be asked if you have met with the instructor. Again, your goal at this step is to resolve the issue. Occasionally, the instructor may be called in to help reach a resolution. Staying calm and focused on resolving the conflict will be to your advantage. In the event that the problem is not solved at this level, your last stop is with the dean of students or vice president for instruction.

TIPS FOR LASTING RELATIONSHIPS

As discussed at the beginning of the chapter, community college students often have a harder time cultivating friendships because of their busy schedules and because they do not typically spend four years with the same group of people. What else can you do to forge relationships in college?

Leave time in your schedule to talk with friends or meet with instructors. If you must leave directly after class to get to work, you will not be as successful in cultivating important relationships. One way to ensure that you connect with your professors is to make an appointment with them during the semester to ask questions or get feedback on your progress. Your ulterior motive is to cultivate a relationship with them. Also, be sure to approach conflict as an opportunity to learn more about yourself, and always act with integrity. Lasting relationships are built on trust and doing what is right.

REFLECTION *exercise* 4.4

From what you have learned about diversity, how can you make changes in your interactions with others that will show that you value and appreciate diverse peoples and situations?

Transfer Tips: FROM COLLEGE TO UNIVERSITY

The Relationships You Foster Now Will Open Doors after Transfer

Your relationships with advisors, counselors, and professors should yield more contacts at your new school. Advisors and counselors will be able to recommend certain programs and administrators. Professors will be able to put in a good word with the people they know at your transfer school, which may mean extra consideration for admission into a program or for a scholarship.

Those same relationships may also prove fruitful if your advisors, counselors, or professors have inside knowledge of little-known internships and aid, or if they know about deadline extensions and special transfer scholarships. The closer your relationships, the better able you will be to use your connections to make a smooth transfer. Advisors, counselors, and professors can also provide advice about the particular challenges you may face once you have completed the move.

Transfer Tips: FROM COLLEGE TO CAREER

Dealing with Diversity Is a Key to Success on the Job

We sometimes think that once we reach our ultimate educational goal and have started our dream career, we will be magically transported to a world in which everyone gets along. Unfortunately, we are brought back down from the clouds as early as the first day on the job.

Certainly, you will never stop needing to make positive connections with others or to redefine the relationships you already have. You will also encounter diversity on a daily basis and will have to rely on what you have learned in college (and life in general) in order to consider others' feelings, beliefs, and attitudes. What you have learned in college about other cultures, time periods, and philosophical and political ideas should provide you with well-rounded views that will make it easier to work with and appreciate your diverse coworkers.

References and Recommended Readings

American Association of Community Colleges. (2010). "Fast facts." Retrieved November 1, 2010, from www.aacc.nche.edu/AboutCC/Pages/fastfacts.aspx

Katz, N. (2005). Sexual harassment statistics in the workplace and in education. Retrieved July 5, 2005, from http://womenissues.about.com/cs/sexdiscrimination/a/sexharassstats.htm

Kuh, G., Kinzie, J., Schuh, J. H., Whitt, E. J., et al. (2005). *Student success in college: Creating conditions that matter.* San Francisco: Jossey-Bass.

Zemke, R., Raines, C., & Filipczak, B. (2000). *Generations at work: Managing the clash of veterans, boomers, xers, and nexters in your workplace.* New York: AMACOM Books.

CHAPTER five

READING, Listening, and Note Taking

IN THIS chapter Whether you love it or find it a challenge, reading will be an integral part of your education in college. Can you imagine getting a degree and *not* reading a page? Technology may have changed the way we read and how we incorporate written information, but it has not changed the importance of reading in becoming an educated individual. Like developing good reading skills, learning to listen and take notes effectively can give you the

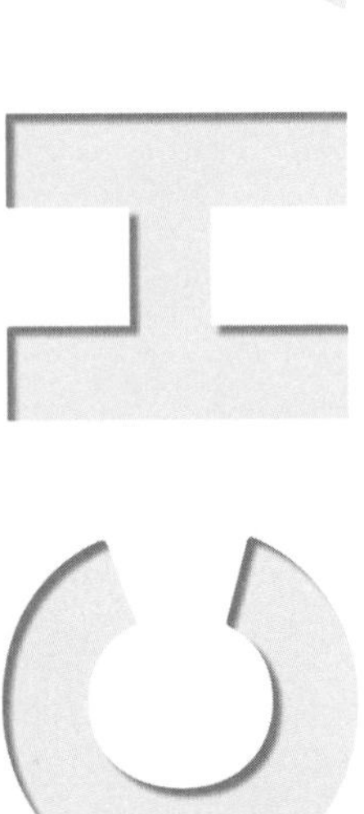

edge in college because you will be able to take in more information and remember it more easily. This chapter discusses reading expectations and skills, various note-taking strategies, and improvements you can make to be a better listener.

More specifically, after completing this chapter, you will be able to do the following:

- Identify college reading expectations and understand different reading strategies.
- Define active reading and critical reading.
- Describe ways to listen more effectively, including eliminating barriers.
- Discuss effective note-taking strategies.

COLLEGE READING Expectations

Reading—and reading effectively—is a crucial part of student success. As previous chapters have mentioned, reading class handouts and college publications as well as your textbooks is essential to success in college. Reading is important to your college education and lifelong learning for many reasons; the following are just a few incentives for making reading an integral part of your daily college work:

- Reading provides you with basic information that you can use to create knowledge of a subject.
- Reading improves your understanding of others and the world around you by exposing you to new viewpoints, ideas, and cultures.
- Reading helps you understand yourself, which will assist you in making better life choices.

Despite this, it must be acknowledged that some students just do not enjoy reading because of bad experiences in school or due to learning difficulties. For these students, reading can be a challenge to academic fulfillment. One common student complaint is that the assigned reading may seem dull and difficult to comprehend. The trick to enjoying your reading assignments—until you get into classes that pertain to your major or career choice—is to think of each reading assignment as an opportunity to improve your comprehension *and* enjoyment of the course content.

In addition to the subject matter that you will encounter in college reading, you will also find the reading load to be greater than in high school or in most jobs. If you are taking four three-credit-hour classes, you can expect to read more than 100 pages a week if each professor assigns a chapter from the textbook. This number does not reflect full-length novels, supplementary articles, required periodical subscriptions, reserved library materials, online resources, and your own notes from class—all of which may be part of your weekly reading load. The truth about college reading is that there will be plenty for you to read and that you will also be held accountable for not only reading, but comprehending and thinking critically about the material.

WHAT TO DO WITH A READING ASSIGNMENT

The majority of your reading in college will most likely be assigned by your instructors. When you first get a reading assignment, you will need to spend a little time preparing to read, which will help you maximize the benefit from the time that you have available. No doubt, in the first week of classes, you will receive handouts, syllabi, and chapters to read in your textbook. How do you manage it all without falling behind and feeling overwhelmed at the start of the semester? First, remember that all written material that your professors give you needs to be read. You will be held responsible for it immediately or at a later date; therefore, you will need to create a process for reading and remembering what you have read.

"I have learned that I enjoy reading the more I do it. I didn't like all the required reading at first, but once I got into some of it, I realized how much the information can help me in everyday life."
—Broderick, 23, student

No matter how big or small the assignment, treat the reading seriously. In other words, make a conscious effort to read and remember important information. A positive attitude about the reading assignment will help make the other steps easier to complete. Before you begin reading, you will also want to organize

TECH TACTICS

Using Technology to Get Ahead

The Internet offers many great resources to help you improve your reading skills. For example, for students who prefer to hear the words rather than read them, there are often audio formats of material you need to read. Some publishers provide additional podcasts that accompany their textbooks and provide summaries of the material; some e-books and databases have audio files of the material in which the works are read by a computer; and software such as JAWS provide students who need assistance reading with audio versions of material on a computer screen.

RECOMMENDED WEBSITES

- www.dartmouth.edu/~acskills/success/reading.html Reading Your Textbooks Effectively and Efficiently is a great site sponsored by Dartmouth College. The page includes helpful links to other sources, such as "Six Reading Myths."
- www.readinga-z.com/more/reading_strat.html Reading and Word Attack Strategies are simple methods for helping students with comprehension issues, including understanding vocabulary. Great tips for any reader at any level.
- www.providence.edu/oas/shop/reading.htm Providence College offers good tips for college students who want to improve comprehension and reading speed.

assignments according to size, importance, and date of completion; start with the most important documents first, and then work your way down the stack. Shorter assignments can be completed first unless their due dates are far off.

To increase your chances of reading effectively, set a definite time and place to read. Just as you would set a time to study or go to work, you will need to schedule time to read, preferably at the same time each day. Finding a comfortable, quiet area to read is also important because it will put you in the mood to focus on what you are reading. Equally important to setting a definite time is to establish routine breaks from reading. Get up, walk around the room, get a drink of water, and get the circulation going in your legs again. Taking breaks in which you physically move around the room will help your concentration and keep you from falling asleep.

In addition to finding the right place, consider setting a purpose for reading. Learning to understand and set purposes for reading will make the assignments easier to comprehend and complete. For example, if your reading purpose is to improve your understanding of networking, then when you sit down with the textbook for your computer networking administration class, you are in the right frame of mind. Conversely, if your reading purpose is to be entertained when you read a chapter in economics, you may be disappointed and less receptive to remembering what you have read.

As noted in previous chapters, writing down goals is the first step to realizing them. The same holds true for reading. If you want to increase your reading speed, vocabulary, and understanding of the material, you should do more than give them passing consideration. Set specific, concrete goals for individual assignments or the whole semester. An example of a reading goal could be to increase the number of pages you can read in one sitting or to learn five new words a week and use them.

Finally, take care of yourself throughout the semester as you do your assigned work. You won't be able to read effectively if you are overtired, hungry, or sick. Don't try to force yourself to read if physical or psychological issues distract you. Too much sugar and caffeine and too little sleep can make reading more difficult; so can certain medications and emotional distractions. If you cannot concentrate, return to the material when you are feeling better, although sometimes, you will just need to dig in and get it done regardless of how you feel.

READING IN THE DISCIPLINES

The following strategies for reading in the disciplines show just a sample of the material you may encounter in college.

Math

Take your time in reading both the written information and explanations as well as the visual representations of problems and steps for solving them. Reading assigned chapters *before* you get to class will help you check your reading comprehension.

Literature

You may find you have more reading in literature classes—novels, short stories, plays, and poetry. Start early with these long reading assignments and take notes along the way. Depending on the complexity of the literature, you may need to read the work a few times, especially poetry, and sound each word out. Although sounding out individual words, or subvocalization, is often considered a reading difficulty, it may be necessary to slow down and read short pieces of literature aloud. Also, pay attention to details when reading fiction and poetry.

Languages

The goal in reading in a foreign language is to improve your comprehension first. Use a dictionary the first time you encounter new vocabulary and work on improving your speed.

Sciences

Reading in the sciences will take time and focus as you encounter new concepts and processes. Look for visual representations of the content in your textbook.

INTEGRITY MATTERS

Integrity has been defined as doing what you say you will do even in the face of adversity. Acting with integrity in college includes making a commitment to complete reading assignments in all your classes even if you face challenges to your commitment.

Reading in college is not optional; rather, it is crucial to success. When you make the commitment to enroll in college, you must also follow through with that commitment by tackling the reading that is part of the experience. You will also need to demonstrate integrity when you do not read—be honest with your instructor, if asked, and be honest with yourself that your progress (or lack thereof) is related to how well you are preparing, through active and critical reading, *before* class.

YOUR TURN Have you experienced the feeling of being confused in class because you did not prepare by reading the assignment beforehand? ■ What was the experience like? ■ What did you do the next time you were assigned readings for class? ■ What did you learn from the experience?

____

____

____

____

____

Social Sciences

Large amounts of assigned material will be part of any social science class. Start reading the chapters early and look for key ideas. People and their theories or their actions (in history) will be key components of the reading. Learning the who, what, when, and where of the material will make it easier to remember.

REFLECTION *exercise* 5.1

How much reading do you expect to do each week while you are taking classes in college? What difficulties, if any, do you anticipate in completing the reading? How are you prepared for the expectations?

READING ACTIVELY and Critically

Active reading, a term that you may hear often in college along with *active listening*, means that you are fully engaged in reading by focusing your mind and body on the activity. Many first-time students read passively rather than actively and do not fully concentrate on the material. Just reading the words is not enough for college classes. Instead, you must be a part of the process by making sure you are comprehending what you are reading.

Critical reading is another term that you will hear frequently in college. Some students may think that critical reading means having a negative reaction to what they have read, but it actually involves a series of steps to react and respond to the reading—either positively or negatively, depending on the material. Your end goal in critical reading is to question and evaluate the material, not to take it at face value. Critical reading, as well as active reading, is a skill that will take practice to develop. The following sections provide specific strategies for improving both skills.

SKIMMING AND SCANNING

You may already be familiar with the terms *skimming* and *scanning* as they pertain to reading. Skimming is reading material quickly and superficially, paying particular attention to main ideas; use this method of reading when you first get a reading assignment because it can help you get a feel for the material, how long it is and how difficult it will be to read. In order to skim a text effectively, you should read the first and last paragraphs and the main headings of the text, as well as the first and last sentences of the remaining paragraphs; of course, if time is a factor, you can delete some of the steps or add more, such as reading the first and last paragraphs of each section. Ideally, skimming should be done before in-depth reading. However, sometimes skimming may be the only chance you have to read the material. If this is the case, be sure to pay attention to the

Your Terms of **SUCCESS**

WHEN YOU SEE . . .	IT MEANS . . .
Active listening	Listening with focus and a purpose.
Active reading	Reading to remember and understand; reading with a purpose.
Bibliography	A list of books or other sources.
Comprehension	The ability to remember and understand.
Context clues	Hints of a word's meaning by how it is used in a sentence.
Critical listening	Listening to evaluate the information.
Critical reading	Reading to evaluate and to question.
Dyslexia	A learning disability that makes it difficult for a person to read, spell, or listen effectively.
Listening barrier	An obstacle, either physical or mental, that keeps you from listening effectively.
Outlining	An arrangement of information that is ordered by how the information is presented.
SQ3R	A reading strategy that stands for Survey, Question, Read, Recite, and Review.
Subvocalization	Sounding out individual words while reading.
T System	A note-taking strategy that involves dividing your paper into an upside-down T. Also known as the Cornell System.
Table of Contents	A list of the chapter titles and section headings in a book; appears at the beginning of a book.

major headings of each section and the first and last paragraphs of the sections. Don't be surprised, though, if you miss major ideas that are sandwiched in the middle.

Although it now has a meaning similar to skimming, scanning is a method of reading that has traditionally meant "examining a text closely." Nonetheless, some reading experts define *scanning* as looking quickly for a specific item or topic as you would scan a phone book for someone's name or a dictionary for a particular word. Scanning also includes examining the table of contents and index of a book to narrow your focus and prepare you to find what you are looking for. Just as with skimming, scanning requires that your eyes move quickly over a page. However, the difference is that you know what you want to find and will slow down once you find it. Scanning is particularly useful when reviewing sources to use for a paper. You can determine rather quickly if the source pertains to your topic or not. Once you scan, you can then skim or read the text actively.

QUESTIONING

Once you have actively read assigned or researched material, your next step will be to read it critically. In most cases, this will mean rereading the material, especially if it is short. Be sure to allow yourself plenty of time for this activity. At this point in the critical reading process, you do not necessarily need to answer the questions you raise—you will just want to look for places within the material where you want to know more, need clarification, or disagree with the author's conclusion.

Questioning the author to find his or her purpose in writing the material is the first place to start. If the material comes from a certain source, whether a magazine or newspaper or blog, you will also want to question the source's purpose. Questions to ask include whether the author is an authority. Is he or she credible? Is there an agenda or bias in the writing? By considering the source, you may ask, "What is the purpose of presenting this material?" If it comes from a newspaper, does the material aim to inform, persuade, or present one side of a debate? If the material comes from a blog or an anonymous website, does the material intend to serve as reliable information, or is it only someone sharing his or her observations with no intention of providing accurate information? Writing these questions in the margins of the text or using a notebook for your questions is a good start to reading critically.

"I now know how important it is not just to read and understand, but also to read and question the author's point of view. I never thought I was supposed to argue with a person whose name is in print until my professors demanded that I do."

Marcus, 19, student

EVALUATING

Another important element of critical reading is evaluating what you have read for its credibility and usefulness; it is also a part of information literacy. By asking the questions suggested in the preceding section, you can use the answers to determine the reliability of the information. For example, if you ask about the author of an article on diet and exercise and you find out that the person has a

Ph.D. in health and has conducted research on eating healthy foods and exercising, you may conclude that the author is credible and therefore the information she provides is reliable. You can also use evaluation to determine whether material has a bias or presents only one side of an issue. If a website, for instance, uses inflammatory language, ignores counter-arguments, or fails to mention any other explanation or reason for its conclusions, then it may be unreliable. There is so much data at our fingertips that anyone who accesses information will need to use evaluation to determine whether it is actually useful.

DEVELOPING Your Reading Skills

Whether you are an expert reader or in need of extra practice, and regardless of your degree, you will definitely strengthen your reading skills while you are in college. The key to improving your reading skills is regular practice reading assigned material such as textbooks, articles, and websites—really anything that your professors require or suggest that you read. The following section provides tips for developing those skills as you read.

BUILDING YOUR VOCABULARY

Increasing your vocabulary is another benefit to reading regularly. Some students get sidelined when they read because they encounter unfamiliar words; few students take the time to look up words that they don't know, and they subsequently miss out on learning new ideas or understanding the intent of the author. It is well worth your time to look up words when you read, but there are some methods you can use to decrease the time you spend flipping through your dictionary.

The first method for learning new vocabulary words is to look for context clues in the sentence. Many times you can figure out what the word means by how it is used in a sentence or by the words that surround it. Consider the following sentence:

> Students often use context clues to *decipher* the meanings of unfamiliar words.

If you didn't know that *decipher* means "to figure out," you could still understand the meaning of the sentence by the words around it and by considering that students are using something (context clues) in order to do something (decipher) the unfamiliar words. You could deduce, then, that students are making the unfamiliar words more familiar by using context clues. Now, try this sentence:

> It was not until we traveled to Beijing that we realized how *ubiquitous* American fast food was. On every street corner we saw a McDonald's or a KFC restaurant.

If you are not familiar with modern-day Beijing, you may not know that American restaurants are plentiful; in fact, you may believe that China has very little American food. Thus, to understand the meaning of *ubiquitous*, the second sentence provides the context clues. The phrase "On every street corner" from the sentence that follows should help you realize that *ubiquitous* means "everywhere."

"I used to be embarrassed that I didn't know what a word meant. I wouldn't feel comfortable looking it up either. Now I realize that the more I learn, the more I need to look up. It is actually fun learning new words."
—Sara, 27, student

Although context clues will allow you to make sense of most unfamiliar words, there will be times when you cannot rely on the other words in the sentence to help you. For example, can you tell what the words *amenable* and *obsequious* mean in the following sentence?

> Charles was *amenable* to going out to eat with Sheila's *obsequious* mother.

In this case, if you don't know what the words mean, the sentence offers little assistance. Does Charles want to go out to eat or doesn't he? Is Sheila's mother someone who is enjoyable to be around or isn't she? To answer these questions, you may need to look up the words. Here is what you may see if you were to look up *amenable* in a dictionary:

> **a me na ble** adj. 1. agreeable 2. open to an activity or idea 3. controllable

Now look up *obsequious* for yourself and see whether you can decipher the sentence.

Another way to figure out what words mean is to know some common Latin and Greek root words, prefixes, and suffixes (see Table 5.1). For example, if your

TABLE 5.1 Common Latin and Greek Root Words

Root	Meaning	Example Word	Definition
Ante	Before	Antebellum	Before the war, specifically referring to the American Civil War
Anti	Against	Antibiotic	Against life, specifically against microorganisms
Auto	Self	Autobiography	Writing about the self
Biblio/Bibl	Book	Bibliography	A list of books
Cede	Go, Leave	Secede	Leave an organization or alliance
Chrono	Time	Chronological	Events ordered by time in which they occurred
Cogn	Know	Recognize, cognizant	To know from before; fully informed
Graph	Write	Autograph	Person's own signature
Inter	Within, Between	Intermission	The period between performances
Phil	Love	Philanthropy	Love of humankind
Photo	Light	Photography	Producing images using light in the process
Pseudo	False	Pseudonym	False name

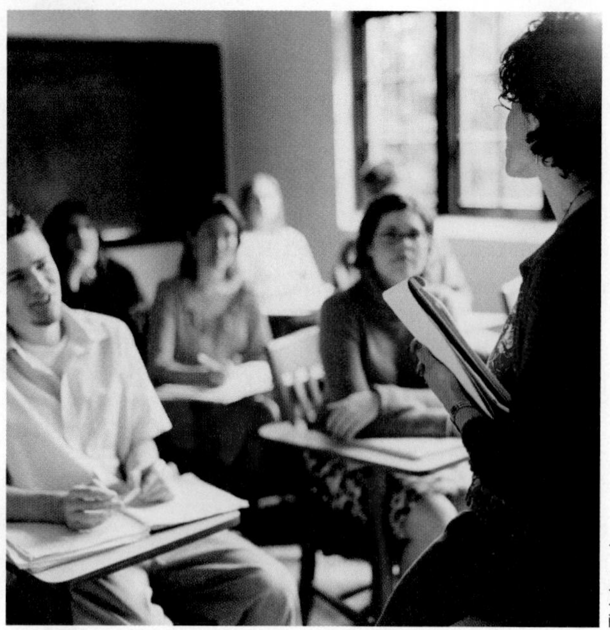
Thinkstock

Prepare for class in advance and get involved in class discussions so that your notes will be more meaningful when you go back to review them.

professor calls astrology a "pseudoscience" and you know that the Greek root *pseudo* means "false," then you will be able to understand that your professor considers astrology not to be a true science. In order to learn the common roots of words that we use every day, you will need to study word origins. Taking a college reading class or looking up words in the dictionary regularly will help you learn to recognize the roots in many words.

CHECKING YOUR COMPREHENSION

The most important aspect of reading is comprehending and remembering what you have read. If your textbook has questions at the end of each chapter that will help you reinforce what you have learned, then get in the habit of answering them when you finish a reading assignment. Even mentally answering the questions will help you understand the material. If your textbook does not have questions, then create your own or write a short summary of the chapter. To reinforce what you have learned, trade summaries with a classmate.

IMPROVING YOUR READING ATTENTION SPAN

Each semester will get more demanding in terms of reading because as you advance in your degree program, you will be encountering more challenging content. Therefore, the more practice that you have in reading effectively, the easier it will be to complete larger reading assignments. If you find that your "reading attention span" is not long, then you can work on lengthening it. First, you will need to figure out how many pages you can read comfortably without getting distracted or tired. Write down the number in your reading log, a notebook, or in a calendar. Each time that you sit down to read an assignment, notice how many pages it is. See if you can "beat" the number in the previous reading session. The more you read and the more you challenge yourself with reading, the better you will get. Just be patient.

COLLABORATION *exercise* 5.2

Working within a group, discuss the reading skills just presented. Which ones will be more challenging for those in your group to build on? What resources does your college have that will help your group members strengthen these skills?

SQ3R Reading Strategy

One of the most popular reading strategies, called SQ3R, was developed by Francis Pleasant Robinson in 1946 and published in *Effective Study.* Although many books and websites since then have interpreted and expanded the strategy, the overall method works as follows:

> **(S) Survey:** Before reading your text closely, start by examining the headings, subheadings, graphics, charts, and references if included.
>
> **(Q) Question:** After finding these major organizational signposts, think of questions that you have. One way to generate questions is from headings and subheadings. For example, the subheading "SQ3R Reading Strategy" can be turned into "What is the SQ3R reading strategy?"
>
> **(R1) Read:** Read each section, making sure you are concentrating on the material.
>
> **(R2) Recite:** After reading each section, say aloud what the section was about and answer the questions that you asked during the Question stage. You may also want to write your answers on note cards to review later.
>
> **(R3) Review:** Anytime after you have completed the first four steps, review what you have read. Some experts suggest reviewing within 24 hours of reading, whereas others recommend reviewing what you have read in short sessions over a period of time.

THE ART of Listening

Listening involves more than just hearing, but is an activity that we often take for granted, an activity that we believe we do well. In fact, John A. Kline (1996), in *Listening Effectively,* reports that people often think they are better listeners than their family members, friends, and coworkers (p. 5). If we believe we are better listeners than others, then we will be less likely to work on the very skill that might prevent so many conflicts, misunderstandings, and hurt feelings—among many other negative effects! It is important to recognize then that, regardless of how you rate yourself as a listener, you will benefit from reviewing basic listening strategies as they relate to gathering information in the classroom. Too often students miss out on crucial information that can help them be successful because of poor listening skills.

PREPARING TO LISTEN AND LISTENING ACTIVELY

We have been listening all our lives—to our parents' voices, to our favorite music and television shows, to our friends on the phone. When something is so common in our lives, why would we need to think about how to prepare to listen? Isn't it as natural as breathing? According to Pauline Rowson (2007) in *Communicating with More Confidence,* we would benefit in preparing to listen by considering the reasons that we may not listen well to begin with: We don't agree with the person speaking; we believe strongly in the topic (and therefore cannot "hear" anyone's perspective that differs from ours); we are tired or distracted; or we want to talk ourselves, which is a frequent reason for poor listening (pp. 152–153).

To help prepare for more effective listening, it is important to understand the different types of listening. *Passive listening,* sometimes called casual listening, is characterized by lack of engaged attention. *Active listening,* on the other hand, involves listening that concentrates on what is being said and taking steps to remember the information. To be an active listener, you must decide that listening is a worthwhile activity and that important information will be shared.

The first step to effective listening is to prepare to listen before you get to class. In other words, you will need to read the assigned pages or chapters ahead of time so that you have some knowledge about the lecture or discussion topic. If you have read the chapters ahead of time, you will be familiar with new words and concepts. Preparing to listen also includes reviewing your assigned readings before you get to the classroom. If you have a few minutes between classes or on the bus, pull out your book and skim the major headings, boldfaced terms, and text boxes that appear in the margins.

"My best defense for listening in class is to read the chapter before I get there. How else will I recognize what a two-factor ANOVA is when my instructor lectures about it?"

—Martha, 52, student

To listen effectively while in class, avoid distractions. First, you will need to sit up front and put away textbooks for other courses, cell phones, pagers, and other distracting items. Your best defense against interruptions is to clear your desk of anything except your textbook, pen, and paper. Stow other items in your backpack or underneath your desk or table. If you need to get anything out during class, such as a dictionary, minimize the disruption by being as quiet as possible.

If you find yourself next to a chatty classmate or one who likes to write notes to you, simply move. Even if you are only politely listening or reading her messages, you will be guilty of disrupting the class by association. Talkative classmates make it difficult for you and others to listen, and they distract you from taking good notes.

Another aspect of listening effectively is to maintain a positive attitude about the class. If you think the class is boring or a waste of time, you will be less likely to pay attention. Even if your beliefs are true—and others bemoan the class as well—pretend that the class is the only one you have left before graduating and that if you don't pay attention and take good notes, then you will have to spend another semester in the course. In other words, do whatever you need to "psych" yourself up and invest in the class.

Minimizing outside distractions is another way to keep a positive attitude. There will be times when you have to work late, stay up all night with a sick baby, or help a friend who has just had a crisis. If not handled well, these stressful experiences could affect your performance in class. As much as possible, leave your personal life at the door and concentrate on the class that you are sitting in. Even if the lecture for the day is overshadowed by a personal problem, remember that you *can* handle both your academic duties and your personal life.

Finally, prepare for class psychologically by preparing physically. Make sure you have eaten something before each class so that you won't be interrupted by a growling stomach. Moreover, dress in layers in case the room temperature is uncomfortable. Nothing is more distracting than being too hot or too cold. Getting plenty of sleep the night before class will also help you pay attention and listen effectively. Although adequate sleep may be a luxury if you work a late shift or you must get up in the middle of the night to take care of a child, be sure to make an effort to get a good night's sleep if possible. You won't be able to maintain high concentration and retention or even good health without adequate rest.

LISTENING CRITICALLY

As previously stated, active listening, much like active reading, involves focusing on the task at hand and concentrating on what is being conveyed, whether words or sounds. Another part of listening effectively is listening critically, or processing what you hear and evaluating it. Listening critically will help you make decisions about what is important and what is not, what is objective and what is biased, and what should be stored for later and what should be discarded.

Listening critically is a skill, one that should be practiced regularly. Your college professors will invite you to think critically and challenge your assumptions (that is learning!). As you get more comfortable with listening actively and critically, you will move from merely listening and taking notes that reflect what your instructors have said to listening to evaluate and ask questions of the notes you have taken. Consider the following questions as you work on listening critically:

- *Speaker.* Is the speaker a credible source? How do I know? What possible biases does he or she have? What is his or her experience with the topic?
- *Message.* What is the speaker's purpose? What are the details he or she uses to convey the message?
- *Details.* Is the speaker using facts or opinions? How do I know? Which type of details work best for what the speaker is trying to convey?
- *Self-knowledge.* What do I already know about the topic? How does what the speaker is saying conflict or support my beliefs and opinions? Do I feel I have learned something new?
- *Larger picture.* How does what the speaker is saying fit into the larger picture? How can I relate the message to something I already know about life or the world at large? Are there any connections between what I have heard and what I have experienced?

Answering these questions will get you started on the right path to listening critically. It is especially important to listen critically and mentally ask questions of what you are hearing, "tuning in" rather than "tuning out," when you hear something that you don't agree with or don't understand.

Remember, too, that *critical* does not mean "negative." If you find that what you are hearing is not holding up to what you know about the subject or the speaker is not credible, you can still ask questions that are respectful and curious. Most people do not mind being politely challenged or debated.

REDUCING LISTENING BARRIERS

Despite your efforts to prepare for class, you may find barriers to listening effectively, barriers that you cannot avoid no matter how well prepared you are.

Problem Solving

Emotionally intelligent people acknowledge their feelings in a situation, stop and think about what is involved, and then choose an act that will help resolve any problems. Read the following common situation and work through the three steps in the boxes.

What emotions do you have in this situation?
FEEL

What is the optimal outcome of the situation for you?
THINK

What attitude and positive action will help you achieve the outcome you want?
ACT

SITUATION

Your ethics class has been quite challenging because some of your classmates openly challenge the professor and divert the discussion toward personal issues; others have side conversations that distract you while you are trying to pay attention, and your professor speaks so quickly and uses so many unfamiliar words that you often feel lost when trying to take notes. You are frustrated with the professor, your classmates, and yourself. You want to be able to do well on the tests and assignments, but you feel lost, and your book isn't helping much because the chapters are long and you find them uninteresting. What do you do?

For example, what should you do if your instructor talks too fast, uses technical jargon or an advanced vocabulary, is unorganized, digresses from the lecture material (tells stories, allows too many irrelevant questions), or does not explain key concepts? Although you cannot coach your instructor in the art of speaking, you can ask him or her to slow down or define terms. Most professors do not mind repeating information or defining specialized language on the board because they want students to understand the material during lecture or class discussion. It may be a little harder to ask the instructor to be more organized or to stay on topic during a lecture. However, one way to get what you need without offending the professor is to ask if she would mind providing an outline before each class. Another method of getting the professor to stay on the subject is to ask a question about the topic or an upcoming exam or assignment. Your nudging may move the lecture back into focus.

There may also be physical or psychological barriers to listening effectively. If you have an unaccommodated learning disability or a hearing problem, you may not be able to listen productively. Talking to a counselor about learning or hearing difficulties can help you listen more effectively. A more common hindrance to listening is students' insecurities about their ability to do well in the course. It is not uncommon for a new student to feel, at first, intimidated by the course, the instructor, or other students in the class. The reason for the discomfort could stem from a student's feelings that he or she is not good enough or smart enough to be in college. A student also may feel that everyone else, except him or her, knows what to do, what to say, and how to act. This fear is common, and usually it subsides after the first week or two.

REMEMBERING WHAT YOU HAVE HEARD

Once you adequately prepare to listen in class and you remove any barriers that inhibit your ability to take in information, you will need to turn your attention to remembering what you hear in class. Taking notes, of course, is one way to retain information. However, there are some other methods that will help you recall information at a later date.

Participating in discussion and activities is an excellent way to remember key concepts. In fact, professors consider student participation as part of active, rather than passive, learning. You are more likely to remember a concept if you have incorporated it into your own thinking. There is a reason that the most talkative students are usually the most successful. They have made the material personally relevant, which makes remembering easier. However, participating in class discussion may be difficult if you are shy or feel out of place in the classroom. Some students refrain from asking questions because they don't want to look ignorant in front of their classmates. Then there is the other end of the spectrum from the silent student—the constant questioner. These students dominate the professor's time by asking questions that sideline the discussion or bring up material that has already been covered. Don't be intimidated by a predominantly quiet classroom or by a student who asks the professor excessive questions. If you have a question, ask it. Some instructors believe there are no "stupid questions."

If you don't feel comfortable asking questions during class, visit with your professor after class or during office hours. Some instructors ask students to write questions down and pass them up before class is over. Take advantage of such a practice; you will be able to ask questions without the fear of speaking up in front of classmates.

Another method for remembering, tape recording lectures, is popular with students who have the time to listen. Listening to a tape recording will work best if you have a long commute or if you go over your notes as you listen. Be sure to ask permission before you turn the tape recorder on, and make sure you have fresh batteries with you in case they are needed.

CRITICAL THINKING *exercise* 5.3

Think about a time when you heard someone speak about a topic that you did not agree with? How did you listen? How did you react to what you were hearing?

NOTE-TAKING Strategies

No matter how much you refine your listening skills, they will not be sufficient for taking in and remembering everything that is said in class. That is where your note-taking skills will help you. There are numerous methods of taking notes for a class. Your goal should be to find the note-taking strategy that works best for you. Remember that you may have to adapt your note-taking style to each course, each teaching style, and each learning style strength. For example, outlining may work well in a history course in which the instructor writes key terms on the board and organizes her lecture around key ideas. If your professor prefers unstructured discussion, you will need to adapt your note-taking strategy to make the most of unorganized information.

Whatever you choose for the particular course, your learning style, and the specific situation, there are a few tips that you need to remember when taking notes.

- *Listen for the main ideas.* Instructors will slow down and emphasize certain information, terms, and definitions. They may even use verbal signposts such as "The most important thing to remember," "This may appear on an exam," or "Two crucial points." If the instructor writes or hands out an outline, you can be sure that it contains the main points of the lecture.
- *Leave plenty of "white space" (blank space on paper) when taking notes.* Don't try to fill your page with as much information as possible. You will need the white space to add more notes or to synthesize ideas once you have reviewed.
- *Review your notes as soon as possible after class.* Waiting for two weeks to review your notes will ensure that you won't remember everything that you have written or how it all fits together. Most experts suggest that you review your notes within two days of the class.

HOW INFORMATION IS PRESENTED

Without a doubt, listening effectively is the first step to taking good notes, but you will also benefit from understanding how information can be presented during a lecture. As you attend more classes, you will probably notice that professors have a certain way in which they present their material. Some will follow the textbook information in the same order. Others will lecture only on new material that cannot be found in the textbook or other course materials. Still others will present a combination of the two methods. Reading assigned chapters and materials before you attend class will allow you to determine which information in the lecture is new and which has been covered in assigned reading materials.

Recognizing the different ways material can be organized will help you stay organized in your notes and will provide you with strategies for revising and reviewing your notes when you begin studying. Table 5.2 provides examples of different ways you can organize your notes.

DEVELOPING A SHORTHAND

As you take more notes in each class, you will find yourself using a few of the same words over and over again. These words are good candidates for abbreviating or denoting in symbols. You can then create your own shorthand. Shortened words such as "ex." for *example,* "w/" for *with,* and "b/c" for *because* are

TABLE 5.2 Types, Definitions, and Examples of Organization of Material

Type	Definition	Example
Chronological	Details arranged in time (first this happened, then this happened, etc.)	1801: United Kingdom of Great Britain is created 1803: Louisiana Purchase is made by Thomas Jefferson 1815: Battle of Waterloo signals end of Napoleon's career
Cause/Effect	Details arranged by presenting a cause and then its effects or an effect and its causes	Cause: Civil War Effects: slavery ended, industrialism began, the nation was brought back together, the federal government proved stronger than the states
Compare/ Contrast	Details arranged by similarities and differences	Similarities between Robert Frost and Walt Whitman: They were males; they used nature in their poetry; and they were considered "poets of the people." Differences between Frost and Whitman: Frost's poetry is more structured, whereas Whitman's is open and loose; Whitman's speakers are more positive and upbeat than Frost's
Most Important/Least Important	Details arranged in order of importance, with the most important detail coming first with minor supporting details to follow or the least important details can start a list that works to a major detail	Self-awareness (purpose of education) Values Goals Mission Personality type Learning style

abbreviations you probably already use in notes and email messages. Symbols that you may already use include % for *percentage*, + for *add* or *and*, and # for *number*. If you use a new abbreviation or symbol for a word, be sure to make a note of what it means; for example, "TR" could mean "Theory of Relativity" in a science course or "Teddy Roosevelt" in a history course.

Here is a list of other commonly abbreviated words and symbols:

At	@
Between	betw, b/w
Decrease	decr
Department	dept
Does not equal	≠
Equals	=
Example	eg, ex
Government	govt
Important	imp
Increase	incr
Information	info
Regarding	re
Significant	sig

Developing a shorthand will allow you more time to concentrate on what is being said. As you get more practice, you will become better at judging which information is worth writing and which is not, and your shorthand will become more efficient. Just remember to read over your notes within a day or two so that your abbreviations are fresh in your mind. It is a good idea also to complete the words or concepts during review so that you won't struggle to remember what all the shortened words mean later in the semester. Moreover, it will reinforce your learning of the material.

OUTLINING

Using an outline is a good method for taking notes if the instructor is organized and offers information in a logical pattern. Some instructors encourage outlining by writing key words and concepts on the board or an overhead projecting device. If your instructor organizes lectures or class discussions in that manner, you will be able to write an outline for your notes quite easily. The key to making your outlines effective will be to provide plenty of space between the items so that you can fill in the blank spaces with extra information. The following example shows an outline for a lecture on effective listening.

Preparing to Listen Effectively

I. Listening Critically
II. Possible Listening Barriers
  A. External
    1. Hunger
    2. Climate discomfort
  B. Internal
    1. Feelings of self-worth
    2. Stress
III. How Information Is Presented
  A. Chronological
  B. Cause/Effect
  C. Compare/Contrast
  D. Most Important/Least Important

ANNOTATING

Writing in the margins of your textbook, also called *annotating*, can be another effective way to take notes, especially if the reading assignment is lengthy. If you don't mind writing directly in your textbook, you can summarize main points that you have read. Writing brief summaries (two- or three-word summaries) or questions in the margins will help you make sense of and remember what you have read. Brief, marginal summaries will also help you review the material before and after class and when you start studying for an exam.

Annotating in your textbook and writing down critical questions are two methods of further reinforcing what you have read and will help you prepare for listening and note taking in class. Examples of critical questions about a reading include "How do I know this to be true?" and "What else should be considered?" Annotating your textbook with your own notes will help you not only reinforce main ideas, but will also help you synthesize the information in new ways that will produce connections between concepts, making the material more memorable and more relevant.

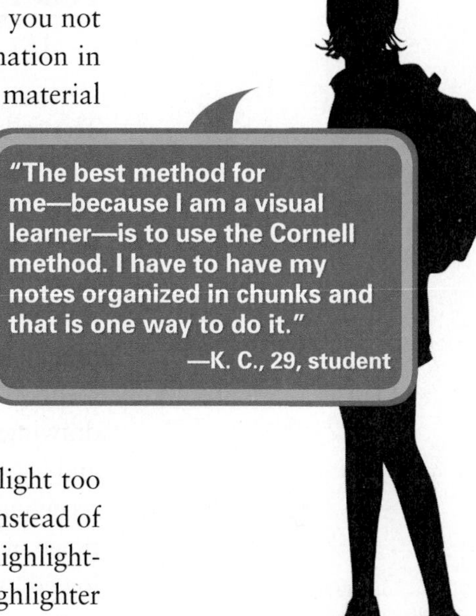

"The best method for me—because I am a visual learner—is to use the Cornell method. I have to have my notes organized in chunks and that is one way to do it."
—K. C., 29, student

If you decide to write in the margins of your textbook, be sure that the book you are writing in is not one that you want to sell back to the bookstore. If you do not want to write in your book but still get the benefits of summarizing the material, you can write your summaries on a separate sheet of paper. Make sure that you label each piece of paper with the chapter title and page number of the book.

Highlighting in your textbook is another method that students use for taking notes on reading material. Mark important concepts for review with a highlighter pen, but be careful that you do not highlight too much information. Over-highlighting the text can defeat the purpose—instead of making it easier to understand key terms and information, too much highlighting can make everything seem of equal importance. Therefore use a highlighter pen sparingly. For example, don't highlight more than two sentences in a row. A better method would be to combine highlighting with written summaries for the greatest effect.

THE CORNELL SYSTEM

Cornell University professor Dr. Walter Pauk developed a system for note taking that has become popular among many students. The Cornell System, also known as the T System, is ideal for those who benefit from the visual impact of organized notes, and it can benefit other types of learners because it is an organized way to take and review notes. The key to the Cornell System is dividing your notebook paper before you begin writing. Draw a horizontal line across your notepaper two inches from the bottom of the page. Then draw a vertical line from the horizontal line to the top of the page about 2 inches from the lefthand margin. The page should look like Figure 5.1.

FIGURE 5.1 Cornell System

The largest area, the righthand column, is used for taking notes during class. The lefthand column is used for asking questions as you take notes about material you don't understand during the lecture or to note possible exam questions that you think about as you are writing. The bottom section is reserved for summarizing your notes as you review them. The act of summarizing should help you understand and remember the information.

NOTE-TAKING STRATEGIES in the Disciplines

The following strategies for note taking in the disciplines are just a sample of what you may encounter in college. Just as we earlier discussed how reading differs in various disciplines, here we offer note-taking strategies for different subjects that will make reviewing your notes and studying easier.

Art

In an art appreciation class, you will need to identify eras (20th century), movements (Cubism), and artists (Picasso) as well as their characteristics, as seen in drawings, paintings, and sculpture. Quickly sketching the works in your notes and listing the characteristic details will help you record the information you are receiving through lectures. You may also notice that in the study of art there are times of intense change (usually coinciding with a world or cultural event) followed by artists who imitate or modify slightly the new style. As you review your notes, look for patterns within groups of artwork and for points of contrast.

Music

In a music appreciation class, use the same suggestions noted for art appreciation when you take notes. Instead of recreating a painting or sculpture in your notes, you may need to write down descriptions of what you are hearing and what the sounds remind you of. Are the sounds fast or slow? Do you hear one instrument or many? Does it sound like a stampede or a trip down a lazy river? "Translating" music samples into written notes as well as reviewing music clips on your own will strengthen your understanding of the material. As with your art notes, during review, look for patterns across movements and eras and denote contrasting ideas and elements.

Literature

Taking notes in a literature class will require you to have completed the assigned readings before class and to have annotated and highlighted your text. Because literature classes, even survey classes, focus more on discussion than on lecture, you will want to be prepared to take notes on the analysis. As with music and art classes, being familiar with basic terminology before you get to class will help you take better notes. As you review your notes, look for ideas that pull the different readings together.

Languages

Foreign language classes center more on speaking and interacting than on listening to a lecture. Taking notes will not necessarily be advantageous, because you will need to focus all your attention on listening actively, processing what is heard, and interacting based on what you have heard. Daily preparation is essential to learning foreign languages; take notes as you encounter new material, and ask questions in class to get clarification on anything you do not understand. Any notes you do take should be reviewed soon after the class. As you review your notes, categorize material such as "irregular verbs" and include any tips for using or remembering the parts of language.

Science

Concepts and processes are key in science classes and should be reflected in your notes. Prepare for class by reading assigned material, making note of new vocabulary words, and studying diagrams and figures in the text and handouts. As with any class, ask questions if you are having trouble following the steps of a process. As you review your notes, consider the different ways that you can represent these concepts and processes visually and physically.

History

History class lectures are usually presented in chronological order. However, you will also be required to move beyond specific dates and events by considering overall themes, ideas, and movements. In addition to chronological order, lectures may also use a cause/effect organization in which you list and elaborate on the effects of a cause or the causes of an effect. An example of a lecture topic in a history class is "The economic and social effects of the end of the Civil War." As you review your notes, look for major themes and be able to recall actions that have led to important events.

Math

Taking good notes in your math classes will require that you prepare and attend each class meeting. As with foreign languages, studying for math should be an everyday occurrence because the skills you learn in each class build on the ones you learned in the class before. When reviewing your notes, you may want to recopy them and make sure that you understand, line by line of each problem, what you are copying. If you have any questions, you can write them in the margins of your notes and try to get answers during the next class meeting.

REVIEWING Your Notes

Notes are only as good as the extent to which you review them. If you never looked at your notes after you took them, they would serve very little purpose. Therefore, to make the most of your notes, you will need to review them. As stated earlier in the chapter, reviewing should be done within two days of the time you took the notes. With this said, it is easy to be lulled into the sense of "studying" by merely reading over your notes again and again. When reviewing your notes, it is best to reorganize the material, make connections between concepts—even across disciplines—and ask questions about what you are learning.

"The best way for me to review my notes is to share them with study partners. I am a social learner and even if I cannot share them in person, I can share them through Google Docs. My study partners add to them and make corrections."

—Helen, 47, student

If you use the Cornell System, then you have a built-in area for adding more information, summarizing, and asking yourself questions. However, if you do not use a particular method, you can still benefit from filling in any blanks or holes in your notes with information you have since learned. As stated earlier, you should also spell out any abbreviations that may cause confusion later. After you fill in any gaps, you should also include questions—either on the same page or a new page—that will help you think about the material on a deeper level. For example, asking "Why is it important to know this?" can help you move beyond demonstrating your comprehension of the material to making it relevant and useful for you.

Find a note-taking style that works best for your learning style preference and the class you are taking.

Shutterstock

Freewriting about the material that you are studying is another way of remembering and learning the information that you have listened to. This technique is often used as a way to generate ideas for writing, but it can also be a way to take advantage of all the thoughts you have in your head about the material. For optimum effectiveness, you will need to freewrite within a day or two of the class lecture. With or without your notes, write down (or type into a word processor) all the information that you remember from the class.

The key to freewriting is continuation; in other words, do not stop writing even if you can't spell a certain word or you get stuck on a particular idea. Give yourself 5 or 10 minutes to freewrite; then, go through your freewriting material (some of it you will be able to use and some of it you will scratch out) and highlight or rewrite into complete sentences the information that pertains to the lecture. In essence, you will be learning the material in more depth as you write about it.

Finally, reciting notes with a friend can be a useful method for reviewing material. You can do this in person or on the phone. The benefits of reading your notes aloud and discussing them include filling in any gaps of information and reinforcing what you have learned. You can also engage in critical questioning of the material and take turns making connections between major concepts.

REFLECTION *exercise* 5.4

What is your experience of listening effectively in college and note taking so far? What kinds of issues do you encounter in each class with regard to listening? What kinds of issues do you encounter with note taking?

Transfer Tips: FROM COLLEGE TO UNIVERSITY

How the Reading Load and Expectations May Change

You have probably noticed that in each chapter's discussion of moving from college to university, the demands always increase, and reading expectations are no exception. Most definitely, the reading load will increase significantly—you may find that you have hundreds of pages a week to read and comprehend. You may also find that you are expected to do more than just recall the information. In addition, you will need to think critically about the reading by asking questions of the author (What does she mean? How does she know? What are the implications of her argument?) and of yourself (Do I agree? Does this argument make sense?). Professors in upper-level classes will also require you to discuss the readings in class. Most definitely, the discussion will move beyond the content of the reading to the formulation of new ideas and opinions about the topic of the reading. The more you are able to contribute, the more you will get out of the reading and the class.

Transfer Tips: FROM COLLEGE TO CAREER

Practicing Critical Listening Skills Will Give You an Edge on the Job

Most of the communication you will do on the job involves listening: to clients' urgent needs, to your employer's plans for the next six months, to coworkers' explanations of how they would complete a project, and to subordinates' questions about how to improve. Being a good listener will involve practicing the critical listening tips that are outlined in this chapter. The reason for cultivating this skill is that you will be bombarded with information from all levels: from your boss above you, from your subordinates below you, and from colleagues around you. Critical listening skills will enable you to filter what you are hearing so that you can act appropriately and avoid making errors in action and judgment. Consider, for example, a coworker who comes to you to complain about a company policy. Without listening actively and critically, you may disregard what the speaker is saying because you don't have time to do anything about it. However, if you took the time to analyze the speaker (Is she a credible source?) and the message (Is the purpose to vent or to change something?) as well as what you know about the situation yourself (Is the policy flawed and in need of change?) and the larger picture (How will this proposed change affect others?), then you are more likely to act appropriately and confidently. On the job, as in life, you will not—and should not—respond the same to all messages you receive from speakers. Practicing critical listening skills will make it easier to determine which messages are critical and which can be acted on later—which in turn will make you a more efficient and effective employee.

References and Recommended Readings

Beglar, D., & Murray, N. (2009). *Contemporary topics 3: Academic and note-taking skills* (3rd ed.). London: Pearson.

International Dyslexia Association. (2009). Dyslexia basics. Retrieved September 18, 2009, from www.interdys.org

Kirsch, I. S., Jungeblut, A., Jenkins, L., & Kolstad, A. (2008). Executive summary of adult literacy in America: A first look at the results of the national adult literacy survey. National Center for Education Statistics. Retrieved May 15, 2008, from http://nces.ed.gov/naal/index.asp?file=OtherResources/ExecSumAdultLitFirstLook.asp&PageId=156

Kline, J. A. (1996). *Listening effectively.* Maxwell Air Force Base: Ala Air University Press.

Pauk, W. (1984). *How to study in college* (3rd ed.). Boston: Houghton Mifflin.

Rowson, P. (2007). *Communicating with more confidence.* Easy Step-by-Step Guides. Rev. Hayling, England: Summersdale Publishers.

Spears, D. (2008). *Developing critical reading skills.* Boston: McGraw-Hill.

CHAPTER six

LEARNING, Memory, and Studying for Tests

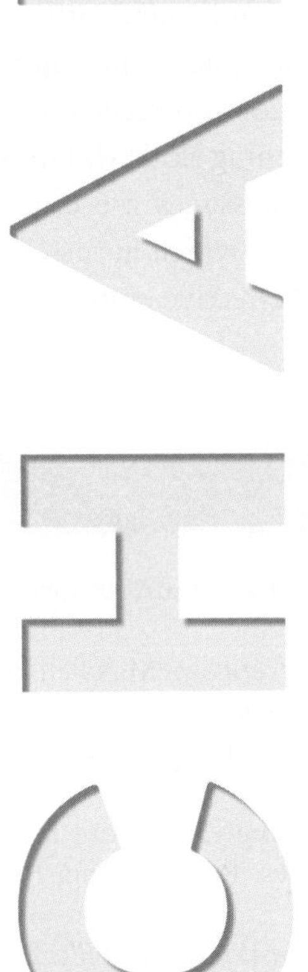

IN THIS chapter To help you improve your learning, no matter where it happens, this chapter focuses on the latest brain research as it relates to learning and memory. It also explains the different types of thinking that will be required of you in college. Finally, it provides you with study and test-taking strategies so that you can effectively demonstrate your learning.

More specifically, after completing this chapter, you will be able to do the following:

- Identify the stages of learning and the process of memory.
- Describe the processes of creative, analytical, and critical thinking, especially as they relate to problem solving.
- Determine the best study strategies for you.
- Identify effective test-taking strategies.

THIS IS YOUR Brain in College

Seems like there are dozens of bumper stickers and T-shirts that broadcast what people are born to do. "Born to Run," "Born to Shop," and "Born to Boogie" are just a few that you may see. But could you add "Born to Learn" to the list? All of us, researchers say, are indeed born to learn. Babies do it without giving the process any thought. The process is simple: The more you do something, say Angus Gunn, Dr. Robert W. Richburg, and Dr. Rita Smilkstein (2007), the

FIGURE 6.1 Dendrite

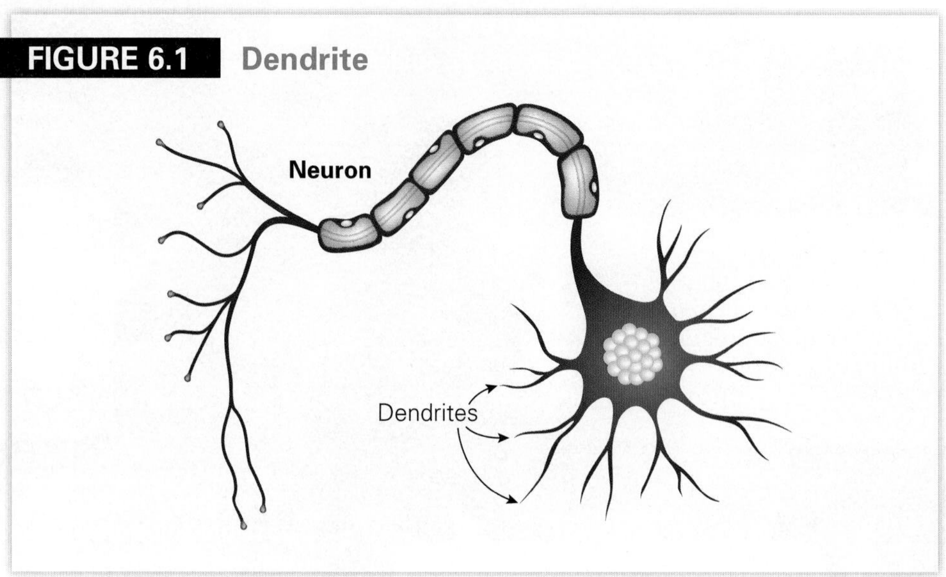

more you create connections in the brain that not only help you remember how to do something, but also help you get better at whatever it is you are learning to do. These brain researchers call this process "growing dendrites," referring to the "tree-like" structures on the ends of neurons, or nerve cells in the brain. The more you practice something, the more those dendrites grow, improving the connections between the neurons in your brain. See Figure 6.1 for an example of what a brain cell looks like.

THE LEARNING PROCESS

The good news about brain research is that spending more time actively learning a subject can translate into deeper learning, and a positive attitude toward challenging learning environments will enable you to learn more. In their book, *Igniting Student Potential,* Gunn, Richburg, and Smilkstein divide learning into six stages that begin with being curious and motivated to learn something new, move to practicing and refining the new skill, and then end with mastery of the skill. Table 6.1 provides an overview of the learning stages. If you think about anything that you are good at, you should recognize the same process that you went through to get better and better at it. We often recognize the need to practice sports and musical instruments, but sometimes we don't make the same connections with other skills such as writing, reading, and math. How much time is needed will be different for different people, but brain researchers contend your skills will increase just as your dendrites will grow.

"Getting students to work through those first few stages of learning—motivation, beginning practice, and advanced practice—is the key to deeper learning in my classes. If I can get them to do those, they usually succeed through the other stages."

—Russ, 29, professor

What happens when you can't get motivated to learn a new skill and make it past the first stage in learning? Dr. Carol Dweck (2006) refers to people who lose interest when learning "get[s] too challenging—when they are not feeling smart or talented" as having a "fixed mindset" (p. 22). People who "thrive when stretching themselves" have a "growth

TABLE 6.1 Six Stages of Learning a New Skill

Stage 1	*Motivation.* Responding to stimulus. Not knowing how to do it or how it works, just trying it.
Stage 2	*Beginning Practice.* Doing it ("practice, practice, practice"), learning from one's own mistakes. Starting to get the feel for it.
Stage 3	*Advanced Practice.* Increase of skill and confidence through more practice, more trial and error, getting comfortable.
Stage 4	*Skillfulness.* More practice, doing it one's own way, deviating from the norm, taking risks, creativity, branching out. Building understanding, skill, and confidence.
Stage 5	*Refinement.* Activity becoming second nature, creativity, learning new methods, strong satisfaction.
Stage 6	*Mastery.* Increased creativity, broader application, teaching it, continuing improvement, expertise.

Source: Adapted from Smilkstein, R. (2003). *We're born to learn: Using the brain's natural learning process to create today's curriculum.* Thousand Oaks, CA: Corwin Press. Used with permission.

mindset" (p. 22). In her book *Mindset: The New Psychology of Success,* Dweck asserts that people with a fixed mindset believe that they are either born smart or not, that there is no changing their "fixed" state of intelligence. People with a growth mindset, on the other hand, believe they can develop talents and skills; even if they fail at a task, they see it as an opportunity to learn more and improve on what they know about the task.

Sometimes one bad experience or several in a row can influence how we see ourselves as learners and masters of a skill. Dweck wants us to know that believing in our ability to learn will result in learning and mastery of whatever task we set our "growth" minds to.

REFLECTION *exercise* 6.1

Think of something you know how to do well. Describe the process by which you mastered the skill. Follow the six steps outlined in Table 6.1 and detail what you did at each step. Then identify a skill or task at which you don't think you could get better. Considering Dweck's theory of the growth mindset, write down a plan for practicing and learning more about how to master the skill or task.

LEARNING IN COLLEGE

How does the information about brain research and learning translate to what you are doing in college? It may be helpful first to identify where, how, and with whom learning can take place. If you think about a clock face in which the big hand is pointing to the 12 and the little hand is pointing to the 3, you can see that for a three-credit-hour class you will be spending 3 hours per week learning in the classroom (see Figure 6.2). As stated in Chapter 3 this means that you will need to spend three times 3 hours learning outside of class.

FIGURE 6.2 Learning in College

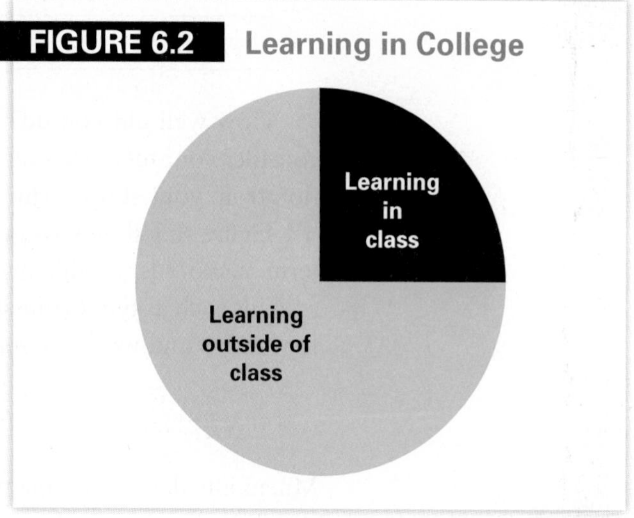

You could easily spend those 9 hours a week per class reading the textbook and studying your notes. However, you will probably have to engage in a variety of other activities as part of learning, such as researching and writing papers, completing homework, visiting with your professor outside of class, studying with a classmate or in a group, or working with a tutor.

Why do you need to do all of that to learn when listening in class, taking notes, and reviewing them before the test worked before? The answer is that in college, you will be responsible for more than just memorizing material and restating it on a test or in a paper. Instead, you will be asked to apply (use information in a new situation), analyze (break information down into its parts and examine it), synthesize (create new information based on what you have learned), and evaluate (judge the information), and you will be graded on your ability to do all of those activities well.

THE MEMORY Game

You will be more likely to remember what you have learned when you have moved it from short-term memory to your long-term memory. Memory is divided into two types—short-term memory and long-term memory. When you meet someone for the first time, you will keep that person's name and face in short-term memory; in fact, according to Harvard psychologist George Miller (2008), you can only store five to nine items in your short-term memory. If you try to put too many items in there, you will find that some of them slip away. Try this by glancing at the following list for 30 seconds. Then cover up the list and write down the words you remember in the space provided; the words do not have to be in the order that you see them.

cup	paper	pencil	magnet	ruler	scissors
spoon	towel	tape	apple	knife	straw

____

____

How well did you do? If you remembered five to nine items, then you can consider your memory average. It takes some work, though, to transfer information from your short-term memory to your long-term memory.

Figure 6.3 shows what areas of the brain are used in memory. Your long-term memory is responsible for storing information like names and dates as well as skills such as tying your shoe. People can have well-developed memory storage for images and words (visual), sounds (aural), and processes (kinesthetic).

MNEMONIC DEVICES

Mnemonic devices are memory aids or strategies that help you remember items, concepts, or a series of events. Usually, mnemonic devices are *not* used for deep

FIGURE 6.3 Parts of the Brain

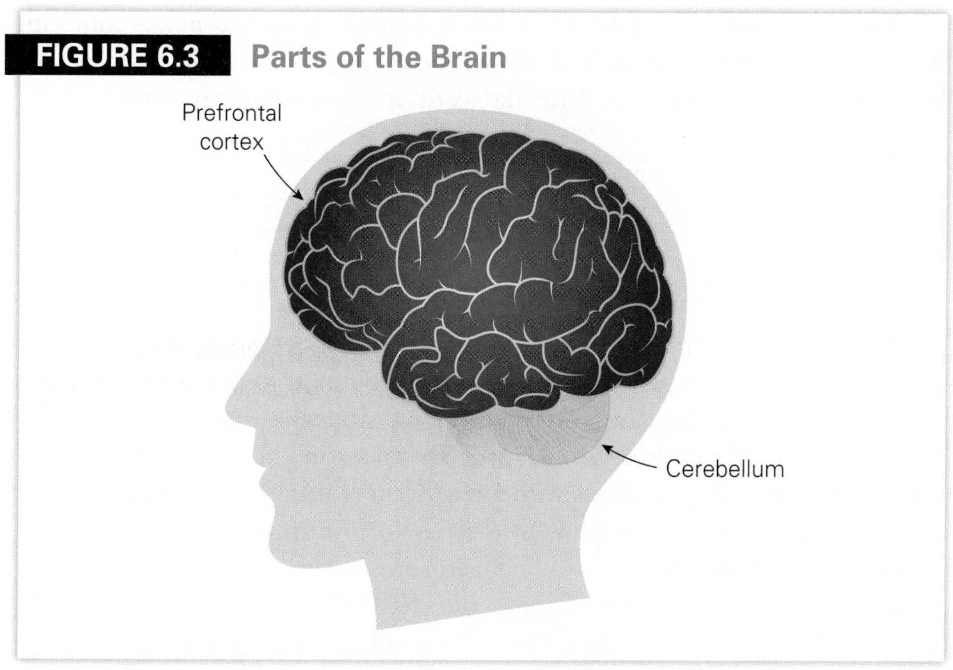

learning, but there will be times during college that remembering the names, for example, of all the bones in the body or all the constitutional amendments must be accomplished before deeper learning can happen. Thus, you may find yourself using mnemonic devices as part of your learning process.

Let's go back to the word list and figure out how you could remember all of the items. Ancient Romans are credited with being able to remember significant amounts of information by using the Roman Room or loci method. This visualization technique can be useful when trying to remember a string of seemingly unrelated items or complex material that needs to be pulled together.

> "My favorite memory aid is the Roman Room. I am a visual learner and I have a hard time remembering things unless I can associate them with a place that I know well. It makes the unfamiliar—like accounting terms—more familiar."
> —Charlten, 20, student

To create a Roman Room, visualize a familiar place, such as a room in your house. If your room is connected to other rooms, then you will have more "places" to put ideas. When you visualize your room, pay particular attention to the items that are already in the room, such as furniture or favorite pictures, and unique details, such as peeling paint. The more vivid the visualization, the better able you will be to remember the items you place there.

To see the Roman Room or loci method in action, take another look at the list.

cup	paper	pencil	magnet	ruler	scissors
spoon	towel	tape	apple	knife	straw

Can you place these items in your kitchen? Put the straw in the cup and place it in the cabinet. Tape the paper on the front of the cabinet. Place the towel on the counter next to the apple, spoon, and knife. Then, put the pencil, ruler, magnet, and scissors in the drawer.

Take 30 seconds to visualize this room or create your own Roman Room with the items listed. Then cover up both the list and the description of the room and see how many you can remember. Write the words in the space provided here.

____

____

____

Did you remember more words this time? If not, then visualization strategies may not be the only type of mnemonic device you need to help you remember lots of information. There are other mnemonic strategies that may benefit different learning style preferences. Acrostic sentences and acronyms are just two methods that may help students with a read/write learning style preference.

Take the first letters of items in a series to form sentences that help you remember the items and their order—acrostic sentences. For example, music students remember the order of the treble clef staff—E, G, B, D, F—with the sentence "Every Good Boy Does Fine." To recall the order of biological groupings used in taxonomy, just remember "Kids Prefer Cheese Over Fried Green Spinach" (Kingdom, Phyllum, Class, Order, Family, Genus, Species).

Take the first letters of items in a series to spell a new word to create acronyms. Examples of acronyms that we use every day include AIDS (acquired immune deficiency syndrome), SADD (Students Against Drunk Driving), REM (rapid eye movement), and SCUBA (self-contained underwater breathing apparatus).

Although there are too many words in our list above to create an acronym, you can create an acrostic sentence (or two) with the letters of each word. Because the order of the items is not important, feel free to rearrange the letters to make your sentence(s).

C P P M R S
S T T A K S

Despite being a little more difficult to compose than acronyms and acrostics, rhymes and songs are another type of mnemonic device that often appeals to aural learners. Who doesn't remember "Thirty days hath September . . ." and "In 1492, Columbus sailed the ocean blue"? Again, simple information works best for these memory strategies. It will take more work to remember the economic effects of Columbus's discovery of the New World.

MEMORY STRATEGIES

When you have the time to explore the variety of memory strategies, try them out until you find the one that works best for the subject matter and your learning style. However, many students need a memory strategy that works quickly when they are cramming before a test. Those students may be successful in remembering information when they get to the test the next day, but the possibility of their remembering it weeks, months, or even a year later is slim. That is why professors and tutors discourage students from cramming—it may work some of the time, and it is better than not studying at all for a test, but it often produces significant anxiety and stress, and the material is less likely to be in your long-term memory when you need it later.

With that warning, there will be times, nonetheless, when despite your best intentions, you will need a fail-safe memory technique to help you remember key concepts in a short period of time. One method, called *chunking,* was developed by Dr. George Miller, the same person who discovered that the human brain can only hold "seven, plus or minus two" items in short-term memory. Chunking is similar to the Roman Room or loci method in that items are grouped together to allow the brain to make connections, making it easier to recall the information later.

To see chunking in action, consider the following 10-digit number:

5114796210

It may be easier to chunk the numbers the way a phone number is divided:

511-479-6210

You probably don't realize that you chunk any time you memorize a phone number or Social Security number. In other words, you are taking the seemingly random numbers and putting them together in groups. The goal in chunking is to reduce a large number of items into only five to nine items. To practice this mnemonic technique, use the following list of key terms. First, however, make sure that you know the definitions of each term. Record your definition next to each item in the list.

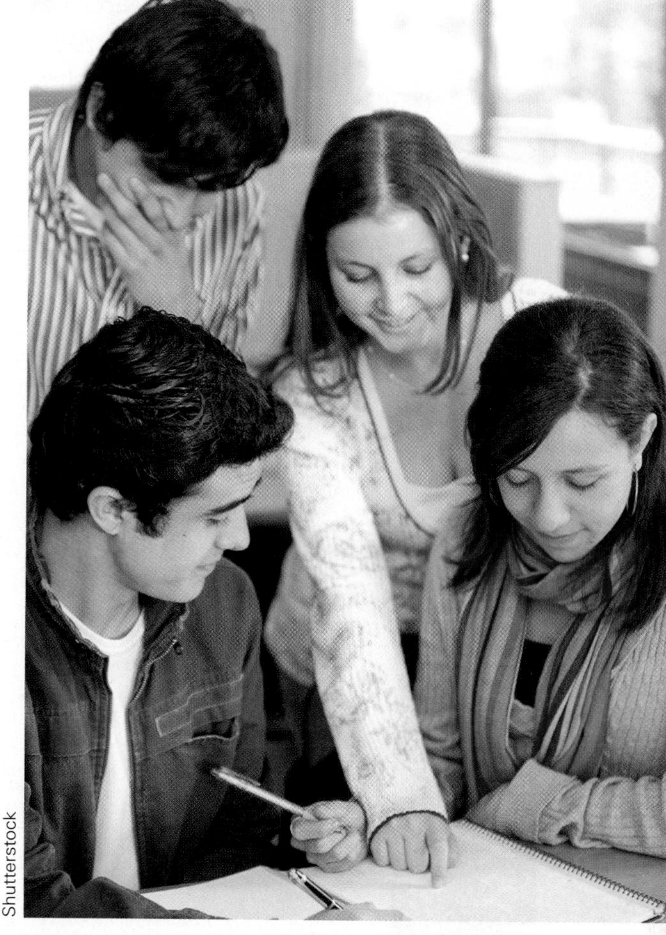

Shutterstock

Studying in groups is a good way to learn the material in more than one way.

Acronym ______________________________

Acrostic ______________________________

Chunking ______________________________

Cramming ______________________________

Loci method ______________________________

Long-term memory ______________________________

Mnemonic device ______________________________

Rhyme ______________________________

Roman Room ______________________________

Short-term memory ______________________________

Teaching others ______________________________

Next, group the items together logically. Then complete the chunking with the remaining terms. For example, one way to group some of the terms could be in a sentence: *Mnemonic devices* are strategies for remembering and they include *acrostics, acronyms, rhymes,* and *Roman Rooms.* How else could the terms be grouped together? Use the spaces below for your ideas.

- ______________________________
- ______________________________
- ______________________________

Your Terms of SUCCESS

WHEN YOU SEE . . .	IT MEANS . . .
Acronym	An abbreviation in which the first letters create a word; AIDS is an acronym for Aquired Immune Deficiency Syndrome.
Acrostic	A mnemonic device in which the first letter of each word in a sentence stands for information or a process; Please Excuse My Dear Aunt Sally is an acrostic for the order of operations: Parentheses, Exponents, Multiplication, Division, Addition, and Subtraction.
Advanced practice	Doing an activity with more skill.
Analytical thinking	Breaking apart information and examining its parts.
Beginning practice	Doing an activity, learning from mistakes.
Cerebellum	Region of the brain that controls sensory perception and motor skills.
Chunking	A method for remembering information by grouping it together in small chunks.
Cramming	A method of studying that involves trying to remember large amounts of material in a short amount of time.
Creative thinking	Thinking that involves generating ideas.
Critical thinking	Thinking that involves reviewing information for accuracy, authority, and logic before considering it useable.
Dendrite	The branch at the end of a neuron.
Loci method	A mnemonic device that uses spatial relationships; information to be remembered is associated with a location or objects within a location.
Long-term memory	Memory that lasts longer than a few days.
Mastery	Doing an activity with expertise.
Metacognition	Thinking about thinking.
Mnemonic device	A method of remembering information.
Motivation	Responding to a stimulus.
Neuron	A cell in the nervous system.
Prefrontal cortex	A region at the front of the brain where complex thinking is believed to occur.
Refinement	Perfecting an activity that has become second nature.
Roman Room	Another term for loci method.
Short-term memory	Memory that lasts only for a few hours or a few days.
Skillfulness	A demonstration of an ability to complete a task.

THINK about It

Think about it. Three simple words that you have probably heard many times, but have you ever thought about how you are thinking? The term for thinking about thinking is *metacognition,* or the act of being aware of your own thought processes. So far in this book, you have thought about what you value, how you spend your time, what college culture is, and how you relate to others. You have also been asked to think about what you are reading and learning in the reflection and critical thinking exercises. In fact, this book has been designed so that instead of passively taking in the information, you are actively engaged in thinking it through and creating knowledge.

CRITICAL THINKING *exercise* 6.2

After reviewing the mnemonic devices, determine which ones would work best for you and use them to create a memory strategy study sheet that would help you remember the major ideas in this entire chapter.

The same activities that have brought you to this point in the book are the types of endeavors you are currently practicing in your classes as well. You are moving beyond only taking information in to send it back out in the same form for a test or paper. Instead, you are building creative, analytical, and critical thinking skills with each course. Strong critical thinking skills will set you apart in the classroom and the workplace: You will be better informed, because you will know to seek out the information you need; you will make better choices, because you have thought through all the possibilities; and you will continue to improve on your chosen solutions, because you will understand that evaluating your conclusions is the key to making better future choices.

CREATIVE THINKING

Creative thinking, or the act of creating ideas for solving problems, is an integral part of education. Without creative thinking, there would be no inventions, new formulas, breakthroughs in technology and science, new art movements, advances in design and architecture—the list is endless. Without creative thinking, there would be no electricity, no indoor plumbing, no automobiles, and no zippers in our clothes. Just getting to your classes would be a totally different experience.

"I wasn't comfortable with being creative until I realized it was fun. There are no wrong answers when you think creatively. The more I do it, the more creative I am."
—Tova, 26, student

In *Creative Problem Solving,* Robert Harris (2002) contends that creative thinking is a skill, a process, and an attitude (pp. 1–2). In other words, creative thinkers are not born with special powers of the imagination; they just use their imaginations more regularly than others. The good news is that you can learn to think creatively by following some basic guidelines, shown in Table 6.2.

Harris states, "Creative thinking creates the ideas with which critical thinking works" (p. 5). To improve your critical thinking and problem-solving abilities, you will need to consider the guidelines in Table 6.2, find ways to practice them, and maintain your curiosity and a positive attitude.

TABLE 6.2 Creative Thinking Strategies

Strategy	Description
Improve your imagination	Find ways to keep your mind sharp and your imagination flourishing. Turning off the TV or picking up a book is an easy way to stimulate your imagination. If you enjoy kinesthetic activities, create something to get your mind active.
Think in all directions	Thinking in all directions means that you consider ideas that have worked before, have not worked before, have worked for other problems, and have not been paired with another idea. Some of the most creative ideas have taken ordinary solutions and reapplied them to other problems. Creative thinking demands that all angles be considered as you generate ideas.
Suspend judgment	For creative thinking, evaluation is not necessary—save it for critical thinking and problem solving. The focus should be on getting ideas down, not on judging them for their practicality or judging yourself as not capable of being creative. "There is no wrong answer" is a common phrase at this point to keep you generating thoughts.
Keep it up	One main difference between people who think creatively and those who choose not to is perseverance, or the determination to see ideas through, and to keep generating them when the ones you come up with don't work.

ANALYTICAL THINKING

Analytical thinking involves breaking down a subject and examining its parts. Students who learn about computer processing or automotive technology use analytical thinking so that they can understand how a machine works. When they master how the parts work together, they are able to diagnose problems that may occur within the processes. The same is true for students learning about the processes in the body: They use analytical thinking to determine how muscles work or how the lungs are supposed to function. Students of literature use analytical thinking to break apart short stories or poems to determine what effect the setting has on the characters or what effect language has on the tone of the text.

Anyone who has tried to figure out why an event has happened (e.g., How did I run out of money before payday?) has used analytical thinking. Just as with any skill, however, it takes practice to become better at seeing the parts of a process or a whole unit and determining how the parts work together to create a unified result. To develop your analytical skills, you can follow the strategies in Table 6.3.

CRITICAL THINKING

The term *critical thinking* is difficult to define, although it has a long tradition. Critical thinkers such as Socrates and Thomas Aquinas, to name only two, have had a tremendous effect on the way we think about the world. But what makes them critical thinkers? Sherry Diestler (1998), in her book *Becoming a Critical Thinker,* defines a critical thinker as "someone who uses specific criteria to evaluate reasoning and make decisions" (p. 2). In other words, someone who thinks critically does not take information at its face value; instead, the information is reviewed for accuracy, authority, and logic before it is considered useable.

TABLE 6.3 Analytical Thinking Strategies

Strategy	Description
Break down a whole into its parts	Ask yourself, "What are the pieces that create the entirety?" Try this by examining a dollar bill. What are the different images on the front and back?
Examine each part for a unique function	If you are still looking at the dollar bill, determine what function each part has on the bill. Does it convey important information about how to use the bill? Does it represent history?
Organize parts by function	What elements can be grouped together? How did you determine which groups to create?
Explore the meaning behind the parts	If possible, find out more information about how each part functions or its meaning. In the case of the dollar bill, you can learn more about the pyramid on the back and what it means.
Reexamine the whole in light of its parts	Look back at the whole and determine what you have learned from examining the parts. Do you have a better understanding of how all the parts work together?

Chapter 5 discussed how to read critically, and that certainly is a start to making informed decisions about what you read, but you will also use critical thinking in other parts of your everyday life. Sometimes you will be faced with an important decision, and you will need to use critical thinking in order to make the best choice.

PROBLEM SOLVING

Problem solving relies on critical thinking as well as creative and analytical thinking. In order to think critically to solve a problem, you will need to go through a process, whether within a group or as an individual. Remember that the more minds working on a problem, the more likely that all sides of the problem can be addressed, which may make the solution better. Although you may not always have an opportunity to work in a group on a problem, you may be able to ask others for their advice during the process.

The process of using critical thinking to solve a problem can be broken into a series of steps.

Step 1: Identify the Problem

Sometimes we assume we know what the problem is, and we try to fix it only to find out that our solution doesn't work because we were fixing the wrong problem. Consider a crying baby who last ate two hours ago. You may assume that the baby is still hungry and wants more to eat. When you try to feed the baby, he rejects the food. Now what? Is the baby not hungry? Have you offered something the baby doesn't like? Is the baby sick, too hot, too cold, tired? You can imagine how much time and energy you will spend trying to find the solution to the problem.

"I used to jump to the solutions before really considering what the problem is and what the solutions could be. I always thought there was only one possible answer."

—Jeremy, 22, student

Identifying the problem's cause is the first logical step before you can begin to solve it. If you do not identify the cause—or at least eliminate possible causes—before starting the next step, either you won't solve the problem or you might create a whole new problem to solve.

Step 2: Generate Ideas

Once you identify the cause of the problem, this is the point where creative thinking will kick in. When you generate ideas, there are no rules except not to eliminate any ideas because they are too far-fetched or too odd. The goal for this step is to get the ideas recorded, and the more you can think "outside the box," the more likely you are considering all possibilities.

When generating ideas, consider using brainstorming, freewriting, clustering, and role playing (if you are able to work with another person) to get ideas flowing. This is a good time to use your learning style strength to stretch your imagination.

Step 3: Analyze the Ideas

More creative and analytical thinking will help you break down the different ideas at this stage. What are the different parts of the possibilities? Are there any that are impossible, impractical, or illogical? Determine the least viable solutions and eliminate them from the list.

Step 4: Evaluate Possible Solutions

Thinking through each solution will involve exploring its benefits and drawbacks. Consider the possibilities, but don't completely discard any at this point.

TECH TACTICS

Using Technology to Get Ahead

Improve your thinking skills by visiting the numerous websites that are dedicated to brain games. Logic puzzles, word games, and visual tricks are all accessible with a little searching. Look also for memory games, which can help you strengthen your memory muscle.

RECOMMENDED SITES

- www.logic-puzzles.org Logic puzzles are a great way to get your mind in shape and help you build analytical skills.
- http://exploratopia.com/memory At this website devoted to memory and improving memory, there are interactive exercises that help you learn more about memory and how to improve it.
- www.fun-with-words.com/index.html This site allows you to explore all kinds of visual and verbal puzzles that can keep your creative juices flowing.

You may need them after you evaluate your final solution and find it to be ineffective.

Step 5: Choose the Best Solution

When choosing the best solution, consider the effects of the solution. Will it cause another problem? What kind of emotional, physical, and financial investment will it take? What will you need to do to implement the solution correctly? Creative thinking to consider all sides of the implementation of the solution will be needed before you make a final decision. Analytical thinking can help you put all the possibilities in a table format so you can examine the consequences.

Step 6: Evaluate the Solution

The final stage of problem solving is evaluation. The ability to evaluate allows you to use what you have learned in the process of solving the problem to solve other problems. Ask yourself whether the problem was adequately resolved. Did the solution only partly solve the problem or was it a complete solution? What, if anything, would you do differently if you experience the same problem again?

STUDY Strategies

Knowing the learning process, understanding how memory works, and practicing the thinking approaches for comprehension and analysis are all great foundations for studying the material you need to master. But you still have to study, and that means making the time to read, write, review, and reflect. The following section will help you identify the strategies that will help you most.

The best advice to give college students is plain and simple: Study for all tests. No exceptions. Sometimes you will find that you do not need to study as much for some classes; however, remember that studying effectively is a habit. To form the long-term habit, you must do it even when you don't think you have to, which is fundamental to making an activity part of a routine.

To understand what you need to study, you will also need to consider what may be on the test. Unless your professor tells you directly what will be on the test, assume that anything that was assigned or covered in class might appear. Just about every college student has a story of a test that covered reading assignments and not what was discussed in class. These students were surprised to realize that studying the lecture notes was not enough. The following list shows the variety of items that you may be tested on for any class:

- Material from lectures, discussions, and in-class or out-of-class activities
- Ideas and concepts provided by a guest speaker
- Information from a workshop or field trip
- Multimedia productions such as video or audio
- Assigned readings, including chapters in the textbook
- Handouts including PowerPoint slides and outlines

You can be assured that you will encounter a variety of test types. Take clues from what you do in class to help determine what kinds of test questions may be used. For example, if your professor spends time applying information from a chapter during class or as an assignment, then you will likely have test questions that ask you to apply the information as well. Listen for clues given by the professor, such as "You should write this down" and "This is a really important point." Other cue phrases include "You may see this again on a test" and "If you saw this on a test, how would you answer it?" When you hear these phrases, write down the information being emphasized and review it when studying your notes. A professor who says these things is begging you to take notice!

A PLACE AND TIME FOR STUDYING

The best time to begin studying is as soon as the semester starts. Be careful of the mindset that because you are not in class every day you don't need to study every day. Some students begin studying the night or day before an exam, which may be too late to review and remember all the material that has been covered over the past several weeks. As stated in Chapter 5, start reviewing your notes within two days of taking them. If possible, you should start studying for future exams right now, today.

"I study in the same place and at the same time each week. While my routine is regular, how I study is not. Sometimes, I reread the material. Other times, I create flash cards. All of this helps me think about the content in a different way."
—Wilson, 25, student

If you are a typical community college student, then your time will be limited. You may not have the luxury of large blocks of time, so you will need to be creative about studying. Because it is more effective to study for short periods of time, consider studying in between classes, during breaks at work, and on the way to work and school (provided you are not driving). Another way to ensure that you study during the day is to get in the habit of always carrying your notes or books with you—this way you'll be able to take advantage of any unexpected "free" time. You can also get up earlier or stay up later so you can spend a few minutes studying before starting or ending your day.

If you have the luxury of choosing when to study, rather than sandwiching it in between work and family responsibilities, pay attention to what *time of day* you are most alert and receptive to learning. The best time of day for you to study is dependent on your schedule, your responsibilities, your age, and your personal preferences. Some people identify themselves as "night owls" whereas others claim to be "morning people." Whatever your peak performance time, be sure to study your most difficult subjects at that time. If you have a predictable schedule all semester, plan to study at the same time each day.

The environment in which you study is just as important as the time of day and the length of time you spend studying. You will need to find the kind of environment that works well for you. Some people need complete silence with no visual distractions, whereas others need a little background noise to stay focused. At the least, create a place that is comfortable, with good lighting, and has space for your supplies and books. It is easier to make time to study when you have a place to do it. If you do not have a quiet and roomy location at home, then

FIGURE 6.4 Tips for Making Study Groups Work

- Start with a small group of three to five people.
- Keep a master list of contact information.
- Be creative about meeting. Try doing some of the work, such as creating sample test questions, through chat rooms or email.
- Schedule a time and place that is convenient, comfortable, and conducive to studying.
- Choose a leader for each meeting.
- Assign each person a role in the group and part of the material to "teach" to the group.
- Do your "homework" before meeting by preparing to "teach" your material.
- Review your notes with each other.
- Take frequent breaks.
- Stay on task.
- Be respectful of others' commitments.
- Quiz each other on the material.

search for a place on campus or at a local library that offers study space. Some people prefer studying away from home because they are not distracted by the television, phone, or family members.

Small children can pose a particular difficulty in finding quiet time. If you have small children, make a concerted effort to find a quiet spot. You may need to hire a babysitter or arrange to trade child care services with a classmate when you want to study. For example, you could offer to babysit a classmate's kids when he needs to study in exchange for watching yours when you have a paper to write. Some college students who are also parents find time to study only when their children are asleep. Therefore, their best studying takes place late at night or early in the morning at home. Do whatever works best for you.

Finally, study groups can be a positive option for students who need support as they work through notes and complete projects. Figure 6.4 provides tips for using study groups effectively.

STUDYING ACTIVELY

The goal of active studying is to make connections between concepts and theories so that you can more easily recall the information and write or speak knowledgeably about it. The information on learning and memory earlier in the chapter can help you understand what you need to do to master the material. To achieve this kind of mastery, instead of simply rereading notes or passively reviewing the major headings in your textbook, your studying should include activities such as the following:

- Rewriting or summarizing your notes
- Rearranging the order of the material from most important to least important or in chronological order

- Making connections between what you have learned in one chapter, unit, or class with material you have learned elsewhere
- Making connections between what you have learned in class and what you have experienced in the real world
- Explaining concepts to someone else who is not familiar with the topic
- Making visual representations of the material

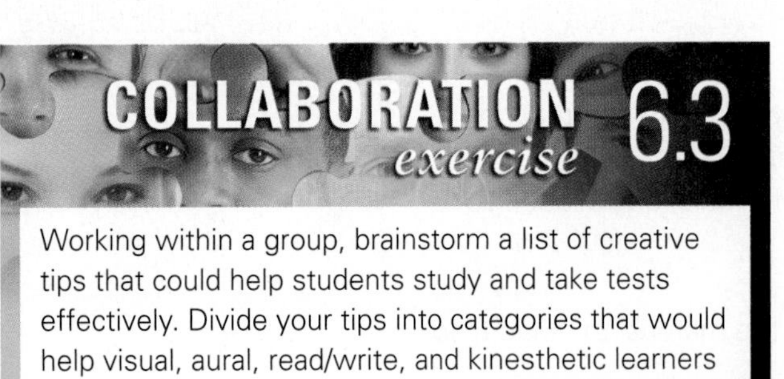

Working within a group, brainstorm a list of creative tips that could help students study and take tests effectively. Divide your tips into categories that would help visual, aural, read/write, and kinesthetic learners

Don't stop with this list of suggestions. Create your own and be aware that different strategies may be needed in different classes.

CREATING "CHEAT" SHEETS

Creating "cheat" sheets was once considered an activity only for those who intended to cheat; however, many educators have seen the benefit they can produce. You may have a professor who tells you that you can bring a three-by-five-inch index card to the exam with anything you want written on it. Students who may not have studied much beforehand usually jump at the chance to cram as much information as possible on that tiny white space. The result is that students retain more of the information than they would if they had not created the cheat sheet. Many times, the cheat sheet is not needed because the student has, in effect, studied adequately in making the sheet.

To create an effective cheat sheet, organization is important. One way to organize the card is to divide it into thirds on both sides so that you have six sections (three on one side, three on the other) to work with. Then, at the top of each section write a specific category such as "Formulas" or "Krebs Cycle." Underneath each heading, write the information that pertains to the category. If you are listing formulas, for example, be sure to write clearly and double-check that all elements of the formula are correct.

Even if you are not allowed to bring a cheat sheet—only bring one if you are given permission—you can still reap the benefits of this technique by closing your books and notes and writing down as much information as you can remember about the subject. For example, if you have a test on genetics, take a blank card and write everything you know about DNA on the front and back. In this case, organization is not important; what is important is to see how much you have learned already. Once you have filled up the card, go back through your notes and books to see what you have missed.

Before you begin to think about what is on a test and how you should study, you must make sure that you are taking care of yourself. Eating and sleeping are fundamental to doing well on tests. If you are not healthy, then you cannot perform at your highest level. Just as athletes prepare for performance days in advance by eating carbohydrates and resting, you should focus on getting regular sleep and eating well days before the exam. At the least, get a good night's rest the night before the test and avoid refined sugar (candy, cakes, and cookies) and caffeine. For more specific information on staying healthy, refer to Chapter 8.

INTEGRITY MATTERS

Numerous recent studies have reported that nearly 75% of college students have admitted to cheating at least once. The reasons students give for cheating are many: Some don't believe that their professors notice or care about their work; some believe that they can justify their cheating because the class or test is unfair; others believe that getting a good grade is the most important goal if scholarships and program admissions (such as nursing school) demand high standards.

No matter what the reason, cheating—and getting caught for cheating—can ruin your college experience. Colleges do take cheating seriously and often have no tolerance for those who cheat. Penalties can range from an F in the course to expulsion from the college.

YOUR TURN Why do *you* think such a high percentage of college students have reported cheating? ■ Do you think colleges create environments in which it is hard to maintain academic integrity? ■ Why or why not?

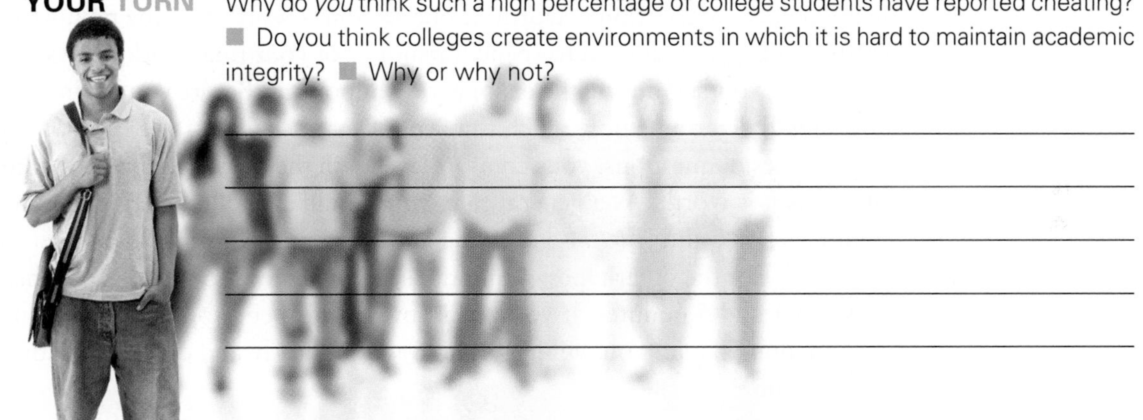

Maintaining a good attitude as you prepare for the exam is another effective strategy. Monitor and eliminate any negative self-talk about your ability to do well on exams. Instead, visualize yourself taking the test successfully and earning a good grade.

TAKING the Test

Once you have prepared for the test, both physically and mentally, you should be ready to take it. Before you leave for class, be sure that you have the appropriate supplies: Will you need a watch, paper, pen, pencil, a calculator, or a dictionary and thesaurus? Are there any approved test-taking aids that you need to bring as well? Will you be able to use your textbook or a cheat sheet with formulas on it?

Once you arrive in class, take a seat away from distractions and where you feel comfortable to spread out and get to work. If you are not wearing a watch, sit where you will be able to see a clock. Cell phone access, which many students use to keep track of time, may be restricted during tests, so be sure to keep track of time some other way. When taking tests that use a bubble form in which you have to pencil in your answers by filling in circles, be sure to bring at least two sharpened pencils.

When you first get the test, read through all the questions, noting which ones will take longer to answer than the others. Taking that time to read all the questions is actually a time saver, because you will know what to expect and how to pace yourself. Turn the paper over and check out the back. Your instructor may have made two-sided copies of the test, which means you will have questions on the back and front of the paper.

As you read through the test, make note of the types of questions and use the tips in this chapter to answer them (see Table 6.4). Read the directions for each section carefully and mark any special instructions. For example, in a matching section, there may be more than one match for an item in one of the columns; in an essay writing section, there may be a choice of topics. Also, be aware of how many points each section is worth. If one section is worth half the points for the entire exam, you will need to spend a majority of your time working that part.

Pacing yourself during the exam is very important. Before you begin the test, you should determine how much time you need to spend on each section based on the types of questions, your comfort level with the questions, and the amount of points it is worth. As a general rule, you should spend less than a minute per multiple choice and true/false question and 15 minutes or more to answer essay questions. For the other types of questions, you will need to spend somewhere in between 1 and 5 minutes. If you get off track and spend too much time on one section, don't panic. You will just need to work quickly and carefully on the rest of the exam.

TABLE 6.4 Test Question Types and Strategies

Test Question Types	Strategies
Multiple Choice	Read the question or statement carefully. Then, mark any special words in the question or statement such as *not, always,* and *only.* Before looking at the choices, see if you can answer the question yourself.
Matching	Read through the entire list and choices to match before beginning. Then, determine if there could be multiple matches to a word in the list. Make sure that you have chosen the correct letter to match with each word in the list.
True/False	Read the statements carefully, noting key words such as *frequently, sometimes,* and *a few.* These words usually indicate a true statement. Words such as *never, only,* and *always* usually indicate a false statement.
Problem Solving	Read the question carefully, marking multiple steps or parts to the directions. Next, determine what information you will need to solve the problem. Then, break the problem into parts and write down what process or operation you will need to perform. Work through the problem, and once you arrive at an answer, check the question again to make sure you have adequately answered it.
Essay	Read the directions carefully. If the essay question has more than one part, be sure to mark each part and answer it in the body of the essay. If the directions specify a length, be sure to meet or exceed it. Before you begin writing, create a brief outline of what you will cover during the essay.

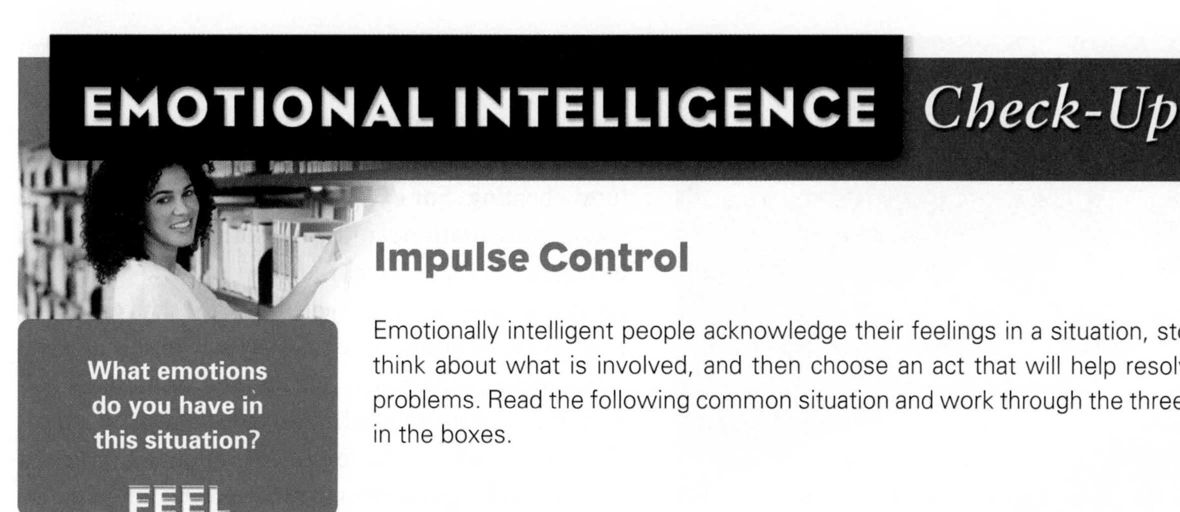

EMOTIONAL INTELLIGENCE *Check-Up*

Impulse Control

Emotionally intelligent people acknowledge their feelings in a situation, stop and think about what is involved, and then choose an act that will help resolve any problems. Read the following common situation and work through the three steps in the boxes.

What emotions do you have in this situation?
FEEL

What is the optimal outcome of the situation for you?
THINK

What attitude and positive action will help you achieve the outcome you want?
ACT

SITUATION

You just failed a major test in your math class. You think it was unfair and covered material that the class had not yet mastered; additionally, you think that you were penalized on some questions on which others were not penalized. You now have only one more opportunity to pass the class, and if you do not pass, not only will you lose your scholarship, but you will also not get into a local nursing program. The more you think about it, the more upset you become. What should you do?

Working the easiest questions first, mark questions that you can't answer quickly or that you find confusing. Don't come back to them until you have completed all the questions that you can easily answer. If you are unsure of an answer, mark that question as well and plan to review it before turning in your exam. If the question or problem has multiple parts, work through as many of the parts as you can. Do not leave questions unanswered. Partial answers may receive partial credit unless you have been instructed otherwise.

Finally, leave yourself 5 to 10 minutes to check your work. If you finish an exam early, always go back through the questions and go over your answers by ensuring that all questions are answered and that all parts are completed. If you have written an essay, read through your response and check for grammatical, spelling, and punctuation errors. Initial each page and number the pages of your essay, if appropriate. Turn in your exam and any paper on which you worked problems or drafted an essay.

MAINTAINING INTEGRITY DURING THE TEST

You may have recently read about the new lengths that students go to in order to cheat on exams or to plagiarize. Advances in technology have made cheating

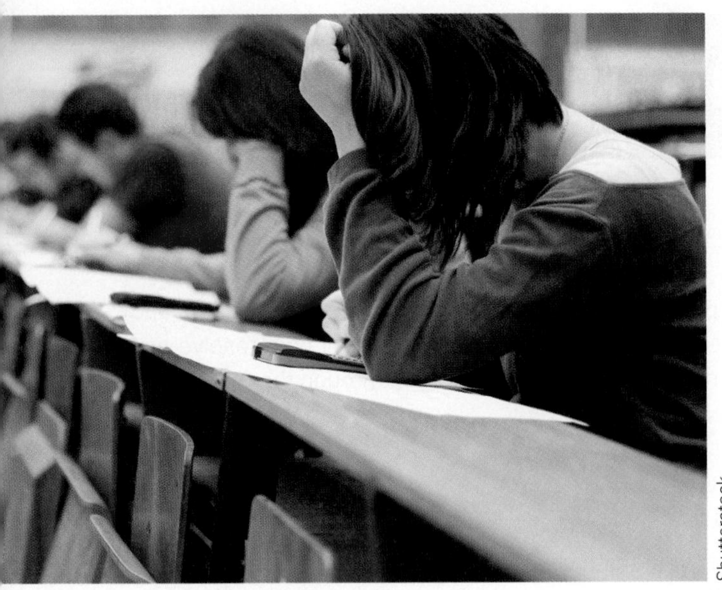
Shutterstock

Learning good test-taking strategies will help you throughout college.

easier and seemingly more widespread, although there is no clear evidence that more students are cheating now than were 30 years ago; however, there does seem to be more confusion about what constitutes cheating. For example, some professors require group presentations and collaboration on projects; however, very few offer guidelines on who should do what and how to document the part that each student does. In addition, collaboration on homework assignments, which was encouraged in high school, may now be prohibited in college. When in doubt about how you should complete homework or group projects, ask your instructor for specific guidelines.

The integrity rules are a little clearer when taking a test. Unless otherwise stated, do not use notes, books, or classmates as references for the exam. Most instructors will ask you to clear your desk of any material except paper and a pen or will ask you to move away from the nearest person. These precautions are to ensure that there are no questions about the originality of the work. Other instructors are more trusting of students and may leave the classroom or give the class a take-home test. An instructor who allows such freedom is sending you a message about integrity: He trusts that his students will act maturely, responsibly, and honestly. Violating that trust can have grave consequences, because not only does the cheating student create problems for herself, but she has also damaged the relationship of trust for the entire class.

CRITICAL THINKING *exercise* 6.4

What types of questions are most challenging for you? What strategies can you employ to master them?

To ensure that you act with integrity when taking an exam, whether supervised or not, do your own work and keep your work surface clear of books, papers, folders, cell phones, pagers, and even drink bottles. If possible, distance yourself from other students so that they are less likely to cheat off you. If you are ever in doubt, however, about your actions or the requirements for an exam, be sure to ask your professor.

BEATING TEST ANXIETY

"I am my own worst enemy sometimes when it comes to test taking. I have learned to tell myself over and over again 'You can do it!' Positive thinking helps me be less nervous."

—Jing-Mei, 45, student

All of the information in this chapter is difficult to put into practice if you have overwhelming anxiety about taking tests. It is not unusual to experience nervousness, anxiety, and fear before or during a test, but extreme anxiety accompanied by excessive sweating, nausea, and crying is not normal. If you are experiencing conditions that make taking and completing tests impossible, you should see a college counselor or other professional. However, if you occasionally experience very mild reactions, there are some techniques that can help minimize your anxiety and fear. Remember that some degree of nervousness is normal and can actually give you an adrenaline boost.

Basic relaxation techniques such as deep breathing and visualizations can take the edge off the tension of taking a test. Taking the time to breathe deeply whenever you feel overwhelmed will help you stay in control. Also, visualizing yourself relaxing or succeeding at a test can help you get beyond self-defeating doubt and stress.

Transfer Tips: FROM COLLEGE TO UNIVERSITY

Different Types of Thinking Will Be Needed to Continue Your Learning

When you transfer to a university, you will continue to use creative, analytical, and critical thinking skills. In upper-level classes, your professors will move away from knowledge and comprehension to synthesis and evaluation. You will spend more time doing research and determining whether the sources you find are reliable and accurate. You will also use those sources to support your own new ideas, developed through creative thinking, about current issues in your major. All in all, you will be more responsible for the depth and breadth of your education, and strong thinking skills will help you deepen your learning.

Transfer Tips: FROM COLLEGE TO CAREER

How Critical Thinking Will Be Used on the Job

Critical thinking on the job is essential to a rewarding and successful career. Your employer, no matter what your position, will value your ability to think critically and solve problems, and you will value the work you do if you are allowed to use those skills to improve yourself and your environment.

How will you use critical thinking on the job? There will be, no doubt, countless opportunities to think critically at work. You may be asked to think critically about a problem in order to solve it. For example, you may realize that the office does not run efficiently and you have evaluated ways to improve the flow of work. No matter how you arrive at thinking critically on the job, keep the steps to problem solving handy.

As you have read in this chapter, critical thinking is a process, not an end. Once you have solved a problem, new issues will arise that require critical thinking. To improve yourself and your progress on the job, you will have to be committed to thinking critically.

References and Recommended Readings

Diestler, S. (1998). *Becoming a critical thinker: A user friendly manual* (2nd ed.). Upper Saddle River, NJ: Prentice Hall.

Dweck, C. (2006). *Mindset: The new psychology of success*. New York: Random House.

Gunn, A. M., Richburg, R. W., and Smilkstein, R. (2007). *Igniting student potential: Teaching with the brain's natural learning process*. Thousand Oaks, CA: Corwin Press.

Harris, R. (2002). *Creative problem solving: A step-by-step approach*. Los Angeles: Pyrczak Publishing.

Miller, G. (2008). The magical number seven, plus or minus two: Some limits on our capacity for processing information. Retrieved March 10, 2008, from www.musanim.com/miller1956

Pink, D. (2006). *A whole new mind*. New York: Penguin.

Von Oech, R. (1998). *A whack on the side of the head*. New York: Warner Books.

CHAPTER seven

WRITING, Researching, and Information Literacy

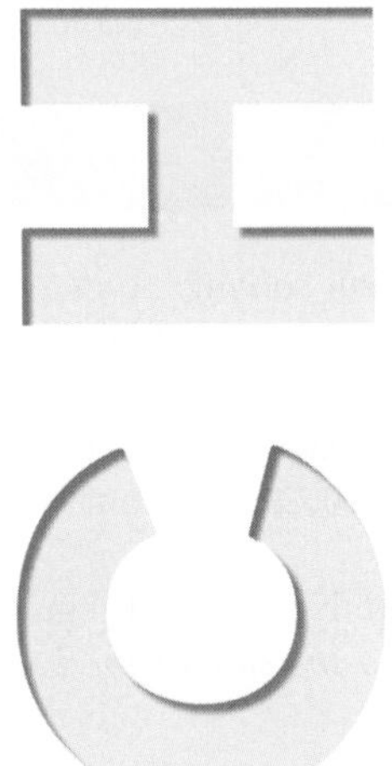

IN THIS chapter Regardless of your major or final career destination, you will be asked to write in college and possibly in your job. As you know from college classes so far, writing well is an important skill, and you will have the chance to improve your writing while enrolled in college.

Although a discussion of all aspects of good writing is beyond the scope of this chapter, it does provide an overview of the basics of writing well. It will also be a good

reference to use when you have completed your composition class and need to refresh your memory about effective writing.

More specifically, after completing this chapter, you will be able to do the following:

- Explain the expectations of college writing and the types of writing assigned.
- Identify the steps in the writing process.
- Discuss the stages of research.
- Describe the process for creating an effective presentation.

COLLEGE Writing Assignments

Homework has a more complex meaning in college than it did in high school. These assignments are more than just reinforcements of what you learned in class, and they certainly are not the dreaded "busy work" that some high school students suffer; instead, the assignments you are given in college will challenge you to think in ways that you may not be used to, and they will demand much more time than you may have needed to complete assignments in high school. For sure, you will encounter familiar assignments such as extra problem-solving

FIGURE 7.1 **Types of Writing and Presentation Assignments**

- Journals
- Portfolios
- Project proposals
- Essays
- Research papers
- Reports
- Demonstrations (lab work, procedures, etc.)
- In-class and out-of-class group assignments
- Formal and informal classroom presentations

questions in math classes and research papers in English classes, but you may also be required to complete a class multimedia project that involves using slide presentation software or even a community-based project that entails working with various agencies to develop a real-world solution to a problem and then presenting it to local politicians. Other types of writing and presentation assignments you may encounter are listed in Figure 7.1.

UNDERSTANDING THE ASSIGNMENT

Before you can revel in the glory of a well-done project or essay, you will have to start with first things first. Understanding the assignment is the first, and sometimes the most crucial, step in succeeding. Too many students jump right in without fully understanding the directions, the requirements, or the time, equipment, and skills that are necessary to complete the assignment.

FOLLOWING DIRECTIONS

Giving yourself the time to complete an assignment will allow you to carefully read and follow the directions. Too often students rush through an assignment sheet only to omit a critical part of the requirements. For example, are you instructed to submit your assignment via email? Will you need to prepare a list of resources you used to complete it? Does it have to be typed? Are you expected to make visual aids? If your assignment has multiple parts, it is important that you complete each part and pay attention to how the parts will be presented. All of these are possible requirements, and if you are unsure of what is expected of you, despite the assignment details, be sure to ask for clarification. Table 7.1 provides an overview of the basic expectations for college writing.

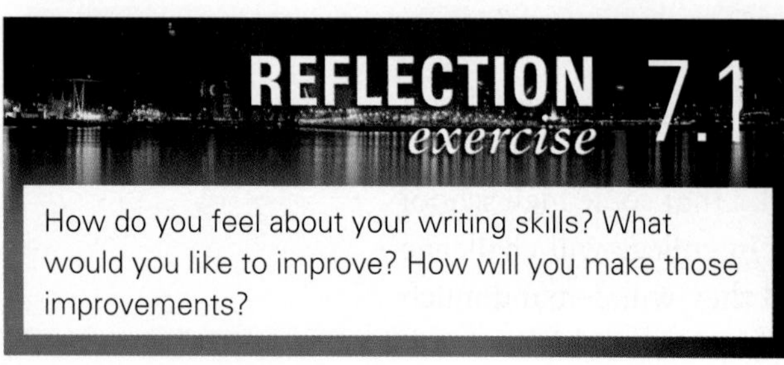

How do you feel about your writing skills? What would you like to improve? How will you make those improvements?

TABLE 7.1 Top Ten Writing Expectations in College

Expectation for College Writing	What It Means
Fulfillment of the assignment	Your paper faithfully follows the assignment guidelines.
Original thought	Your paper presents your own viewpoint of the topic.
Main point or idea	Your paper conveys one major idea.
Organization	Your paragraphs and the details within those paragraphs are presented logically.
Focused paragraphs	Your paragraphs present one minor idea at a time. Each minor idea supports your overall main point.
Concrete, specific details	Your concrete details appeal to the reader's senses; your specific details provide a clear picture of your point.
Neat presentation	Your paper is neatly word-processed and printed on clean, quality paper.
Grammatical sentences	Your sentences are complete and error-free.
Correct spelling	All of your words are spelled and capitalized correctly.
Punctual	Your assignment is turned in on time.

LENGTH, AUDIENCE, AND PURPOSE

Length, audience, and purpose are other key factors in understanding writing assignments. For many assignments, you will be given a required length, such as a two-page paper or a 1,500-word essay. Instructors assign lengths to help you gauge the development that you need in order to fulfill the assignment adequately. For instance, if your instructor assigns you a one-page review of a website, then a ten-page paper will not be appropriate because too much information will be included. Conversely, if you have a 2,500-word research paper to write, a 750-word paper will not suffice because there will not be enough information and reflection to fulfill the assignment. If you worry that you cannot meet the length requirement of an assignment, talk with your instructor as soon as possible. He or she will be able to help you narrow or expand your topic so that you will have enough material.

The audience for your assignment includes any potential readers of your paper. When creating a writing assignment, many instructors assume that the audience is your classmates or people who are interested in the subject, but many students assume that the only person who will read their papers is the instructor. If an audience is not specified for your assignment, imagine that you are writing to college students who have been studying the same subject—such as your classmates. How you present your ideas and the words you use should be appropriate for other college students. However, there may be times when you will be assigned a particular audience as part of the requirements for a writing project. The reason that instructors do this is to help you focus your ideas, language, and argument. Consider, for example, an assignment that may be part of a health class:

Writing Assignment for Concepts of Health and Wellness

In a three-page paper, discuss the latest information about sexually transmitted diseases.

This is a straightforward assignment that can be completed by anyone who has access to current information. However, how would the assignment change if your audience were 12-year-old public school students? What information would you add or eliminate? What kind of language would you use? Would you include diagrams and definitions or cartoons? How much detail would you provide? These are all new considerations you will have to make because your audience will have certain limitations. Unfamiliar vocabulary, technical terms, detailed information, and photographs may be inappropriate for these students. Simple terms, diagrams, and personal stories about kids their own age may be a better way to convey the more complicated information.

Now, consider the same topic with a different audience: 70- to 80-year-old men and women who live in a nursing home. Again, you will have the same questions: What information would you add or eliminate? What kind of language would you use? Would you include diagrams and definitions or cartoons? How much detail would you provide? Obviously, this audience will have different needs than young students. Because your audience is more mature, you will need to think about how to approach a topic that they have definite ideas about. Some may be resistant to hearing about the topic because they believe it is not appropriate to discuss, or others may feel they know enough to make their own decisions. Still others will not see the relevance for them. As our two examples show, certain challenges are unique to your audience—changing *who* you are writing for changes *how* you present the information.

"Learn the process of writing an essay and learn it quickly. Once you get that nailed down, the writing assignments won't seem so intimidating."
—Nora, 22, student

A final consideration for your assignment is the purpose. Your purpose for writing will be closely connected to the assignment (see the assignment types noted in Table 7.2), but there are additional purposes for writing. For example, in addition to evaluating a website, your purpose could also be to make your audience laugh. Or in comparing two popular diet plans in a paper, your purpose could be to persuade readers that one of the plans is a healthier choice. The purposes for writing are endless, but it is important to ask yourself why you are writing and what you want to accomplish besides completing an assignment or getting a good grade. The answers to those questions will be your purpose for writing, and knowing that purpose will help you complete your assignment ef-

FIGURE 7.2 Example of Assignment Directions

Topic Proposal

Due: Wednesday, April 18

Before you begin work on your research paper, you will submit a proposal to me for approval. This process is much like proposals that scholars submit to determine if they will be accepted for a conference. Your proposal must be typed and must contain the following, all on one or two pages:

- Your name
- Working title of your research paper
- Working thesis of your research paper
- A 75-word abstract (summary) of your topic
- A 100-word description of how you plan to research your topic

fectively. See Figure 7.2 for an example of what a typical college writing assignment can look like.

TYPES OF WRITING ASSIGNMENTS

Many students underestimate the importance of reading and understanding the writing assignment before they begin writing. Carefully reading and taking note of what you are asked to do will save you time in the long run. The key to fulfilling any assignment is to know what your instructor wants you to do. Table 7.2 presents different types of writing assignments and how to fulfill each one. Note how the verbs used relate to the type of assignment.

FORMATS AND OCCASIONS

Research papers and essays will not be the only way you are asked to show your professors how well you write and think. You may also be asked to show your writing ability in other formats and for different occasions. Essay exams and portfolios are the two most popular types of assignments that will require an ability to write well, but you may also need to demonstrate your writing skills in group projects and multimedia presentations. One of the benefits of writing well is that you can easily move from one type of assignment to another. The key to success is to learn what additional writing skills are necessary for these different formats and occasions.

PORTFOLIOS

A writing portfolio is a collection of your writing throughout the semester. This type of project is popular with instructors because it allows students to work on their writing continuously. Instead of getting a grade on the first draft that is turned in, students can revise papers until they meet the minimal standards for

TABLE 7.2 Writing Prompts, Definitions, and Explanations

Writing Prompt	Definition	Explanation
Summary	A brief retelling of a subject.	In a summary, you will cover the main points of an event or a text, without offering your opinion on the subject.
Evaluation	Asks for your opinion.	You will need to consider the subject's strengths and weaknesses, and you will need to provide specific examples to support your ideas.
Discussion or description	Provides specific details about the topic.	The more specific details you can provide, the more likely you will adequately describe or define the subject.
Analysis	Breaks a subject apart and looks at its components carefully.	Once you have investigated the parts, you must put the subject back together again.
Comparison and contrast	Examines two subjects more carefully to make a significant point about them.	Before you describe their similarities and then their differences, you will set up the reason for the comparison and contrast.
Synthesis	Combines two or more sources into an essay.	A synthesis uses your perspective or argument as the foundation and provides the reader with ideas and support from other sources.
Persuasive argument	Takes a stand about a topic and encourages readers to agree.	A persuasive argument is most effective when specific, accurate details are presented. Effective persuasion requires that you treat your readers with respect and that you present your argument fairly.

the course. A benefit of the portfolio method is that students can focus on the process of writing instead of the final product—the polished paper.

"Find out what the expectations are in each class as soon as you can. Ask for sample assignments that were high quality. Don't go into a writing assignment with no clue what the expectation is . . . or you may not meet it."
—Curtis, 39, student

The best way to handle a writing portfolio is to first review the requirements, including due dates and policies on completing final drafts. If you have questions about expectations, especially if you have never completed a portfolio before, ask your instructor and schedule periodic meetings to make sure that you are completing the components successfully. Finally, take advantage of the opportunity to submit multiple drafts and receive feedback on them. Revising essays for a portfolio takes time, but the rewards are extensive feedback and help with improving your writing.

EVALUATION OF WRITING

Your college professors may vary widely in how they evaluate your written assignments. Some professors look for and reward key words and concepts in an essay exam, whereas others mark and count off for grammatical, mechanical, and organizational problems even if the key concepts are easily identifiable. You will soon learn, if you have not already, that each professor has his or her own criteria for grading written assignments, and the sooner you learn what the criteria are, the better able you will be to complete assignments satisfactorily.

If your professor does not give you a list of grading criteria, you should ask for a sample assignment or a list of what the professor will be looking for. Talking with the professor before and after the assignment is graded is the best way to know what to expect. Asking other students who have taken classes with the professor is another way to get an idea of how you will be evaluated.

Remember that professors expect you to write at a college level and that your writing assignments will reflect the characteristics that have been discussed in this chapter. You may find that although you received good grades on papers in high school, you have to work much harder for those same grades on college papers. In addition to higher standards, you should be aware that your professors' job is to make you a better thinker and writer, no matter what the subject.

GETTING HELP with Writing

There may be times when a writing assignment is confusing or overwhelming. If at any time you don't understand what you are supposed to do or you feel stressed about the assignment, contact your instructor as soon as you can. Stressing out about the assignment will only make it seem impossible to complete. Instructors know you have other responsibilities and classes and are often willing to work with you if you have planned ahead and asked for help early.

When getting help with an assignment, be sure to ask your instructor first—he or she is the one who will best know what needs to be done. If your college has a writing center, you should make an appointment with a tutor as soon as you realize you need some help. Writing center tutors will be able to explain what you need to do to complete the assignment.

Other students in the class and friends who are not in the class can be other sources of help, but use their support cautiously. Your classmates may not know much more about the expectations than you. Moreover, your instructor may prohibit any kind of collaboration, even if it is to better understand what you need to do. Getting help from anyone who is not in the class or not taking college courses should be your last resort because they are even further removed from your instructor's expectations.

No matter who helps you with the assignment, be sure that you are doing the assignment rather than letting

You will use critical thinking for all kinds of situations while you are in college.

Stockdisc

INTEGRITY MATTERS

One major consideration when beginning and completing your writing assignment is maintaining academic integrity; that is, when writing papers that require no research, follow one simple rule: Do the work yourself. Unless your instructor explicitly states that you can work together with a classmate *and* can share answers or help while completing the assignment, avoid collaboration when completing written assignments.

At no time should you copy the answers that another student has written. Just as you would not share answers during a test, it is best not to share your answers on work that is assigned out of class. If you have taken a class in a previous semester, you will also want to keep your assignments from being shared. Instructors may use the same assignments from semester to semester, and you don't want to put a fellow student in an awkward or potentially bad situation.

YOUR TURN In what ways do students compromise academic integrity, perhaps without even knowing it? ■ What safeguards do you put in place to ensure academic integrity when working with others, helping classmates with assignments or getting help, or using resources other than those required or suggested by your professors?

someone else do it for you. Some students, out of fear or frustration, have found others to complete part or all of their assignments. The most obvious reason to not allow someone else to help too much is that your instructor could penalize you for not doing the assignment yourself. More important, if you do not complete the assignment yourself, you are robbing yourself of an opportunity to learn more about the subject that you are studying and about yourself.

PEER REVIEW

Peer review is a process that you may go through in your composition classes or in classes that have an important group project as part of your grade. Peer review is defined as a procedure in which a classmate evaluates your work. This may occur in a peer review workshop, common in writing classes, in which you and a classmate exchange papers and assess how well each of you has met the assignment requirements. You may also be looking for grammatical and spelling errors, which can be corrected before your final draft or project is submitted.

Peer review, especially if assigned as part of your work in a class, can be extremely helpful to you. It can show you what others in the class are writing about and how they are completing assignments, which can in turn help you gauge how well you are doing. It can also help you learn how to correct mistakes, because you may find it easier to see errors in others' papers than in yours. Finally, it can help you get your paper in shape before you complete it for submission.

CRITICAL THINKING exercise 7.2

Think about an instance in which getting substantial help on a writing assignment can actually help a student learn important concepts. What kind of instance would it be? Why would it actually be an advantage? Are there any disadvantages that the student would experience as well?

TUTORING

Another form of assistance available to you as you write your papers is tutoring. Most colleges have a learning assistance center or tutoring lab where other students or professional tutors are available to help those who need it. Tutoring is especially valuable if certain skills, such as grammar or spelling, need to be practiced and refined. The tutors at your college are usually trained to help students with the most common problems, and they have the added benefit of having completed the very courses they tutor in, so they know what to expect in terms of assignments and grading. Tutors, just as peer reviewers, however, cannot assure a good grade on an assignment that is reviewed. They can, though, point out areas that need to be improved and provide resources to help you become more aware of your strengths and weaknesses as a writer.

HOW MUCH IS TOO MUCH HELP?

How do you know when you have received too much help on a writing assignment? If someone else writes whole sentences, paragraphs, and pages for you or supplies you with many main ideas and examples that you use in your paper, then you have probably received too much assistance on your writing assignment. Some professors disapprove of editing and proofreading services as well. When in doubt, check with your professor and explain what kind of help you are getting.

THE WRITING Process

Once you have read and understood the writing assignment, it is time to use one or more prewriting techniques to get your ideas down on paper before you start organizing them and writing your rough draft. You probably have your own way of writing, but it is worth investigating some of these proven methods for generating ideas.

There are three common prewriting techniques that you can use to generate details for your paper. *Freewriting* is a simple way to get ideas down on paper.

The only rules in freewriting are to start with an idea and stop only after you have filled a page or after a certain amount of time has passed. When freewriting, you can allow your mind to wander off the subject; you must, however, write down everything that comes to mind. Later, when you start organizing your details, you can eliminate anything that does not pertain to your subject. If you are a good typist, you can freewrite by typing into a blank document. Don't worry about spelling, grammar, or punctuation when you freewrite—the purpose is to free your mind of that little voice that censors everything you think.

Clustering is another method of prewriting that works well for those who learn better by visualizing concepts. Clusters, or think links, are visual representations of ideas and their relationship to each other. The key to clustering is to start in the middle of a sheet of paper, write down your topic, and circle it. Draw a line from your subject and write down a related topic that is part of the subject. For instance, "types," "prevention," and "treatment" are all parts of the topic "sexually transmitted diseases." In addition, subtopics branch off "prevention"—for example, "abstinence" and "condoms." The words and phrases that surround a topic or subtopic must be connected to it, both logically and literally, by drawing lines.

Another effective method for generating ideas is *brainstorming,* a process that involves writing down ideas as they come to you. The goal in brainstorming is to get as many ideas as possible down on paper, no matter how ridiculous or off-topic they are. The more details you generate, the more you have to work with as you begin organizing your paper. To brainstorm, simply write your topic at the top of a sheet of paper, or type it into a new document on your computer, and then start listing any and all ideas that come to mind in the form of a list.

CREATING A THESIS AND ORGANIZING DETAILS

Once you make a list of details that you would like to use in your paper, give some thought as to what your main point will be, a topic sentence if it is a paragraph or a thesis if it is an essay, before you decide how you would like to organize the details. Your main point will be at least one sentence that tells the reader what the whole piece will present or argue.

There are a variety of ways that you can organize a paper effectively. You can arrange the details from most to least important or vice versa. Details can also be arranged chronologically, especially if you are writing about an event that needs to follow a specific time line. Or your points can be arranged from general ideas to specific or specific details to general. It is important to organize your points logically; how you arrange the supporting details will depend on your purpose and audience, as long as each detail builds on the previous and leads to the next while supporting your thesis.

WRITING ESSAYS

The word *essay* has its origins in French and means "an attempt" or "a trial." For college students, writing essays is an attempt, or a trial, in some sense, to meet the assignment without going crazy! In the context of college, an essay is

EMOTIONAL INTELLIGENCE *Check-Up*

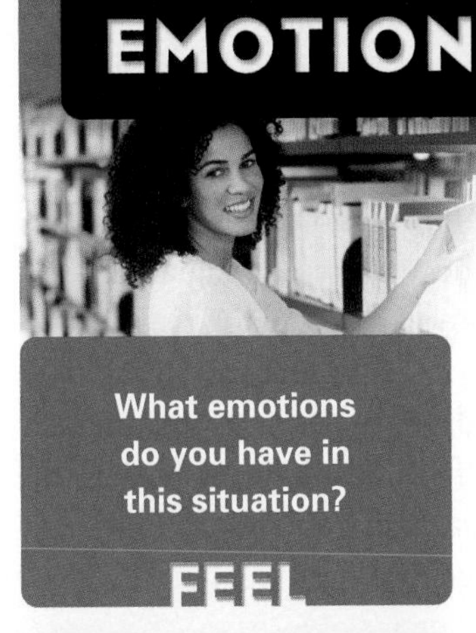

Problem Solving

Emotionally intelligent people acknowledge their feelings in a situation, stop and think about what is involved, and then choose an act that will help resolve any problems. Read the following common situation and work through the three steps in the boxes.

What emotions do you have in this situation?

FEEL

What is the optimal outcome of the situation for you?

THINK

What attitude and positive action will help you achieve the outcome you want?

ACT

SITUATION

In two of your classes, you have to write a research paper in the next three weeks. In your sociology class, you get to choose the topic, but you have to tie your research and conclusions to a sociological concept you have learned. You also have a paper to write in your health class about community health centers and their impact on improving the health of the community members. You don't feel as though you have time to write both well. In fact, you wonder if you can write one paper for both classes. What should you do?

---

a written composition on a particular subject that offers the author's view. If, for example, you are asked to write an essay on the death penalty or obesity in children, then you will need to present your viewpoint on the subject. Essays do not usually contain research; instead, they are built on your observations, details, and opinions. They are, in essence, an attempt by you to convey your viewpoint on a subject and perhaps to learn something more of what you think about that subject.

When you are assigned an essay for a class, you need to include some basic components. Without all of them, your essay is simply a piece of writing, just as a few bones do not make up an entire skeleton. At the least, you will need a title, introduction, thesis, body paragraphs, and a conclusion.

AVOIDING PLAGIARISM

No word strikes fear and confusion in academic writers more than *plagiarism.* Simply defined, plagiarism is the use of another's words or ideas without proper acknowledgment. Put another way, if the information or the expression of the information comes from another source besides your own brain, then you must let the reader know what that source is. Proper acknowledgment can be as simple as naming the source or it can be as complex as using a documentation system such as MLA (Modern Language Association) or APA (American Psychological Association). Penalties for plagiarism can range from redoing the assignment to facing expulsion from college. Because most colleges do not distinguish between intentional and unintentional borrowing, it is in your best interest to learn how to avoid plagiarism.

"Plagiarism is a really serious offense in college. You could get an F in a course from submitting a plagiarized paper."

—Tashonda, 20, student

You may ask yourself, "If I don't know what plagiarism is, can I still be penalized if I don't mean to do it?" The answer is that your professors will expect that you already know how to distinguish between your own and others' ideas. If you don't know how to do that, or if you are unsure how you can avoid plagiarism, you should talk with your professors or seek assistance from the writing center.

INFORMATION Literacy

It has been estimated that we have access to more than 100 million websites in seconds. With so many choices and so many outlets for information sharing, many of us get lost in all the possibilities from a simple Google search! Fortunately, there are some tools that you can use to help you find and use information more efficiently and effectively. Those tools are the basis of what is known as *information literacy,* which, simply stated, is the ability to find, understand, evaluate, and incorporate information from a variety of sources or media. The Association of College and Research Libraries defines information literacy as the ability to "recognize when information is needed and . . . the ability to locate, evaluate, and use effectively the needed information." No matter what the research assignment, you will learn to use information literacy skills to help you manage the process more successfully.

"Students have to have good information literacy skills to complete assignments. Without them, they may assume that any kind of information they find is acceptable to use in an assignment. There is good information and there is bad information out there. They need to know the difference."

—Kara, 30, professor

RECOGNIZING WHEN INFORMATION IS NEEDED

Before you can begin to find sources, however, you will need to consider length, audience, and purpose of your assignment, and you will need to pay close attention to the requirements for your research. Instructors may insist that you use certain journals or databases, or they may ask for survey results or literature reviews. As with any writing assignment, you should start early and break it up into manageable parts. For a research paper, you will need to invest a considerable amount of time and energy.

The assignment information you are given may help you determine what your topic will be. In some cases, your professor will be very specific; for example, an assignment may state, "Write a research paper in which you present three methods for teaching preschool children to read." Other professors may be less direct—for example, "Write a paper on an important historical event." If you are ever unsure as to what your topic should be, always ask well before the assignment is due. Oftentimes, you can get ideas for narrowing the topic from the professor or your classmates.

Before you settle on a topic to research, consider the assignment's purpose and length. If you are writing a ten-page paper, your topic will need to be broader than a five-page paper. Also, if you are required to argue a point rather than provide basic information, your topic, and your subsequent research, will be focused differently. Determining your topic first, regardless of what it is, will save you time when you begin to find sources for your paper.

FINDING AND EVALUATING INFORMATION

Once you determine your topic, you can then begin to search for sources for your paper. You will definitely want to learn how to use your library's catalog and databases beforehand. Oftentimes, the library will provide an orientation to students or you can get one-on-one assistance from a staff member. Never waste valuable time by being confused—ask someone for help if you are not sure how to find information.

Your assignment and topic will influence what kinds of sources you need for your paper. If your education class requires that you find websites that provide

TECH TACTICS

Using Technology to Get Ahead

Your college's website can provide you with links to resources, such as the tutoring center or the library, that can help you with your assignments. Many colleges place their tutoring center hours on the website as well as some electronic resources for students who cannot come to campus to access the services. Likewise, more and more college libraries provide accessible information that can help students in the research process. Visit both and see what information and assistance is available at your fingertips.

RECOMMENDED SITES

- www.ccc.commnet.edu/mla/index.shtml Capital Community College provides a thorough resource for college students to follow the research process.
- http://owl.english.purdue.edu/owl/resource/658/1 Purdue's Online Writing Lab (OWL) is a well-established "go to" site for all things related to writing in college.
- www.aresearchguide.com/3tips.html Making presentations just got a little easier with the strategies provided at this site.

information on cyberbullying in elementary schools, then you will know to look at online sources for your paper. However, if your education class requires that you write a research paper on the latest studies about cyberbullying, you will most likely need to access journals in your library's databases to find scholarly articles on the subject.

"Finding sources and using them properly is an important part of writing and it *takes time!* Most of the students I tutor want to rush through this part. You have to give yourself time to do it right!"
—Terry, 23, tutor

Once you find your sources, you will need to spend time deciding if they are reliable, credible, and useable for your paper. Again, look to your assignment or to your professor for guidance if you are unsure whether a source is acceptable for your paper. Most likely, if it is a source that you have found in the library's catalog or databases, it should be a credible source.

USING INFORMATION EFFECTIVELY

Deciding what to put into your paper is the next step in the research process. How you do this will depend on the *documentation style* that your professor requires. Two of the most common are MLA (Modern Language Association) and APA (American Psychological Association), but there are more that you will need to be familiar with, such as Chicago Manual of Style (CMS) and Council of Biology Editors (CBE) formats. A documentation style simply means the format in which you acknowledge your sources within the paper and at the end in the references or works cited page.

Regardless of which style you use, using sources in your paper requires that you provide essential information, usually the author's name and the title of the source, whenever you first use it in your paper. This means that whether you are quoting directly or paraphrasing, which is putting the author's ideas into your own words, you will need to let your reader know the origin of the information. Proper acknowledgement and documentation are essential to incorporating your sources correctly. Your professor will certainly want to hear *your* thoughts on the topic, but she will also expect you to have found sources and documented them properly to support your ideas.

COLLABORATION *exercise* 7.3

Working in a group, discuss the steps to writing a research paper outlined in the preceding section and determine why students usually have trouble with research papers. What part of the process is most difficult? What can students do to make the process easier?

MAKING SPEECHES and Presentations

Learning to speak and present on a topic effectively in college is a skill that will benefit you not only on the job but also in life. For example, you may need to speak on behalf of the parents at your children's school as president of the Parents and Teachers Association, or you may be asked to make weekly announcements at your church. In your college classes, you will more than likely get a specific assignment (Give a 5-minute persuasive speech on a current event) or a specific topic (cloning). However, not all speaking experiences will begin with detailed directions. You may be asked to introduce someone or to "talk for about 10 minutes about whatever you think will interest the audience." Regardless of how you are assigned a speech, the process will be the same: You will need to plan, prepare, deliver, and assess.

PLANNING A SPEECH OR PRESENTATION

Choosing a topic is the first step to preparing to speak, just as it is in the writing process. At times, you will be provided a topic, but in some of your classes—or for some occasions—you will be allowed to create your own. Topics for speeches can come from your personal experience, current events, or from in-depth research. If you are not sure which personal experience, current event, or research topic you want to explore, it is a good idea to use brainstorming or another method of generating ideas (discussed earlier in this chapter) to determine which topic interests you the most.

Deciding your purpose will be your next step. You may need to inform, persuade, or entertain your audience. If you will be informing them of your topic, you will more than likely use details and language that present the information in an unbiased manner. If you will be persuading your audience, you will probably employ examples and language to change their attitudes or beliefs. Entertaining your audience will involve including information, details, and language that will get a laugh or amuse. Your speech can have more than one purpose—and sometimes all three—but one will be the most emphasized.

Just as writers need to identify their audience before they begin writing, speakers must also consider whom they will be addressing. Audience analysis is the process by which speakers determine who will be the recipients of the message. Audience analysis questions include the following: How many people will be in the audience? What are the characteristics of the audience (gender, ages, race, culture, educational background, learning style, etc.)? What are their attitudes toward your topic? What do they know about the topic?

"Practice, practice, practice. It is the only way to be a better speaker and to lessen your anxiety."
—Robb, 50, instructor

Occasion analysis questions include the following: When are you speaking? How long will you have to speak? What is the space like (if you can find out in advance)? What else will you need? Visual aids? Handouts? Time for questions or discussion?

VOCAL DELIVERY

What if you crafted a fantastic speech and no one ever heard it because they couldn't understand what you were saying? Sound impossible? It has, unfortunately, happened before: A great speech is lost because the speaker didn't project his voice or mumbled through the words. Vocal delivery, then, is the most important aspect to getting the words out successfully. Consider the following suggestions when practicing and delivering a speech:

- *Pay attention to tone and pitch.* Is the vocal quality of your voice soft or harsh? Do you sound angry or giddy? Audience members prefer voices that are easy to listen to.

Your Terms of SUCCESS

WHEN YOU SEE . . .	IT MEANS . . .
Analysis	To break apart a subject to examine its parts as they relate to the whole subject.
Audience	The person or persons who will be reading your paper or listening to your speech.
Brainstorming	A prewriting technique that involves writing down everything that comes to mind in a list.
Clustering	A prewriting technique that involves visually representing how a subject is related to other subjects; also called mind mapping.
Conclusion	The last paragraph of an essay, presenting your overall points and final thoughts.
Concrete details	Details or examples that appeal to a reader's sight, taste, smell, touch, or hearing.
Description	Explaining the characteristics of an object, subject, or experience.
Documentation style	The style used to document the sources in your paper; many professors require either MLA (Modern Language Association) or APA (American Psychological Association) documentation and format for papers.
Essay	Literally "an attempt"; a type of assignment that has an introduction, a thesis, body paragraphs, and a conclusion.
Freewriting	A prewriting technique that involves writing freely and without consideration of punctuation, grammar, or spelling.
Organization	How your details for your essay or paper are placed.
Outline	The essential parts of a paper or speech; usually presented in a specific outline format using Roman numerals for each major part.
Peer review	A process in which a peer, or classmate, evaluates your paper or project.
Persuasive argument	Presents a debatable idea in order to convince an audience.
Physical delivery	The bodily and facial movements that enhance or distract from a speech.
Plagiarism	The use of another's ideas, words, or images without proper acknowledgement.
Prewriting techniques	The processes by which details for an assignment are generated.
Portfolio	A collection of separate assignments or of drafts of an assignment.
Reflection	To provide a thoughtful consideration of a topic.
Research	The act of finding, evaluating, and incorporating sources into an assignment.
Rough draft	An unpolished attempt at an assignment.
Summary	To provide an overview of what an entire work or subject is about; does not contain original thought or evaluation.
Synthesis	Combines two or more ideas together.
Thesis	An essay's central idea that is supported throughout the writing.
Transitions	Words or phrases that signal a change in thought or additional ideas.
Visual aid	An object that is used to engage an audience or emphasize a point.
Vocal delivery	How the voice is used in a speech.

- *Speak slowly and deliberately.* Make sure that you are properly pronouncing words (check the dictionary) and using correct grammar (consult a writing handbook). Open your mouth and move your lips to ensure that you are enunciating. Speaker credibility is lost when words are not used properly or poorly pronounced.
- *Use variety when speaking.* Vary volume, pitch, and speed to create interest. Pause between points for effect. Do you remember the monotone teacher in the movie *Ferris Buehler's Day Off?* He didn't vary his volume, pitch, and speed, and his students were either asleep or not paying attention.

PHYSICAL DELIVERY

Appropriate nonverbal communication while you are speaking can mean the difference between an effective and an ineffective speech. Paying attention to and practicing your body movements will help you develop good physical habits when speaking. Here are just a few to consider:

Image Source/Getty Images

Part of the college experience is presenting your research in front of your classmates.

- *Dress appropriately.* If you look professional, you appear more credible. Unless you are making a point by dressing down or wearing a costume, dress up. A neat and clean appearance also suggests attention to detail and understanding the importance of all aspects of presentation.
- *Smile at your audience.* It demonstrates a positive attitude and puts your audience at ease.
- *Plant your feet.* Place them firmly on the floor and stand up straight. Slouching or slumping lessens your effectiveness.
- *Act naturally.* The more you practice, the more comfortable you will be with your body movements and less likely to use unnatural, mechanical hand gestures and head movements.
- *Move from the waist up only.* However, make sure it is natural and not stiff and awkward like a robot. Shuffling and pacing are distracting.
- *Step out in front.* Get in front of the podium when speaking to smaller groups of 30 or fewer because it helps create intimacy and connection.
- *Use hand gestures appropriately.* Keep arms and hands close to the body; avoid pointing your finger to emphasize an idea; instead, use a closed fist with thumb slightly up; open hands work well, but avoid banging on the podium or table.
- *Maintain eye contact.* Use the "Figure 8" method of scanning the room so that each area gets your attention throughout the presentation. Think of an 8 lying on its side and trace the curves and lines with your eyes, starting either on the right or left of your audience.

VISUAL AIDS

In addition to considering your delivery methods, both physical and vocal, you may also want to keep in mind how you will use any visual aids. According to Arthur Bradbury (2006), "for a truly powerful *and memorable* presentation you will need to include some form of visual aid" (p. 84). A visual aid can be anything from an object, such as a doll or book, to an elaborate poster or handout emphasizing certain points that the audience can view while you are speaking. Slide presentation software can also provide your audience with a visual representation of your topic.

When using visual aids, remember that they are most effective when they help the audience remember your key points, see a point you are making more clearly, or enliven your presentation without distracting from your words. Here are a few tips for handling your visual aids:

- *Less is always more with visual aids.* They should be simple and easy to understand.
- *Make sure that your aids can be seen clearly by a person at the back of the room.* To be seen and not heard was once a virtue, but you will want both in a presentation with visual aids. Clear writing or large font on a slide presentation will help the audience get your point.
- *Be the center of attention even with a visual aid.* You don't want it to take away attention from your speech or dominate your presentation. A well-considered prop or visual aid should enhance rather than become your speech.

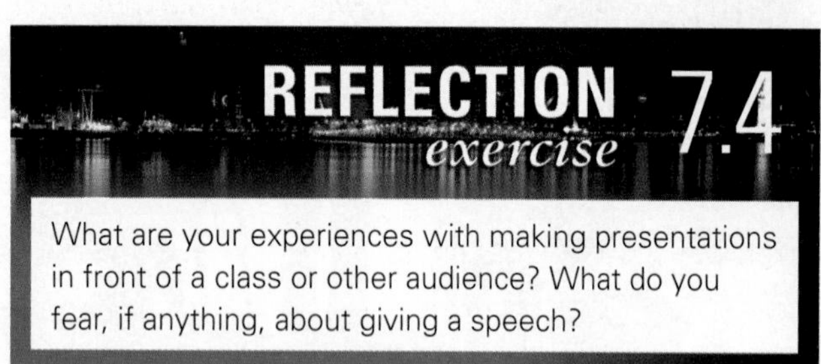

What are your experiences with making presentations in front of a class or other audience? What do you fear, if anything, about giving a speech?

Transfer Tips: FROM COLLEGE TO UNIVERSITY

How Writing Assignments and Expectations Will Change

Most definitely, when you take upper-level courses at the university, you will write more and the expectations will be higher. Your professors who teach at the junior and senior levels will assume that any writing challenges you had in your first two years of college have been overcome. Your professors will be more concerned with the strength and originality of your argument and the depth and breadth of your research than with grammar, punctuation, spelling, and mechanics. Instead, they will expect these lower-level issues to have been mastered, and they will want you to expand on the higher-level issues such as presenting a successful academic argument.

Certainly, you will be writing more to discover what you think about a particular topic. You will also find writing and research more enjoyable as you settle into a major course of study. Most students who transfer and take courses in their major learn that they enjoy writing about subjects that will help them in their careers. This kind of satisfaction comes over time, and although you may not enjoy every writing assignment that you must do in your first two years in college, realize that with each paper you complete, you will become a better writer and thinker, which will help you make your transition to a four-year university that much easier.

Transfer Tips: FROM COLLEGE TO CAREER

Why Strong Speaking Skills Will Set You Apart at Work

Don't think of your speech communication class as the last occasion that you will speak in front of peers and superiors. No matter what career path you take, chances are likely that you will need to use those communication skills to work in groups, relate to your boss, and instruct or present information to your coworkers. Examples of when you will need to rely on what you learned in class include making a presentation to a client, summarizing the company's goals and projects to new employees, or presenting a new idea for efficiency to management. These will all be instances in which you will be able to use what you learned both in class and by frequently practicing your speaking skills for other occasions besides Public Speaking 101. Just as good writing skills are essential to on-the-job success, solid public speaking skills will set you apart from your coworkers as someone who can communicate even the most complicated or mundane aspects of the company's policies. That kind of ability will garner respect and admiration from those who work with you.

References and Recommended Readings

Bradbury, A. (2006). *Successful presentation skills* (3rd ed.). London: Kogan Page.

"Information literacy competency standards for higher education." (2010). Association of College and Research Libraries. Retrieved April 7, 2010, from www.ala.org/ala/mgrps/divs/acrl/standards/informationliteracycompetency.cfm#f1

Strunk, W., & White, E. B. (1999). *The elements of style* (4th ed.). Boston: Allyn & Bacon.

Tracy, B. (2008). *Speak to win: How to present with power in any situation.* New York: AMACOM Books.

Wilder, L. (1999). *Seven steps to fearless speaking.* New York: John Wiley & Sons.

Zinsser, W. (2006). *On writing well* (30th anniv. ed.). New York: Harper Paperbacks.

CHAPTER eight

MAKING Healthy Choices

IN THIS chapter For most of us, minimizing the negative effects of stress and maximizing good health is a matter of making appropriate choices. How to decrease stress, how to increase energy, what to eat, how much to exercise, and how to reconnect with ourselves are judgments we make every day, yet so many of us make inappropriate choices. The choices we make now are decisions that we will literally have to live with for decades to come. We will be living longer than our ancestors did, but will our lives and our health be bet-

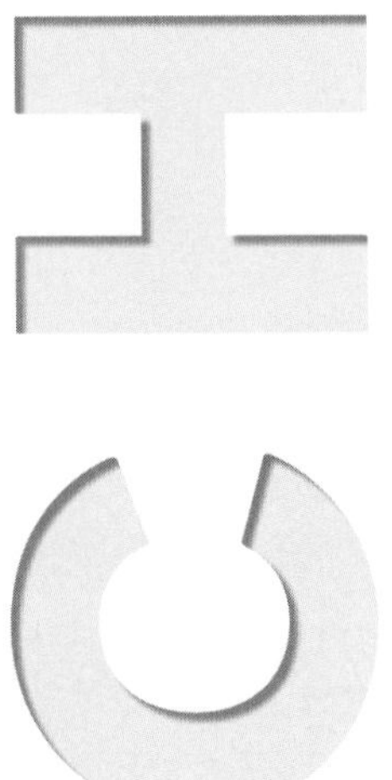

ter? Some experts are seriously worried that we are making decisions about our health without thinking through the consequences.

The purpose of this chapter is to provide you with information so that when you know better, you will make better choices for your physical, mental, and sexual health, which will in turn help you handle stress more effectively.

More specifically, after completing this chapter, you will be able to do the following:

- Define stress and where it can appear in your life.
- Describe methods for reducing stress and minimizing stress-related illnesses.
- Determine which health issues are important to consider while you are in college.
- Identify methods to make better choices about your overall health.

UNDERSTANDING Stress

Stress is a physical and psychological response to outside stimuli. In other words, just about anything that stimulates you can cause stress. Not all stress, however, is bad for you. For example, the stress you feel when you see someone get seriously hurt enables you to spring into action to help. For some students, the stress of an upcoming exam gives them the energy and focus to study. Without feeling a little stressed, these students might not feel the need to study at all.

WHAT? ME WORRY?

Not everyone, however, handles stress the same way, and a stressful situation for you may not produce the same reaction for someone else. How we handle stress depends on our genetic makeup, past experiences, and the stress-reducing techniques that we know and practice. There are ways to reduce stress or change our reaction, both physically and psychologically. First, though, it is important to be able to identify causes of stress. The list in Figure 8.1 is not exhaustive, but it can start you thinking about different ways that you experience stress.

Each of us has certain triggers, such as the ones listed in Figure 8.1, that stress us out. Usually, however, the same situation doesn't stress us out the same way each time it occurs. Take waiting in line at the bank. One day, you might be extremely angry at waiting 15 minutes in a line to cash a check because you are late for a job interview. The next time that you are in the same line waiting the same amount of time, you may be calm and relaxed because you are enjoying a little quiet time to think while your mother waits in the car. Thus, it is not necessarily the situation or action that causes negative stress, but more likely other factors that are involved.

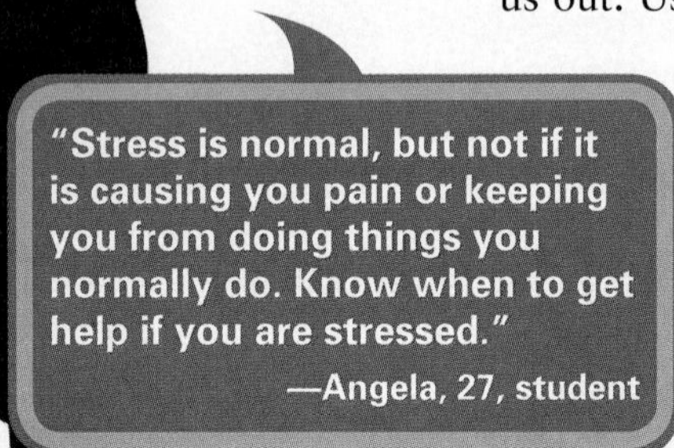

"Stress is normal, but not if it is causing you pain or keeping you from doing things you normally do. Know when to get help if you are stressed."
—Angela, 27, student

When you are suffering from lack of sleep, you may be more likely to react negatively to people and situations that usually would not bother you. When you are feeling unsure of your abilities to be successful in college, you may take constructive criticism as a personal attack. Being aware of times and situations that cause you the most stress is one step to helping manage stress better. If you

FIGURE 8.1 **Possible Causes of Stress**

- Self-doubt
- Fear of failure or the unknown
- Congested traffic
- Uncomfortable situations
- Life experiences such as the death of a loved one, having a child, getting married, or moving
- Waiting in lines
- Pressure to succeed (from yourself or others)
- Speaking in public
- Lack of support—financial, physical, or psychological
- The demands of a job such as a promotion or demotion, deadlines, and evaluations
- Too many activities and not enough time to complete them
- Computer problems

ACTIVITY 8.1 What Stresses You Out?

Situation	Stresses Me	Does Not Stress Me
Starting a big project		
Paying bills		
Being in a messy environment		
Receiving graded papers and exams		
Not getting enough sleep		
Taking a personal or professional risk		
Getting out of bed		
Not getting feedback on my work		
Being distracted by other people		
Thinking about the future		
Taking tests		

realize that you are sensitive to others' feedback because you are feeling insecure, then you may be less likely to react negatively.

In Activity 8.1, place an X next to situations that are negatively stressful for you. Consider other situations or people that cause you to react negatively. The goal is to recognize a pattern of stress and then work to overcome it.

STRESS IN COLLEGE

Because you will encounter stress at college, work, and home, it is important to be able to identify the different stressors in each environment and work toward minimizing the negative stress in each area. Some weeks, you will have to contend with negative stress in only one area, but there will be times when it seems as though each part of your life is making you miserable. The more you understand what you can and cannot control, the more likely you will be able to work through stressful times and stay on track with your goals.

Stress in college is inevitable, but it doesn't have to be overwhelming if you know what you can do to minimize negative stress in the first place. There are several ways that students unknowingly cause themselves stress: failing to read the catalog and student handbook about course prerequisites and descriptions as well as degree program requirements; registering for more hours than they can handle; trying to do too much at work and home; missing deadlines; arriving late for class or appointments; and keeping the same social schedule despite more academic demands.

INTEGRITY MATTERS

Have you ever promised someone that you would do something for her, only to break your promise? Have you ever offered to help someone, only to let him down when he needed you most? We all have had moments in our lives when we were not true to our word about what we would do. No matter why we fail to see our promises through, the end result always causes us some stress in our lives because such actions, or inactions, can damage our relationships with others.

One way to eliminate stress and anxiety is to make integrity a top priority in your life. Only promise what you know you can deliver. Tell someone no or do not even offer in the first place if you know you won't be able to keep your word. Even though it may seem less stressful to take the easier path, in the long run, your negative stress will decrease when you maintain your integrity.

YOUR TURN When have you let someone down by not delivering on a promise or an offer to help or when has someone let you down? ■ How did you feel about not honoring your word or about the other person's broken promise? ■ In what ways did your relationship change?

____

____

____

____

____

The information in this chapter and throughout this book should help you minimize your stress in college by providing you with information and strategies for accomplishing your goals. Even if you avoid the stress-producing behaviors just noted, you may still find that things don't go your way in college. If you accept that there will be times when you or others will make mistakes, then you will be more likely to bounce back from problems. Minimizing the negative effects of stress can include commonsense activities such as reading all information that you receive from the college; paying attention to flyers on doors, bulletin boards, and tables; and talking to your advisor, instructors, and counselor on a regular basis.

You will also want to regularly check the college's website for announcements and updates. Be sure, too, to read publications such as newspapers and newsletters that the college sends to the community. As always, ask questions when you are not sure of something, and make an effort to get involved with campus organizations and clubs because people in these groups often know what is going on around campus.

STRESS AT HOME

Reducing stress at home will, no doubt, be the first step for minimizing your overall stress. Because your family and friends are likely to be your most important supporters, what they think of you and the demands they place on you will need to be discussed. Some family members may be unsure of what you are doing or worried that your schoolwork will leave little time for them. Your friends may feel the same way, especially if they are used to hanging out with you after work and on the weekends. The key to minimizing stress at home is to communicate your needs. Talk to your loved ones about what you and they can expect when you are taking classes.

Some other tips for making your home life a sanctuary rather than an asylum include telling your family when you have exams or major projects due and informing them of your breaks and vacation time. They may be excited to count down the days until you are finished with the semester. Remember to explain how your responsibilities will change when you are in college. Also, be aware that you are a role model for your family—you may be inspiring other family members to go to college.

STRESS AT WORK

For some, stress on the job can be the most difficult to deal with because of the fear of performing poorly and being fired. Stress on the job can also be particularly tough to manage because you may feel uncomfortable confronting coworkers and being honest about your feelings. There are ways, though, to cope with the negative effects of stress at work. To help minimize the amount of stress at your job, consider talking to your employer about your educational goals. Your boss may be very encouraging about your determination to increase your knowledge and improve your skills. Your employer may allow you flextime to take classes, which means you may be able to arrive at work early, skip a lunch break, or stay late in order to take classes during the day.

As you would with your family, let your boss know when you have finals or other activities that may interfere with your regular workday, but avoid studying on the job. Be sure to handle any conflict that may arise from your schedule as soon as possible. Coworkers may be jealous of your success or they may misunderstand the arrangements you have made to work and go to school. If you have any concerns, address them to the appropriate person.

There is no cure-all for stress. It is an integral and important part of life and can actually be thrilling and exciting. Nonetheless, preventing unnecessary stress in the first place can keep you happier and healthier, which will make you better able to achieve your goals.

"I went to the doctor recently for stomach pain. She said it was stress-related. Since I have been learning to relax and meditate, I've noticed I don't get sick as often."
—Courtney, 30, student

STRESS-RELATED ILLNESSES

Stress can cause a variety of health-related problems, such as sleep deprivation. Stress-related illnesses can vary from person to person, but there is one common denominator: With information and techniques for reducing stress, you can decrease the negative health effects. Although some of the following illnesses can be caused by other factors such as heredity and environment, they can be signs that stress is making you ill:

- Digestive problems including upset stomach, heartburn, constipation, diarrhea, and ulcers
- Severe headaches and migraines
- High blood pressure, heart attack, and stroke
- Muscle and joint pain
- Cold, flu, respiratory, and sinus infections

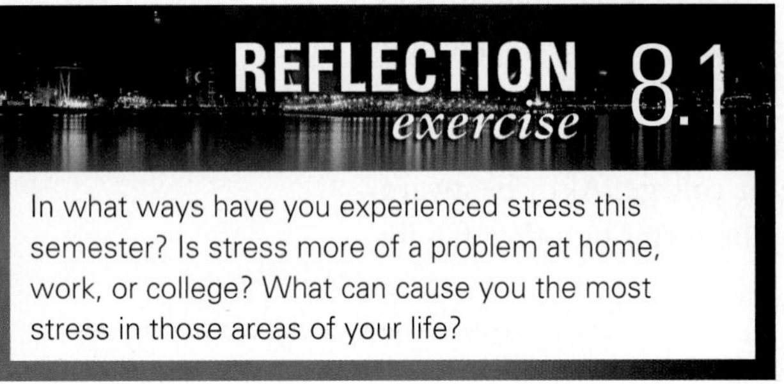

In what ways have you experienced stress this semester? Is stress more of a problem at home, work, or college? What can cause you the most stress in those areas of your life?

Staying healthy by eating well, exercising, and getting adequate sleep are all ways to help prevent stress-related illnesses. Be careful, especially at stressful times such as the beginning and end of the semester, that you do not neglect both your physical and mental health, for you will be more susceptible to stress-related illnesses that could keep you from doing well in college.

HANDLING Stress

No doubt you have felt stress since enrolling in college. You wouldn't be human if you didn't at least worry at the beginning of the semester how you will manage it all—family, work, college, and personal life. Stress is normal, but it can seriously derail college students from achieving their goals if they cannot manage it successfully. Looking for ways to minimize—not eliminate, because you can't—stress and to maximize balance in your life will make your college experience more enjoyable, if not completely stress free.

REDUCING THE NEGATIVE EFFECTS OF STRESS

Because you cannot eliminate all stress, you will need to develop methods for reducing the negative effects that your body and mind experience when they are stressed out. One of the quickest, easiest ways to reduce the negative effects of stress is to take a deep breath. You may have even told someone who was upset to breathe deeply in order to calm down. Proper breathing is, as many cultures have known for thousands of years, an important part of life; for example, in yoga, the ability to control the breath is essential to controlling the mind and body and to bringing fresh air to the lungs and other organs.

Visualization is another method for reducing the effect that stress has on the mind and body. In order to visualize a more relaxed time and place, all you need to do is to find a quiet, comfortable spot, sit down, and close your eyes. Relaxation experts suggest that you visualize a place that makes you feel warm and relaxed. Many people think about a beach because the mood there is often relaxed and the sound of the ocean is comforting. You will need to find your own special place.

Once you decide where you want to go mentally, you should start noticing the details in your chosen place. If you are at the beach, then you should feel the sunshine's heat. Next, listen to the waves crashing on the surf and smell the salty air. Depending on how long you need to visualize this special place, you may want to stick your toe in the water or lie down on the beach and soak up the rays—leave your stress in those designated beach trash cans. The goal in this method of relaxation is to stay there as long as you need to; when you mentally return to your present location, you should feel refreshed and renewed.

Sometimes physical activity can be a better stress reliever than mental exercises. Getting outside or to the gym to work out your frustrations and stress is an excellent way of maintaining your health. By exercising, you can eliminate the physical side effects of stress while you take your mind off your troubles. If you do not usually exercise, take it slowly. Start with a 15-minute walk around the block or do some simple stretching exercises on the floor. Overdoing exercise can lead to more stress, so start small and increase the time you spend getting your blood circulating as you get stronger.

If you happen to exercise too much, you can look toward massage therapy to reduce all your stress. Although it is a little less conventional than other methods of reducing stress, a massage can improve circulation and alleviate muscle soreness. You can seek professional massage therapy or ask a family member to rub your neck, shoulders, or feet. Massage therapy can give you the rejuvenation you need to tackle the rest of the week.

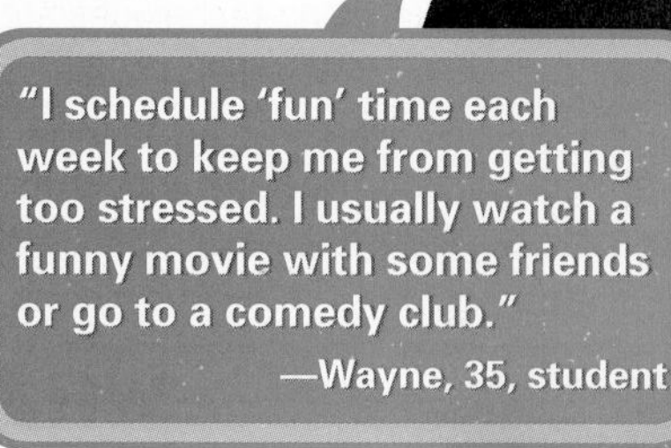

"I schedule 'fun' time each week to keep me from getting too stressed. I usually watch a funny movie with some friends or go to a comedy club."
—Wayne, 35, student

The cliché "Laughter is the best medicine" is another way of saying it is an ideal way to eliminate stress. Have you ever been in a very stressful situation when someone made you laugh and you thought, "Boy, I needed that"? You probably felt all the tension melt away as you doubled over giggling. Surrounding yourself with people who make you laugh is one way to keep stress at a minimum. Other ways include renting comedies or reading funny books. Of course, good, old-fashioned acting silly can relieve stress and anxiety as well.

Last, you can comfort yourself with familiar favorites to eliminate the negative effects of stress. A special meal or a visit with your best friend can put you at ease. Looking at old photographs, reminiscing about family trips, and watching your favorite movies can be great stress relievers. If you have enrolled in college in a new town or you have moved out on your own for the first time, you may find comfort in the familiar, whether an old pillow or a favorite movie. Make sure, though, that your methods of reducing negative stress are healthy. Drugs and alcohol may temporarily relieve stress, but they cause more problems in the long run.

STAYING FLEXIBLE

An important method of managing stress is to remain flexible. If you try to control too many aspects of your life, you will quickly discover you can't do it all.

Although it is important to manage your time and mark progress toward your goals, you still need to plan for the unexpected and be willing to make adjustments. Good time managers plan for problems by keeping their schedules loose enough to make room for adjustments. For example, if you have a doctor's appointment at 2:00, you shouldn't schedule a job interview at 3:00. Delays in the doctor's office or traffic problems could keep you from your interview and cause more stress. Instead, you should give yourself plenty of time in between scheduled tasks, especially if you will have to rely on others' time management skills.

KNOWING WHEN TO GET HELP WITH STRESS

If you ever feel as though you cannot cope with the amount of work and responsibility that you have—despite attempts to reduce your stress—seek professional help. Excessive crying, difficulty breathing, inability to get out of bed, and suicidal thoughts are severe reactions to stress. Knowing when to reach out to other people will be crucial in your recovery.

When asking for help, find someone you trust who will be objective about your experiences. Sometimes, close friends and family members can be your best allies to combat stress, but other times an outside party, who will listen to what you have to say without judging, can be extremely helpful. When you talk to someone, be honest about what you are feeling. Don't try to minimize any fear or anxiety. The more the person knows about what you are experiencing, the better able he or she will be to help.

CRITICAL THINKING *exercise* 8.2

What stress-relieving techniques are most helpful to you and why? How will you make sure to find time to relieve stress while you are in college? What possible effects will *not* managing your stress have on you?

WHAT'S Good for You

Think about this scenario: You have just bought a brand-new car and are about to drive it off the lot. Before you do, the salesperson provides you with an owner's manual and begins to tell you how often you will need to fill the tank, replace the oil, check the brakes, and rotate the tires. You tell the salesperson you don't need to know any of that stuff, and you drive the car off the lot. Besides, you know that the car needs to be filled up whenever the light on the dashboard comes on. What else is there to know?

For those who own and drive cars, you can imagine what will happen next. One day, maybe in a few months or a few years, you will find the car stops working regularly or stops working at all. In some cases, the repairs are minimal; in other cases, major repairs must be made to get the car into shape. The costs could be astronomical, so much so that you find yourself without a car and without hope for getting another one anytime soon.

Now, consider that the car is your body. You know when you are hungry and when you are tired, when you feel happy and when you are stressed, but do

EMOTIONAL INTELLIGENCE *Check-Up*

Impulse Control

Emotionally intelligent people acknowledge their feelings in a situation, stop and think about what is involved, and then choose an act that will help resolve the problems. Read the following common situation and work through the three steps in the boxes.

What emotions do you have in this situation?

FEEL

What is the optimal outcome of the situation for you?

THINK

What attitude and positive action will help you achieve the outcome you want?

ACT

SITUATION

You are stressed out at the end of the semester, and your friends think they know exactly what will make you feel better—a night out with them partying. To be fair, you used to unwind with your friends by getting together at a restaurant and bar and then dancing all night, but since you have been in college, you have barely left the library each night before 10 P.M. You do want to hang out with your friends even though you need to start studying for finals, but you don't know if it will end up the same way it used to—with your not feeling well in the morning and regretting your actions. What should you do?

---

you know how to take care of yourself? Maybe you do know that exercising will improve your health and help you manage your stress, but you won't make the time to include fitness as a part of your weekly routine. Just as a car will eventually have problems without regularly scheduled maintenance, there will come a day when neglect will keep your body from running properly or at all.

Learning to take care of your physical and mental health is crucial to getting where you want to go. To continue the car analogy, you won't be arriving at your destination if the vehicle is not in proper working order. One of the benefits of higher education, as stated earlier in this book, is that you must learn to make better choices, including better choices about your health. You can do that by understanding what you can control and how to get information to stay physically and mentally healthy.

EAT WELL

One key to living a healthy life is making it a priority to eat nutritious food. Getting the recommended daily allowances of fruits, vegetables, whole grains, proteins, and fats is a commonsense approach to healthy eating, but as a society, we are choosing less healthy foods that are quick and easy—and loaded with calories, fat, salt, and sugar. Some of the reasons for poor nutritional choices include lack of time, information, and access to healthy alternatives. Increased stress is another reason that students make poor food choices; they may choose comfort food over nutritious alternatives.

To make healthier choices, arm yourself with information. As with any aspect of your health, the more you know, the better choices you can make. Learn what healthy foods are and seek them out. Read about and pay attention to serving sizes; too much of even a healthy food can add unneeded calories and contribute to weight gain. Read and learn to interpret food labels and ingredient lists that provide information about what is in the food and how much of it represents recommended daily values. The U.S. Food and Drug Administration (2004) provides detailed information on their Web page, titled "How to Understand and Use the Nutrition Facts Label," which can be accessed at www.cfsan.fda.gov/~dms/foodlab.html.

"Plan, plan, plan to eat healthy. Don't leave your dinner up to what is in the vending machine at school. Take fruit, nuts, and water with you in case you need a snack in between classes."

—Stella, 25, student

Another way of getting nutritional information is to talk with a physician or a nutritionist to get a better idea of what kinds of food will be best for you to consume. Regular doctor visits will determine if you have any potential health risks, such as high blood pressure or diabetes, which will make your food decisions even more crucial to good health. Keeping chronic illnesses in check with monitoring and medication will not only help you feel better, but it will also keep you healthy for the long term.

Eating healthy means eating regularly. Most experts recommend eating smaller meals more frequently rather than heavy meals 5 to 7 hours apart. At the very least, as nutritionists recommend, start the day with a healthy breakfast, even if you don't have enough time to sit down and eat a full meal. You will feel more alert and energized throughout the early morning. However, what you eat for breakfast is just as important as whether you eat at all. Powdered doughnuts and a sugary, caffeinated soda will not provide you with the nutrients you need to be at your best. A piece of fruit and a cup of yogurt, for example, would be a better choice if you have to eat on the run. In addition to smaller, frequent nutritious meals, drinking plenty of water throughout the day has numerous health benefits, including regulating body temperature and assisting digestion.

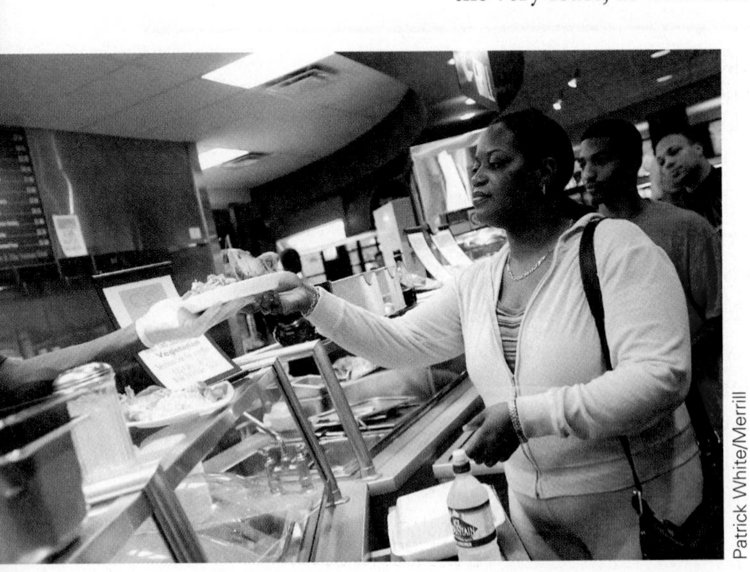

Patrick White/Merrill

One of the most important things you can do to improve your health is to eat nutritious food.

Avoiding fad diets is another strategy for staying healthy. Although they may promise increased energy and weight loss, the results may be short lived and potentially harmful. A better approach to eating healthy is to stick to the recommended guidelines from the Food and Drug Administration or a health expert. Be aware, too, of the potential for eating disorders such as anorexia and bulimia. Anorexia, a condition in which people strictly control how much food they eat,

FIGURE 8.2 Tips for Healthy Eating in College

- Find and read reliable information about health issues.
- Eat consciously and take time to appreciate the nourishment you are receiving from healthy foods.
- Plan your meals *and* snacks ahead of time so that you are not susceptible to last-minute poor choices.
- Take bottled water in your backpack and drink it throughout the day.
- Take healthy snacks with you to eat between classes to avoid making unhealthy choices at the vending machines or at the student union.
- Pay attention to serving sizes and eat what you need to stay healthy, not the amount that you want to eat.
- Make wise choices at vending machines by avoiding food that is high in fat, caffeine, sugar, or salt content.
- Make any changes gradually. Think long-term health, not short-term results.

and bulimia, a condition in which people cycle between overeating (binge eating) in a short amount of time and then purging (through vomiting or abusing laxatives), are two eating disorders that can cause serious physical and psychological harm. Students who suffer from anorexia or bulimia, or believe they do, should see a health professional as soon as possible.

Why should you be concerned about what you eat and how much? One benefit of eating healthy is that it improves your body's functions. You may find that eating better enhances your ability to sleep or reduces the fatigue you feel by the end of the day. Eating well also improves your mental abilities. Studies have shown that eating certain foods, such as fish, can improve your test-taking abilities. Finally, eating healthy without overeating helps keep stress under control, which in turn keeps stress-related illnesses at a minimum. See Figure 8.2 for more tips.

GET MOVING

We all know that making good choices about nutrition and exercise is part of a healthy lifestyle, but busy students often find it difficult to squeeze in time to work out. Take into consideration that as a student, you will spend many hours sitting down studying or working on the computer. Even if you previously had a regular exercise routine, you may find that you have to make studying a higher priority.

Because you may have less time for exercise, it will be even more important that you find time to include some physical activity in your busy schedule because of the numerous health benefits. At the very least, getting regular exercise will help you relieve stress.

Regular exercise can lower blood pressure, increase your metabolism, improve muscle tone, and lessen your chances of suffering diseases that are directly related to a sedentary lifestyle. It can also improve your mood and self-confidence. Experts vary on how much exercise is ideal, but most agree 30

TECH TACTICS

Using Technology to Get Ahead

The Internet provides many quality resources for maintaining your health and wellness. Look for government-sponsored sites, such as the Food and Drug Administration's website, and other reliable sites that are affiliated with organizations that are truly trying to provide the most accurate health information. If you have a serious health issue, do not, though, try to diagnose yourself using website information. Seek sound face-to-face medical advice from your physician.

RECOMMENDED SITES

- www.mypyramid.gov My Pyramid.gov provides important nutritional information and allows you to analyze your diet and make a personalized plan for eating healthy.
- www.mayoclinic.com/health/stress-management/MY00435 The Mayo Clinic provides numerous resources for understanding and minimizing the negative effects of stress. This site allows you to assess your stress levels.
- www.webmd.com/fitness-exercise/guide/default.htm Web MD offers exercising information for everyone, including the beginner. The site even debunks some myths about exercising.

minutes of sustained activity three or four times a week will provide you with health benefits.

If you have trouble getting started or staying in an exercise routine, consider setting fitness goals that are reasonable and achievable. Reward yourself whenever you meet your goals, and don't get discouraged if you fall short now and then. Regular physical activity should be a lifestyle, not a short-term effort, so think of your progress as part of a long-term plan to live better. See Figure 8.3 for tips, but as with any exercise program, see a doctor before you begin and start gradually if you are not usually physically active.

SLEEP SOUNDLY

Getting an adequate amount of sleep each night is as important to maintaining good health as what you eat and how often you exercise, but most Americans, especially college students, do not get enough sleep to maintain their health. Experts say that adults should get 7 to 9 hours of sleep a night to function normally

FIGURE 8.3 **Tips for Exercising in College**

- Take a physical education class at your college.
- Use the exercise facilities and equipment on your campus.
- Take advantage of walking trails or paved walkways on your campus.
- Park farther away from the buildings and get extra steps in.
- Join a gym and go regularly.
- Ask a friend to exercise with you.
- Incorporate short sessions of exercise into your studying routine by taking walking or stretching breaks in between reading or writing papers.
- Learn how to play a new sport or investigate a new form of exercise.

throughout the day, but millions regularly get 6 hours or less. While you are in college, you may believe that 6 hours a night sounds like a luxury as you juggle your multiple responsibilities. For sure, there will be times that, because of circumstances, you will not be able to get enough sleep, but those times should be few and far between. Maintaining a regular schedule of going to bed and getting up will help you get the amount of sleep you need. Despite the myth of what college life is like, pulling "all-nighters" to study for tests or complete assignments is strongly discouraged, because it will make you less likely to perform well the next day.

For some students, the idea of keeping a regular sleeping and waking schedule seems impossible because of other factors that limit their ability to sleep. The reasons for sleep deprivation are varied, but include health problems such as breathing obstructions and stress. If you believe your lack of sleep is the result of medical problems, consider seeing a health care professional. For stress-related sleep problems, practicing the stress-relieving strategies discussed early in this chapter will help alleviate the symptoms; however, if you find that relaxation techniques do not improve your ability to sleep well, then consider seeing a general practitioner or mental health professional for issues regarding stress.

What you put into your body can affect your sleeping habits. Eating high-fat and high-sugar foods near bedtime can slow you down, even if they seem to speed you up at first. Good sleep can also elude you if you consume alcohol and caffeine—even in small amounts—close to the time that you go to bed. Drugs, including medications for common illnesses, can deprive you of sleep or make you feel sluggish after you take them. Avoid consuming food, drink, or medications that overstimulate or make you drowsy right before bedtime. Never abuse prescription, over-the-counter, or illegal drugs to stay awake.

In addition to what you put into your body, what you do to it will affect your ability to get a good night's rest. Exercising too close to your bedtime will make it harder to fall asleep. However, too little physical exertion during the day can also contribute to difficulty falling and staying asleep. Experts suggest exercising early in the day—an activity as easy as walking for 30 minutes will suffice—in order to sleep more productively at night. Regular exercise will also help you alleviate the negative effects of stress. If you find, though, that you cannot "shut off" your mind because thoughts overwhelm you, consider writing down your worries—anything you may stay up thinking about after the light is off—in a journal, which will help you unwind and put away your day's thoughts.

Because sleep deprivation can contribute to irritability, depression, and physical health problems, it is important to make getting enough sleep a priority throughout the semester. If you have difficulty sticking to a regular sleep schedule, treat it like any other goal and write down what you want to do. Make it easier to achieve your goal by keeping your bed and bedroom free of clutter and by avoiding using your bed as a place to do homework or watch television. In other words, creating a sanctuary in your bedroom, a place where you can truly relax, may alleviate stress and anxiety that contribute to sleeplessness. Finally, avoid taking naps during the day, even on weekends, because they can throw off your sleep schedule. If you have an irregular schedule because of working different hours each day of the week, find a system that is relatively regular and that works for you. You may have to be creative about how you get enough sleep each evening or day.

"If I don't get enough sleep, my brain doesn't work well. There is no way I could do well on a test if I didn't get a good night's sleep the night before."
—May-Lin, 19, student

The bottom line is that sleep deprivation can be dangerous and deadly. How little sleep you get should not be a medal of honor that demonstrates how much you work or how dedicated you are to meeting your goals. Getting enough sleep

Your Terms of SUCCESS

WHEN YOU SEE . . .	IT MEANS . . .
Acquaintance rape	See date rape.
Active lifestyle	Maintaining regular exercise.
Alcohol abuse	Using alcohol excessively or to the impairment of your senses.
Balanced living	Finding balance in one's personal, academic, and professional life that provides you with a sense of well-being.
Date rape	Rape, or forced sexual contact, between two people who know each other or who are dating.
Mental abuse	Harmful treatment of the mind or intellect.
Mental health	The condition of one's mind or mental processes.
Physical health	The condition of one's body.
Sedentary	Sitting in one place, not active.
Sleep deprivation	The condition of not getting enough sleep.
Spiritual health	One's religious or spiritual outlook on life.
STDs	Sexually transmitted diseases.
Stress	A physical and psychological response to outside stimuli.
Stress-related illness	An illness that is caused by the body's reaction to stress.
Verbal abuse	Harmful treatment of someone through yelling, name-calling, or insults.

is a necessary part of living well, enjoying what you *do* accomplish, and being enjoyable to be around when you are awake.

DRUGS AND ALCOHOL

There are some habits that we know are potentially hazardous to our health, and yet some people still indulge in them. Smoking and using tobacco products, taking drugs, and consuming too much alcohol are known risks, but college students sometimes pick up these poor health habits because of peer pressure, a desire to fit in, and a need to find a way to relax or escape.

According to the American Heart Association (2009), about a quarter of Americans smoke, and people with the least education (9 to 11 years in school) are more likely to smoke than people with more education (more than 16 years in school). Smoking or chewing tobacco carries with it increased risks of heart disease, stroke, high blood pressure, cancer, and emphysema. The more educated you become about the health risks that are associated with smoking and using smokeless tobacco, the more it will be obvious that using tobacco products can cause serious health consequences. There are a variety of methods for quitting. It is worth investigating what your college and community offer if you are a smoker or a user of smokeless tobacco. Your college may provide information, support groups, or physician referrals for students who want to quit.

Alcohol and drugs are two other health issues that affect college students—sometimes even before they get to college. Having parents, partners, or friends who have abused drugs or alcohol is one way students can be affected. They may feel that they have to take care of others who drink too much or take drugs, which can take a toll on their time and emotional well-being. Students may also suffer from abusing drugs and alcohol while in college—and the effects can be far reaching. According to Facts on Tap (2009), a website that offers drug and alcohol education and prevention information, 159,000 first-year college students will drop out of college because of issues related to drug and alcohol abuse.

Being drunk or high can have grave consequences, the least of which is that you will do something you later regret. You increase your risk of having an unwanted sexual experience and causing physical harm to yourself and others. Death from overdosing on drugs and alcohol can happen even for those who are first-time users. Whether they are consumed for recreational purposes or because of other, more serious health reasons, abusing drugs and alcohol should not be a part of your college career because you will find it more difficult to reach your educational and personal goals. See Figure 8.4 for tips on avoiding drugs and alcohol.

In addition to abusing alcohol and illegal substances, taking medications for purposes other than their prescribed uses can have grave consequences, including death. Excessive consumption of medications that contain amphetamines and narcotics may seem like a good idea at first if you have trouble staying awake or going to sleep, but continued use beyond the prescribed period can lead to dependency.

FIGURE 8.4 Tips for Avoiding Drugs and Alcohol in College

- Educate yourself about the effects of abusing drugs and alcohol.
- Cultivate relationships with people who have healthy habits.
- Avoid situations in which you know drugs and alcohol will be present.
- Take walking breaks instead of smoking breaks.
- Find other ways to relax that are healthy, free, and legal.
- Talk with a counselor or health care professional if you feel you are about to make a poor decision regarding the use of drugs and alcohol.
- Appeal to your vanity, if all else fails: Drugs, alcohol, and tobacco make you look and smell bad.

SEX

A discussion of health issues would not be complete without talking about sexual health. Most colleges and universities strive to educate their students, especially those who are recently out of high school, about sexual responsibility and common sexually transmitted diseases (STDs). Gary Gately (2003) reports the alarm of many experts and college officials at recent statistics showing that 73% of students report having unprotected sex while they are in college. More disturbing is that 68% of those having unprotected sex do not consider themselves at risk (Gately, 2003), pointing to a major reason why students, despite sex education in high school or elsewhere, continue to engage in risky sexual behavior. Students, especially those 18 to 24 years of age, believe they are immortal and that nothing they do will have negative consequences. Because most STDs lack immediate visible or physiological symptoms, students who are at risk for contracting a sexually transmitted disease rarely ask to be screened for signs of infection.

Risky behavior, which includes having sex with multiple partners and having unprotected sex, opens the door to possible infections and illnesses such as chlamydia, gonorrhea, genital herpes, HIV, and AIDS (see Table 8.1). Some diseases can be transmitted in ways other than sexual intercourse. Hepatitis B and C are both diseases that can be contracted through shared razors or toothbrushes, body piercing, or tattooing.

If you are sexually active, it is important to be screened regularly for STDs even if you do not have symptoms. Your long-term health and the health of those you come in contact with are at risk if you do not. As with any health issue, educate yourself with the facts about risk factors and symptoms. Then, monitor your behavior, practice safe sex, and see a doctor regularly to maintain good health.

DEPRESSION AND SUICIDE

The pressures to succeed while juggling multiple priorities can lead to negative stress and feelings of being overwhelmed. Often, feeling a little stressed during the semester is normal, but there are times that students can feel as though they

TABLE 8.1 Common Sexually Transmitted Diseases

STD	Symptoms	Treatment
HIV and AIDS	May have no symptoms; extreme fatigue, rapid weight loss	No cure, but prescribed medication can keep the virus from replicating
Chlamydia	May have no symptoms; abnormal discharge, burning during urination	Antibiotics
Genital herpes	May have no symptoms; itching, burning, bumps in the genital area	No cure, but prescribed medication can help treat outbreaks
Gonorrhea	Pain or burning during urination; yellowish or bloody discharge; men may have no symptoms	Antibiotics
Hepatitis B	Headache, muscle ache, fatigue, low-grade fever, skin and whites of eyes with yellowish tint	No cure, but prescribed medication can help guard against liver damage

are in over their heads, with no hope of getting out. It is no wonder that one of the most common mental health issues on college campuses is depression.

In an online article about college students and depression, Neil Schoenherr (2004) reports that Alan Glass, M.D., the director of student health and counseling at Washington University–St. Louis, claims problems students face often start before they enroll in college: "Students arrive already having started various medications for depression, anxiety and attention deficit disorders." Signs of depression include loss of pleasure in activities, feelings of hopelessness, inability to get out of bed, increased use of alcohol or drugs, changes in appetite or weight gain or loss, altered sleep patterns (sleeping too little or too much), extreme sensitivity, excessive crying, lack of energy or interest in participating in activities, and indifference to taking care of oneself.

Suicide is another mental health issue associated with depression. With the startling statistic that 25% of college students have contemplated suicide, it is no wonder that college health and counseling centers strive to educate students about the signs of severe depression that may lead to suicide attempts. Thoughts of ending your life should always be taken seriously and you should seek help immediately. Call a college counselor, an advisor, a hospital emergency room, or 911 if you are thinking about committing suicide.

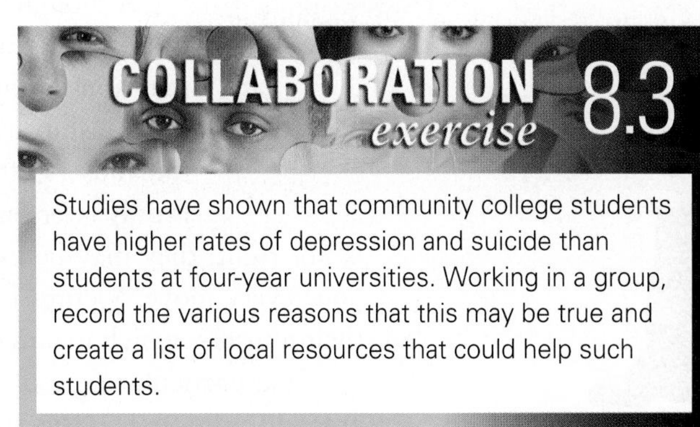

Studies have shown that community college students have higher rates of depression and suicide than students at four-year universities. Working in a group, record the various reasons that this may be true and create a list of local resources that could help such students.

HEALTHY LIVING for Life

There is more to life than just eating well and exercising. Healthy living is a practice that involves all parts of your well-being: physical, mental, and spiritual.

LIVING A BALANCED LIFE

Living a balanced life means paying attention to and improving all areas of your life—from relationships to cardiovascular health to your inner peace. If one area is overdeveloped, then the other areas will suffer from the lack of balance. There will be times when you will need to put in more hours at work and school, throwing the balance off slightly, but be careful that you make some time for the other areas that have been neglected.

A great way to stay balanced is to strive to create relationships with people on campus. Having healthy relationships with professors, advisors, and classmates will not only enable you to stay connected with your college work, but it will also provide you a personal support network in case you feel as though you need help with the stresses of being in college.

Balancing your life to eliminate stress also entails evaluating your values and priorities whenever you begin to feel stressed. You can then identify areas in your life that are getting out of balance and put those areas higher up on your list of priorities. For example, if you value exercise and are stressed because you realize that you have been spending most of your time at work or at school, you can make working out a higher priority, creating better balance in your life.

MAINTAINING HEALTHY RELATIONSHIPS

Maintaining healthy relationships is as much a part of your good health as eating nutritious foods and exercising, but relationships can also be unhealthy and even dangerous. One sign of an unhealthy relationship is abuse: physical, mental, verbal, and sexual. Being in a relationship with someone who is abusive is not healthy. Although the previous statement seems like common sense, take time to think about it. No one deserves to be hit, controlled, or humiliated, *ever*.

"I was once in a really unhealthy relationship and didn't realize how much stress it was causing me until I ended it. Now, if I am in a relationship that makes me feel angry or sad more than happy, I either change it or end it."

—Todd, 29, student

Although we know that someone who makes us feel bad physically or emotionally can prevent us from being our best, studies find that abused men and women find it difficult to get out of abusive relationships. One reason people stay with abusive partners is that the abusers often are—at first—charming, attentive, and loving. It is only later that abusers begin to show subtle signs that something is not right; they may be extremely jealous, verbally insulting, and focused on your every move. Victims may also be dependent financially or emotionally on their abusers, which makes eliminating their influence difficult at best.

One particular type of unhealthy relationship that occurs most frequently among traditional college students is date or acquaintance rape. Simply defined, rape is a forced sexual act in which one party does not actively consent; often, the two people involved are not complete strangers—hence the terms "date rape" and "acquaintance rape." Although men and women can be victims of date rape, women make up most of the victims. Alcohol or a "date rape drug" such as Rohypnol may be involved in the incident. Many experts warn college-age women and men about the risk factors for date rape and encourage them to get to know whom they are going out with, avoid getting intoxicated, make sure their food or drinks are not handled by others, and communicate loud and clear if they find themselves in an uncomfortable situation.

Maintaining a healthy relationship takes time and energy, but there are many ways to make sure your relationships are positive experiences. For example, get to know people well before spending time alone with them. Learn to communicate your wants and needs effectively. Say no loud and clear when you do not want something to happen. Watch for signs of abusive and controlling behavior; sometimes, people show you signs of their true selves in smaller, subtler ways early in a relationship. If a situation makes you uncomfortable, get out of it immediately. Last but not least, do not abuse alcohol and drugs, which can impair your ability to judge situations. If you feel as though you have no options in removing yourself from an abusive relationship, seek professional help.

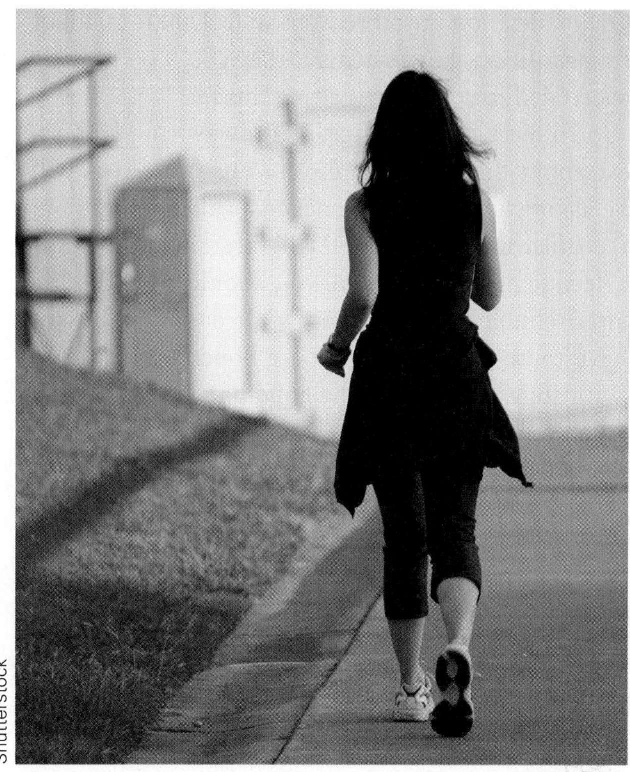

Shutterstock

Walking is an easy way to exercise each day.

GETTING HELP WHEN YOU NEED IT

An important part of making good choices and staying healthy is to get regular checkups and to see a health professional whenever you experience pain, difficulty, or even uncertainty about a health issue. Your college may provide access to a health clinic or health fairs. Free screenings, health seminars, and dispensing of over-the-counter medications are possible services that your college clinic may offer. Take advantage of these types of services, such as blood pressure checks or information about handling diabetes, because they may provide you with life-improving or life-saving information. If your college provides only limited access to health services, then you will need to find other ways to monitor your health. Regular checkups are part of taking care of yourself both in the short and the long term.

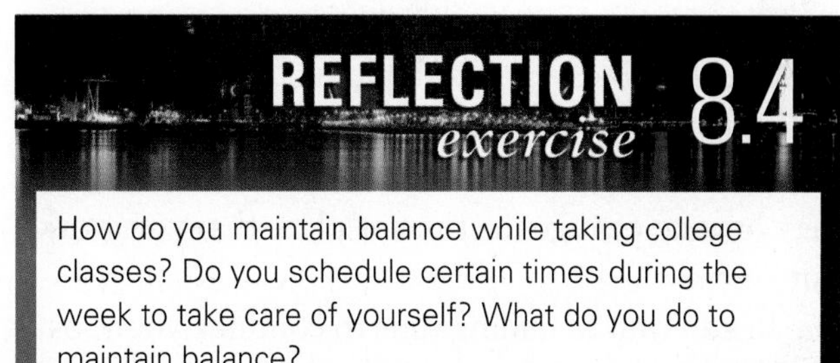

REFLECTION *exercise* 8.4

How do you maintain balance while taking college classes? Do you schedule certain times during the week to take care of yourself? What do you do to maintain balance?

Transfer Tips: FROM COLLEGE TO UNIVERSITY

How Your Stress Will Change and How to Handle the New Pressures

There are many possible stressors awaiting you when you make that move from your community college to university. Increased tuition, higher expectations, more difficult workload, impending graduation, and goal realization are all reasons to feel anxious about the transition, but remember that you have already succeeded in college by getting this far.

To meet the challenges that await you, be honest about them. For example, your professors will be asking more from you academically. In addition, recognize the fact that you will be graduating in just a few semesters and that you should plan for life after school. These realities, while daunting, do not have to be defeating if you are honest about them. With some work—and the good habits you form at your community college—you can handle them with the same success.

Regardless of the new challenges, once you transfer, it will be even more important to have a solid support structure at work and at home. In addition, you will be making connections with people whom you hope will help you get a job after college. All of these relationships can provide you with a system for handling the demands of a four-year university. You will also need to be mindful of the stress-reducing strategies that work best for you. Practice them regularly and seek assistance in achieving your goals; you will then be more relaxed and more confident in your abilities.

Transfer Tips: FROM COLLEGE TO CAREER

Making Healthy Lifestyle Changes Is a Good Long-Term Strategy

Making healthy choices in college certainly has short-term results in that you will feel better and handle the negative effects of stress more effectively. However, the purpose of making better choices should be a long-term strategy to create a better life for you and your family. Therefore, when you complete your certificate or degree and enter into or return to the workforce, you may need to revise or reinforce your health goals. For example, you may have had time after classes to work out or play a sport as part of your exercise routine, but after graduation, you may have to change the time or place that you work out.

In addition to finding time to continue your positive health choices from college, you may also need to consider making your mental well-being part of your overall health plan. Maintaining healthy relationships with those who have positive influences on your life is one way to keep stress levels at a minimum and to create a safety net of friends and family when you may need them. Avoiding drugs, alcohol, and other poor health choices will be crucial to performing your best on the job. Some employers have strict policies about the use of drugs and alcohol on or off the job.

Because of the importance of good health, some employers have made keeping their employees healthy a top priority—it saves time and money in the long run when employees do not miss work because of illnesses. Talk with the human resources department about what your company offers employees to support healthy habits. They may provide free screening, free or reduced-cost vaccinations, time off for doctors' appointments, health insurance, discounted gym memberships, and planned physical activities such as softball or basketball games.

References and Recommended Readings

American Heart Association. (2009). Cigarette smoking statistics. Retrieved September 6, 2009, from www.americanheart.org/presenter.jhtml?identifier=4559

Facts on Tap. (2009). Alcohol and student life. Retrieved September 6, 2009, from www.factsontap.org/factsontap/alcohol_and_student_life/index.htm

Gately, G. (2003, August 23). College students ignoring risks of unprotected sex. *Health Day News*. Retrieved August 29, 2005, from www.hon.ch/News/HSN/514968.html

Schoenherr, N. (2004). Depression, suicide are the major health issues facing college students, says student health director. *News & Information*. Washington University–St. Louis. Retrieved September 6, 2009, from news-info.wustl.edu/tips/page/normal/4198.html

U.S. Food and Drug Administration. (2004). How to understand and use the nutrition facts label. Retrieved May 16, 2008, from http://www.cfsan.fda.gov/~dms/foodlab.html

CHAPTER nine

PLANNING for Next Semester

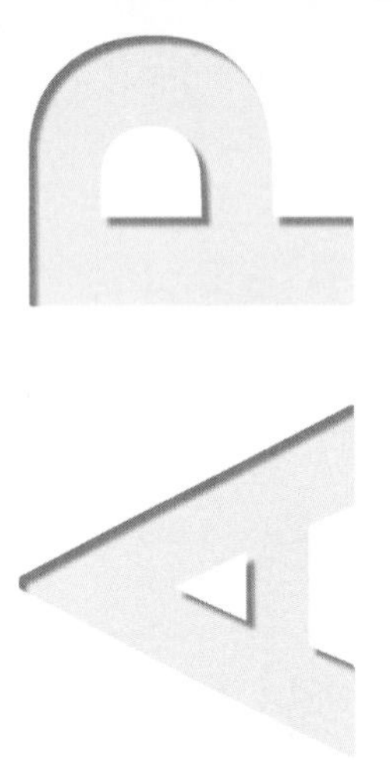

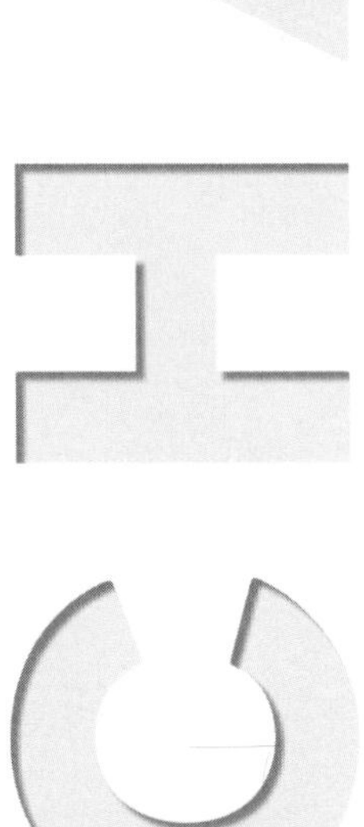

IN THIS chapter The purpose of this chapter is to help you navigate the last few weeks of classes and plan your semesters to come. The last weeks of your semester will be filled with decisions to make about finances and coursework, but once you have successfully completed a certificate or degree program you will be able to say, "I did it!"

More specifically, after completing this chapter, you will be able to do the following:

- Determine the steps to complete your education at this college or another.
- Understand how to prepare for the end of the semester and what to expect.
- Identify methods of paying for college.
- List the benefits for staying in college or returning after a break.

PLANNING FOR Your Educational Future

It is never too early to begin thinking about your educational future, especially if it involves completing a certificate or degree at your current college. Understanding what you need to do—in addition to passing your courses—may mean the difference between graduating on time and staying another semester to finish just one class. Visiting your advisor regularly can help you stay on track; so can reviewing the college catalog and reading the college's website and other information for updates.

A DIFFERENCE OF DEGREES

You probably discovered when you enrolled that community colleges offer a variety of certificate and degree options, but you may not be entirely clear about the differences between programs. Certificate programs usually last a semester or two semesters (sometimes referred to as "one year" programs) and require about 15 to 30 credit hours. Students enroll in certificate programs either to gain skills to enter the workforce or to complete training requirements for a job.

Most certificate programs are not transferable, which means they do not necessarily meet the requirements of an associate's or bachelor's degree. Instead, they usually serve a specific purpose of providing graduates with a set of skills that they can readily use on the job. If you plan to use a certificate program as a stepping stone for an associate's or bachelor's degree, be sure that you check with the department or college (if it is not the same as the one in which you are currently enrolled) where you will complete your final degree plan. For example, if you want to pursue a bachelor's degree in nursing, but you are thinking about completing a nursing certificate first, talk to an advisor in the bachelor's program to determine what, if any, courses they can take from your certificate program. Although you may choose, for personal or professional reasons, to earn a certificate first and then take additional classes to complete another degree, knowing what will be accepted and what will not can help you make the best educational decisions now.

"At first, I couldn't decide between getting an AA or an AAS. Then I realized that the AA was better for me because I want to get a four-year degree in business."
—Reneasha, 22, student

In addition to certificate programs, community colleges offer associate of arts (A.A.), associate of science (A.S.), and associate of applied science (A.A.S.) degrees (see Table 9.1). Unlike certificate programs, an associate's degree usually requires a student to take twice as many credit hours—at least 60 credit hours. An associate of arts and an associate of science degree closely mirror the first two years of a bachelor's degree program and are often transferable to a four-year university with little problem. Nonetheless, as with any degree program, always check with the institution where you intend to transfer to make sure that the classes you take in your associate's degree fulfill the requirements of the bachelor's program. Other associate degrees include associate of fine arts (A.F.A.) and associate of arts in teaching (A.A.T.).

TABLE 9.1 Program Types

Program Type	Length/Requirements	Purpose
Certificate	One semester or two; 15–30 credit hours	To obtain skills necessary for a job-related or personal goal or for direct entry into the workforce; not intended to fit into a higher degree
Associate of Applied Science	Four semesters; about 60 credit hours	To obtain knowledge and skills for direct entry into the workforce; usually not intended to fit into a higher degree
Associate of Arts/ Sciences	Four semesters; about 60 credit hours	To obtain knowledge and skills for transfer to a higher degree program or for direct entry into the workforce

The associate of applied science degree is different because it is a 60-hour (at least) program that is intended for students who plan on entering the workforce after graduation; it is not usually intended for students who want to transfer to complete a bachelor's degree, although some four-year universities are beginning to accept courses that are completed in this degree program. An associate of applied science in accounting degree, for example, is meant for students who want an entry-level job in bookkeeping. To earn a bachelor's degree in accounting, however, a student would earn an associate of arts degree that will fit into the bachelor of science in accounting degree at a university.

Choosing the right certificate or degree program will take some thought and discussion with college advisors, people in the career you want or already have, and your instructors. Ultimately, your career and life goals will determine which program to choose. Remember that no matter which certificate or degree you complete, you can always return to college at any time to continue your education. With fluctuations in job requirements, changes in industry, and longer lifespans, you may find yourself back in college again at some point in your life to learn a new skill, change your life's direction, or dabble in a hobby.

TRANSFERRING TO A UNIVERSITY

You may find that you want to complete a degree at a different institution. Even if you feel sure that it's possible, investigate what you need to do for a successful transfer. There may be special scholarships for transfer students, and there will certainly be admissions requirements such as completing an application, providing transcripts of your work at your current college (and any other college you have attended), and submitting financial aid forms (if you are receiving financial aid). To make sure of a smooth transfer, it is strongly encouraged that you visit the campus and speak with an advisor in the department in which you will ultimately get a degree.

DEADLINES AND IMPORTANT DATES

Once you decide on your schedule and the classes you want to take, you should take advantage of early registration periods and due dates. If there is even a small chance you will return next semester, consider registering for courses just in case. Depending on your college's policies, you should be able to drop courses by a certain date without penalty, and it will be easier to drop classes than build a schedule from classes that are still open. In addition to being aware of registration periods, take note of payment due dates. Some colleges require that you pay soon after you register, even if that means paying for tuition and fees a few months in advance. If you do not pay on time, your classes may be dropped, and you will have to start all over right before the new semester, which could mean that you don't get the classes for which you originally registered.

What are the important due dates that you need to know for the rest of the semester (e.g., last day to withdraw from classes)? What are the important due dates that you need to know for the next academic year (e.g., financial aid application deadline)? How will each due date move you closer to your educational goal?

COMPLETING the Semester

The end of the semester is a good time to start assessing how you have done and where you want to go. Begin planning for next semester while not neglecting any loose ends from your current classes. You should now know what to expect at the beginning of next semester, and with that additional information, you should be able to make better choices and prepare yourself for what lies ahead.

PREPARING FOR FINAL EXAMINATIONS

Another traditional "ending" to the semester is final exams. Surviving "finals week" is often considered a well-earned badge for a college student. The reasons that finals are so stressful for some college students is that they often carry more weight than any other tests during the semester, they contain questions about material from the entire semester, and they are all scheduled around the same time.

To help you survive finals, go back to Chapter 6 and review the material about taking tests. There are additional steps you can follow to get ready for them quickly in these final weeks of the semester. First, be sure to note the day, place, and time of each final and write it down on your calendar. Double-check this information a week before the exam. Be aware that where and when you take your finals may differ from where and when you took your classes during the semester.

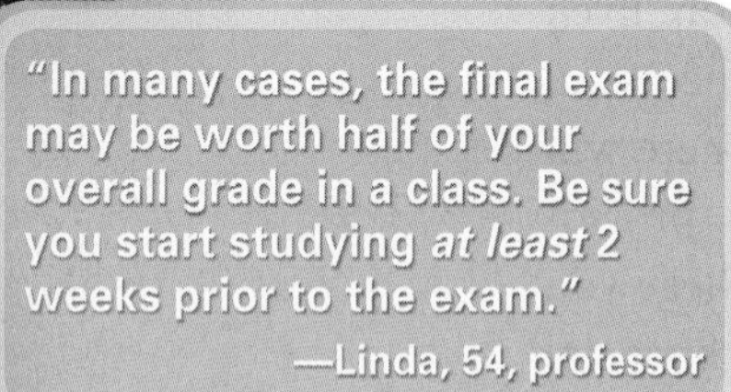

"In many cases, the final exam may be worth half of your overall grade in a class. Be sure you start studying *at least* 2 weeks prior to the exam."
—Linda, 54, professor

A few weeks before the final, ask questions about the exam. What will you be allowed to use? What do you need to bring? What should you study? Is photo identification required? Get plenty of rest during the days that lead up to the exam. When you take the exam, use your time wisely. Final exams usually take longer to complete than regular tests, so be sure you use the entire time that you are allotted (one to three hours). Be prepared by bringing ample writing supplies and any approved items such as a calculator or dictionary.

CHOOSING CLASSES FOR NEXT SEMESTER

Even if you have not completed your classes this semester, you can start planning for next semester. By now, you should be familiar with the college catalog and can identify the courses that you may want to take by reading their descriptions and checking your degree plan. Both the description and your plan will help you determine which classes you need to take in what order. Figure 9.1 is a typical catalog description for a developmental math course.

In addition to reviewing the catalog descriptions for a course, you will also want to determine whether there is a required course you must take beforehand. In the example of Elementary Algebra in Figure 9.1, a student will need to either provide a test score that meets the minimum requirement or she will need to complete successfully the *prerequisite,* or the course required before it.

FIGURE 9.1 Catalog Description

DEVE 0336. Elementary Algebra

This course includes, but is not limited to, the following concepts: operations on integers and rational numbers; solving linear equations and inequalities in one variable; graphing linear equations and inequalities in two variables; operations on exponents and polynomials; and problem-solving techniques. Prerequisite: DEVE 0334 with a grade of C or better, or a COMPASS Algebra placement test score from 23 to 32, or a score of 16 or 17 on the mathematics section of the ACT. Final grade will be A, B, C, or NC (no credit) (3 credit hours).

Courses may have *corequisites,* which are other courses that must be taken before or at the same time as the course. For instance, a Chemistry I course may have a corequisite of Intermediate Algebra, which means a student can complete the course before enrolling in Chemistry I or can take the course during the same semester.

Course Formats

In addition to which courses to take, you may also want to research your options for the design of courses. Many colleges are now offering classes in a variety of formats. You may have the opportunity to take classes in a *learning community,* which means that two or more classes are linked together by a certain topic. The students in the learning community classes stay together for each course. For example, a class of 25 students may take a morning speech communication class and then the same students take an afternoon college writing course. Even though each class is taught by a different professor, they may study similar topics or the students in the learning community may be required to work on a project that links both courses together.

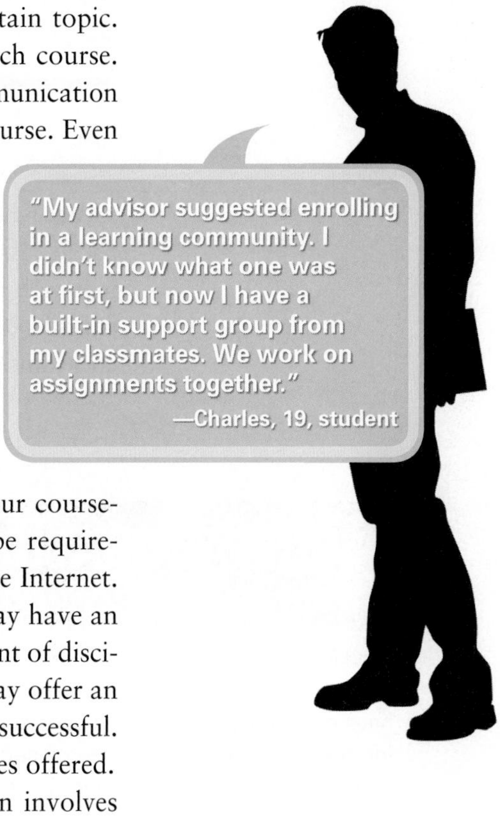

"My advisor suggested enrolling in a learning community. I didn't know what one was at first, but now I have a built-in support group from my classmates. We work on assignments together."
—Charles, 19, student

Web-enhanced classes are another format that you may want to consider when registering for next semester. The term *web-enhanced* usually means that some part of the class will be online and that you will be required to complete work via a computer. *Hybrid* is another common name for a class that requires computer work. In the case of hybrid classes, though, you may only meet once a week, instead of two or three times, on campus and then do the rest of your coursework online. Good computer skills and access to a computer will be requirements for this type of class. Fully *online classes* are completed via the Internet. In some cases, such as proctored tests, labs, or performances, you may have an on-campus or on-site requirement. Online classes take a certain amount of discipline and technology skills on the part of the student. Your college may offer an orientation or other special information for helping online students be successful. Check out that and any other useful information about types of classes offered.

Among the numerous types of course formats, a popular option involves *alternative pacing.* These courses can also be called *accelerated* classes, in which you are able to complete your work at a faster pace than a regular 16-week semester. There can also be *self-paced* classes in which you work at your own

TECH TACTICS

Using Technology to Get Ahead

Online classes and degrees are growing in popularity and now there are more to choose from than even 5 years ago. Some colleges offer a few online classes, which can give students more flexibility in completing their degrees whereas other colleges have complete degree programs available online. If you have an opportunity to take a class online, do it. You may have to take some online classes to complete a degree or to get additional training after college.

RECOMMENDED SITES

- www.ion.uillinois.edu The Illinois Online Network offers 10 tips for online students to stay on track when taking a class online.
- www.distancelearn.org The Distancelearn.org site provides more tips for students who are taking classes online.
- www.spcollege.edu/ecampus/help/tips.htm St. Petersburg College offers ideas for its students to stay on track, but the advice is easily applicable to any online student.

speed, whether over a semester or more than one. Usually, accelerated and self-paced classes require online work and testing to ensure you are mastering the material. Finally, *intersession* classes, as the name implies, are offered during the period between semesters, functioning much like accelerated classes in that a large amount of material is covered in a short period of time.

Learning Formats

As if a course's presentation is not enough to consider when building your schedule for next semester, you may also want to think about how classes may require you to learn. *Service learning* is gaining popularity at many colleges, and it involves community service as part of the learning process. The course's service learning project may involve working at a homeless shelter, designing a neighborhood playground, or testing area drinking water. The project will depend on the course and the hours needed to complete the project will depend

COLLABORATION *exercise* 9.2

Working with a group, discuss the different learning and course formats presented. Which ones do you have experience with? Which ones seem the most interesting? Of the formats mentioned—and the ones your own college provides—which are the best fit for your learning preferences?

on the instructor's assignments, but such a course offers a unique opportunity for students to apply the concepts they learn in class to help solve a community issue. *Cooperative learning* is another type of format that requires students to work in small teams to learn the material in a course. Cooperative learning groups work all semester to help their teammates learn concepts and complete projects. Different from small group work that you may participate in for other classes, cooperative learning is sustained and deliberate—the teams work together for the entire semester.

> **"Before I choose which professor to take, I make an appointment to 'interview' them about their teaching style and requirements. I have been able to make great choices for me because of this."**
>
> **—Laurie, 38, student**

Professors

Just as important as which classes you take next semester, and in which formats, is with whom you take those classes. By now, you should realize that choosing the right instructor could make the difference in how much you enjoy and learn in a class. If you have the option of choosing an instructor, then you should start talking with other students about them. Ask specific questions of a variety of people. Remember that each student has his or her own view of what makes a good instructor, a view that might not match your own. Questions you should ask need to move beyond "Is she a good teacher?" Instead, you should ask about her teaching style, the types of assignments she gives, and how available she is during office hours. Be wary of Internet sites that rate professors. They are not reliable because anyone can post just about anything they want without regard to accuracy, or sometimes decency. There is no mechanism to keep the same people from posting multiple positive or negative comments, which can present only part of the picture.

An even better way to determine which instructors are the best for you is to talk with them before enrolling. Make an appointment with a potential instructor and ask pertinent questions: How much reading is involved? How do you teach the course? Do you require a research paper? What do you expect students to know when they complete the course? The benefits of interviewing your instructor before signing up for the class include determining whether the instructor is a good fit with your learning style and making a good impression by demonstrating your maturity and interest in your education.

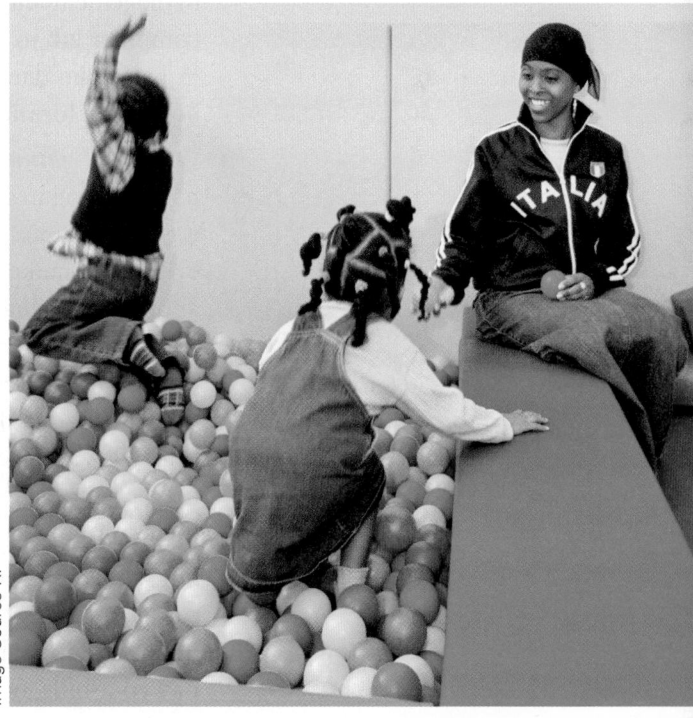

Handling other obligations, such as family, will be a part of your considerations when planning your schedule next semester.

Image Source RF

Building Your Schedule

What worked this semester and what didn't? Why? What will change for you next semester? Did you have enough time in between classes? Did you waste time that could have been spent more productively? All of these questions will need to be answered before you set your schedule for next semester.

When planning your next semester (and beyond), consider five factors: how many hours you need to take, how many hours you need to work, what support is available, what other obligations (planned trips for work or with family, for example) you have, and how much stress these factors will cause.

- *Number of credit hours.* To determine how many credit hours you need to take, be sure to review your financial aid, scholarship, and degree plan information. If you are receiving financial aid, you may be required to take a full load, which often means at least 12 hours. In some cases, you will need to take 15 hours each semester in order to finish a degree in four semesters. If you have to take developmental classes, then it could take longer to complete a degree.
- *Number of work hours.* If you will not be working next semester, you can skip this section. However, even if you are only working a few hours a week, you will need to schedule your work hours so that they do not overlap with the times you are in class. You also need to allow plenty of time to get to and from work and school. Be realistic when calculating this time and plan for delays. An accurately planned schedule will help keep your stress levels at a minimum.
- *Amount of learning support and learning opportunities.* If you know or anticipate a need for learning assistance or tutoring, be sure to build that time into your schedule. You may also need to see each of your professors on a regular basis, some more than others, which should also be a consideration when creating a schedule. If you leave little time for meeting with your instructors, it will be difficult to get the help and advice you need. Good time management and a flexible schedule will allow plenty of time for visits to the computer lab to get help with technology issues, to the library for assistance in using the databases or locating material, and to the tutoring lab at the hours and locations that are most convenient to you.
- *Other obligations.* Working, going to school, taking care of a family, and participating in social and community activities all require your time and energy. To balance all your activities, you will need to keep an eye on upcoming events and make sure you plan accordingly. For example, if you are thinking about registering for the fall semester and you know that you must take a weeklong trip for work in October, you should contact potential instructors to see what their policies are for missing class. Likewise, if you like to participate in your child's school activities, you will need to consider how much time you can give if you are also studying for classes. You may find that you need to cut back on social and volunteer commitments or at least postpone them until after the semester.
- *Stress levels.* Your work schedule, course load, and other responsibilities can lead to high levels of stress. For example, if you have to take 15 hours of courses to maintain your financial aid and you have to work 40 hours to pay your bills, but you feel overwhelmed and anxious about balancing it all,

then you are not likely to handle both well. If you find yourself in this situation, you will need to reconsider your plans before you get in over your head. Getting locked into a rigid schedule that doesn't allow you to drop a course that is too difficult or to decrease your hours at work will lead to frustration and high levels of negative stress.

What should you do if you cannot work a schedule out despite your efforts to make it all fit together? There may be a semester that a course you need is not offered or the class is filled before you can register. Should you throw up your hands and quit when faced with these problems? Of course not. Instead, you should take advantage of the relationships you have cultivated at college. Now is the time to talk with fellow students, instructors, and advisors. They may be able to offer solutions that you have not considered. If, however, there is an academic need for you to get into a class or rearrange your schedule, you should point that out. Some college officials are willing to bend the rules if you need one more class to complete your degree and transfer on time.

EMOTIONAL INTELLIGENCE *Check-Up*

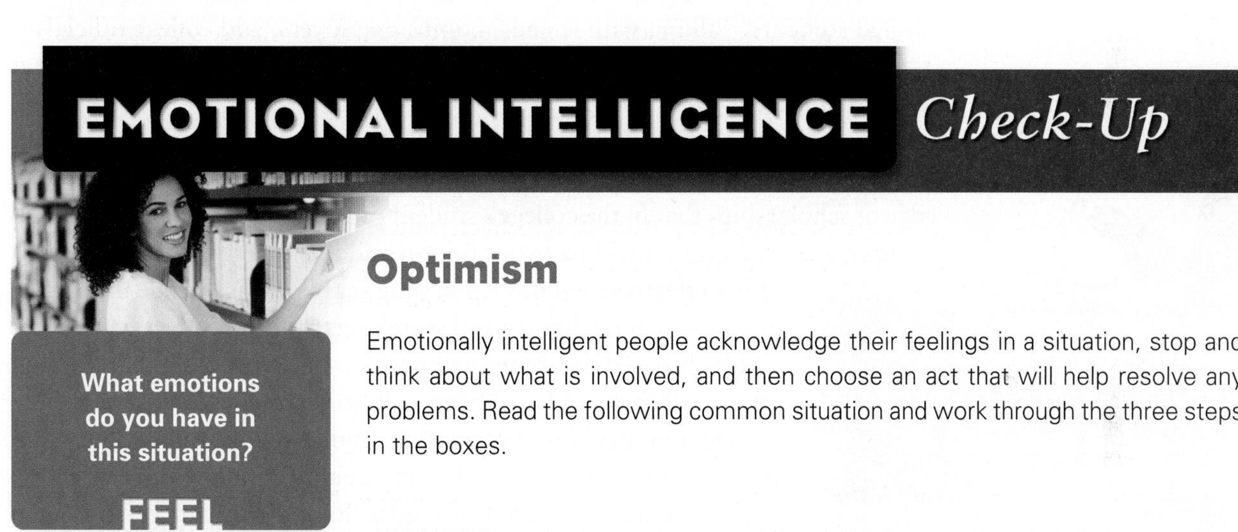

Optimism

Emotionally intelligent people acknowledge their feelings in a situation, stop and think about what is involved, and then choose an act that will help resolve any problems. Read the following common situation and work through the three steps in the boxes.

SITUATION

Your ultimate dream career is to be a pediatrician, and you have chosen an associate of science degree as your first step. However, you have been out of school for a while and when you enrolled in college, your test scores placed you into developmental classes for reading and math. You believe that your test-taking skills are low, not your abilities. Your advisor, though, has expressed concern that you have too many challenges in front of you to reach your goal—it will take at least 10 years of college! He wants you to consider a degree in social work instead because there are fewer math requirements. What should you do?

What emotions do you have in this situation?
FEEL

What is the optimal outcome of the situation for you?
THINK

What attitude and positive action will help you achieve the outcome you want?
ACT

FINANCING Your Education

When thinking about your financial future, most likely paying for college will be at the top of your list. Even if you have a solid plan for paying tuition, fees, and books, it will be worth your time to investigate other methods in case your current approach falls through. Despite what many think about the costs of college, community college tuition is a real bargain and perhaps one of the reasons that you enrolled. Regardless of where you choose to go to school, it is likely that you will need to decide how you will pay for the costs you incur.

SCHOLARSHIPS

Winning a scholarship is by far the most rewarding (financially and psychologically) way to pay for college because it is literally free money—you don't have to pay it back. There are thousands of scholarships out there for needy and accomplished students. Talking with friends, family, employers, and college officials is a great way to start the process. They may know of obscure scholarships that will fit your needs perfectly.

Another way to get information about scholarships is to talk with the financial aid officers and counselors at your college. They have access to and knowledge of scholarships that fit the college's student profiles such as single parent and transfer scholarships that will pay your tuition and fees at a four-year university.

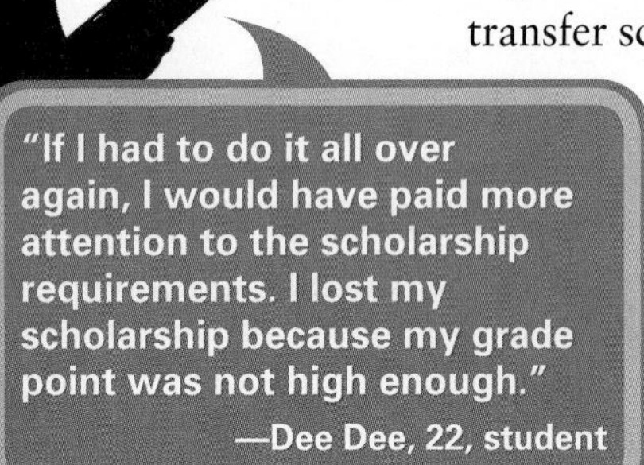

"If I had to do it all over again, I would have paid more attention to the scholarship requirements. I lost my scholarship because my grade point was not high enough."
—Dee Dee, 22, student

Other effective methods for finding scholarships include investigating sources at the library and searching the Internet. Searching print and Web-based databases will provide you with more than enough information; the only problem will be narrowing your focus.

Do not pay for information about scholarships. There are services that claim to match your qualifications with scholarship qualifications, but charge a fee to do so. You can get free help from high school and college counselors as well as libraries and Internet searches. No reputable scholarship will demand a fee to apply, and very few scholarship services will demand payment. There are legitimate scholarship searching services out there, but be careful. The website FinAid! (www.finaid.org) provides information about different types of financial aid for college students as well as tips for avoiding scholarship services scams.

According to this site, any service that guarantees to match you with a scholarship or that offers you an award that you did not apply for is likely to be a scam. Many colleges recommend the website Fastweb! (www.fastweb.com) as a great starting point for finding scholarships that match your accomplishments.

GRANTS

By definition, grants are financial assistance that does not need to be paid back. A common federal grant is the Pell Grant, which can be awarded for full-time or part-time enrollment. To determine your eligibility, talk with your financial aid counselor or visit any of the various websites that provide governmental information about financial aid. Pell Grants do have a limit to the amount of the award ($5,550 for July 1, 2010–June 30, 2011).

Another type of grant that a student can receive is the Federal Supplemental Educational Opportunity Grant (FSEOG), which is available to those who demonstrate an exceptional need. According to the U.S. Department of Education (2010), the difference between a Pell Grant and an FSEOG is that "each participating school will receive enough money to pay the Federal Pell Grants of its eligible students. There's no guarantee every eligible student will be able to receive an FSEOG." The procedure for receiving an FSEOG is similar to that for receiving a Pell Grant; your eligibility will determine the amount that you receive.

When you are awarded grant funds, your college will receive the money and then disburse it to you once classes start. Because of recent federal requirements about grants and student loans, colleges may wait several weeks before paying students, and they may provide more than one disbursement throughout the semester. If you are expecting to receive your grant the first day or week of classes, you should make alternative arrangements to pay bills (including your bookstore bill).

To remain eligible for grants each year, you will need to maintain good academic standing at your college. If you apply for a grant, be sure to make note of the minimum GPA that you must have in order to ensure your eligibility to receive future grant money. One last tip for continuing to receive grant funding: Make sure that you adhere to the college's attendance policy. You may be penalized (and lose your grant funding or have to pay it back) for missing too many classes or for dropping a class. As always, check with your financial aid officer to make sure that you clearly understand the expectations for receiving grants.

STUDENT LOANS

In the event that you are not eligible for grants, be sure to investigate student loans. The idea of taking out a loan to attend college makes many students shudder with fear because they don't want the added pressure that they must pay back what they borrow. If you can avoid a student loan, then by all means do so. However, receiving a student loan sometimes makes more financial sense in the long run.

Federal student loans typically carry low interest and can be paid back over 10 years. For families that would otherwise have to deplete their savings or borrow against retirement or their mortgages to pay for college, a low-interest student loan is a good option. Most loan programs allow you to defer payment (but you may accumulate interest) until after you graduate, or you can sometimes defer payment if you remain unemployed after you graduate.

One type of federal loan is the Stafford Loan, which comes in subsidized and unsubsidized versions. A subsidized loan is one in which the government pays the interest for you while you are in college. Once you graduate and start making payments on your loan, you will accrue interest as well. The government does

INTEGRITY MATTERS

Student loans, because they are low interest and have a long-term payment plan, are often a good way to pay for college if you do not have the financial means to do so otherwise. However, there are serious consequences if you do not pay them back when required to do so. Defaulting on student loans can make you ineligible for future federal aid and can have negative consequences on your credit rating.

Before you sign to receive a student loan, be sure that you have a plan to pay it back after you graduate. If you find yourself unable to make a payment after your loan payments become due, notify your lender immediately. Sometimes, the lender can work out a repayment plan for you if you have an unusual hardship.

YOUR TURN What are your concerns about paying for college? ■ What would be your plan for repaying a loan should you take one out? ■ What is your back-up plan if you were to find yourself unable to pay it back when it came due?

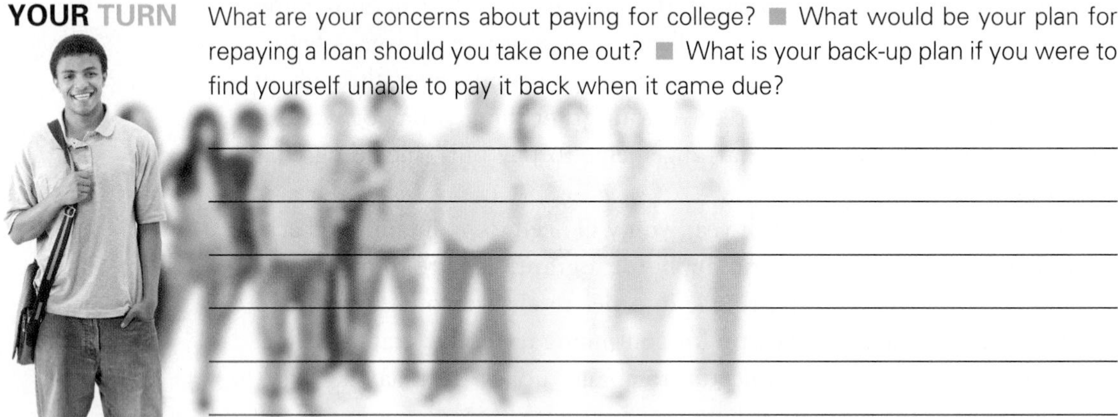

not make interest payments for an unsubsidized loan; however, you may, instead, pay the interest while you are in college (usually a small amount), or you can wait until after you graduate to make any payments, although your interest will be capitalized. In other words, the interest will be added to the principal amount of the loan, which makes your monthly payments higher.

A federal Perkins Loan is a loan between you and your college. The Perkins Loan allows you to borrow thousands of dollars (check www.finaid.org for specific amounts) over 5 years, and you don't have to repay it until 9 months after you graduate or drop below at least part-time status. One benefit of a Perkins Loan is that you may be able to cancel up to 100 percent of the debt if you meet certain criteria. For example, on graduation, if you choose to teach in a "teacher shortage" area or if you serve as a full-time nurse, you may be eligible for cancellation of your loan.

PLUS, which stands for Parent Loan for Undergraduate Students, is another method for receiving money to help pay for college. If you are fortunate enough to have parents willing to take out a loan to help you pay for college, PLUS is a possible option. To qualify, you must be a dependent student, which means your parents support you financially. A PLUS can be provided by the government or by private lenders. Parents who take out a PLUS are usually trying to make up the difference between the cost of tuition and the financial aid package that their children receive. Nonetheless, it is the parents who are ultimately responsible for repaying the loan, which can begin as early as 60 days after they receive it.

MILITARY AND VETERANS FINANCIAL AID

Being a member of the military can be especially helpful when you are paying for college. There are numerous benefits for active members and veterans as well as their dependents. To find out about military benefits, talk with a financial aid officer. If you have served in the military, you may want to contact a local service branch for more information as well.

WORK-STUDY

Work-study is a program that allows students to earn money while they work on campus. The reason it is called "work-study" is that the job may allow for you to study when you work, although most work-study positions are similar to office assistant jobs and will keep you busy for the majority of the time you work. To work in such a program, you must be eligible for federal work-study money, and you will be limited to a certain number of hours you can work per week. Not everyone who is eligible for work-study will be able to find a position on campus, however. Each department and area of the college advertises, hires, and manages work-study positions; sometimes, hiring can be competitive. There may be specific requirements (such as computer skills) that a candidate must meet before being hired. Because some positions require working with students' personal information, work-study students must also abide by the college's privacy standards.

The benefits of participating in work-study include earning some money that will help pay your expenses and also working closely with college employees. By getting to know professors and administrators better—and by working for them—you may have access to valuable advice and information. To investigate whether or not work-study is available for you, talk with your financial aid officer. He or she will review your eligibility and help you apply for on-campus employment.

TUITION WAIVERS FOR EMPLOYEES

Another source of financial help is your employer. Large corporations sometimes offer financial assistance for employees, although there may be stipulations that you work for a certain amount of time after graduation. If your employer doesn't offer scholarships to employees, you should still ask if he or she is interested in doing so; employers will benefit from employees who further their education. Finally, your college may offer tuition waivers for its full-time employees. Some students seek jobs offered at colleges so that they can take classes for free or at a reduced cost. If you need a part-time or full-time job while you are in school, you may want to check out the openings at your college.

APPLYING FOR FINANCIAL AID

Each college is different in how they handle the application process, but it is worth talking generally about what to expect when applying for financial aid. Even if you receive financial aid for this academic year, there may be some information that you need to know before applying again. The first step in the process is obtaining a Free Application for Federal Student Aid (FAFSA), which can be picked up from the financial aid office of your college or can be accessed online at www.fafsa.ed.gov. Financial aid applications must be renewed each academic year; the time line for receiving aid for a year starts in August and ends in July. Thus, if you applied for financial aid in November and received it for classes that started in January, you will have until July to use that aid; then, you will need to reapply for aid for the fall semester.

Purestock/Getty Images

Figure out how to pay for college expenses without getting into extreme debt.

As part of the FAFSA application process, you will need to determine whether you are considered "independent" or "dependent." The federal government defines a student's independence by certain criteria such as age, marital status, or whether both parents are deceased. Students who fit the definition for dependent status, but with extenuating circumstances, may be able to appeal that their status be changed to independent.

In addition to determining your ability to pay for college, you will also be asked to provide an Estimated Family Contribution (EFC) amount; for example, if you receive child support payments or Social Security payments, you will have to report that income as part of your EFC. One other consideration when applying for financial aid is that each year a certain percentage of loan applications get identified for verification. This means that a number of student financial aid applications may take longer to process because of the requirements of verification.

RENEWING FINANCIAL AID AND PAYING IT BACK

In order to continue receiving financial aid, you will need to make sure that you understand and follow the requirements of your college. Many colleges maintain a satisfactory academic standing policy that states you will need to stay enrolled in a certain number of credit hours and maintain a minimum grade point average to continue to receive grants and loans. Sometimes, the required GPA is higher than the GPA to remain in college. For example, you may have to maintain a

2.7 GPA to continue to receive financial aid but need only a 2.0 GPA to stay in college.

If you do not meet the requirements for a semester, your college may place you on financial aid probation, which means you must meet the college's requirements for the next semester to be removed from probation. Failing that, the next step after probation can be suspension from financial aid, in which you no longer receive financial aid, although you may still be able to enroll in classes as long as you pay for them yourself. If your suspension involves extenuating circumstances, some colleges have an appeals process. To appeal your suspension, you may request a review by a committee who will determine whether you can reapply for financial aid.

Whenever applying for loans, you need to consider how you will pay them back after completing your degree or otherwise leaving college. Student loan default is a common problem nationwide and there are stiff penalties for failing to pay back the federal government. On the other hand, loan forgiveness programs are often available for students who major in fields that are in high demand in their community. To find out more about these types of programs, be sure to talk to someone in the financial aid office at your college.

Working within a group, make a list of possible ways to pay for college. Discuss the costs and benefits of each type of financial aid.

THE DECISION to Continue

There is tremendous pressure on those who do not have higher degrees to get them. Frequently high school students hear this pitch from parents, counselors, and teachers: Success in life is dependent on obtaining a college degree. People who have been in the workforce know, as well, that a college degree can be the difference between doing the same job until retirement and being promoted.

But does everyone need to go to college? College is a great place to continue your education and to make your career dreams a reality. There are also indirect benefits to pursuing higher education, such as improving your health and financial well-being because you know more about yourself and the world around you. Nonetheless, going to college is not the only key to success. There are many vibrant, intelligent, successful people who have not completed a college degree.

IS COLLEGE RIGHT FOR YOU RIGHT NOW?

How will you know if college—either your community college or a four-year university—is not right for you? It may be difficult to tell, but you shouldn't quit going if you are unsure. The best way to discover how you feel about being in college is to ask yourself a series of questions. Then talk about your responses with a college counselor, advisor, or trusted friend who can give you good advice.

- Who wants me to be in college?
- Do *I* want to be in college?
- How do I feel when I am in class?
- How do I feel when I am studying?
- How do I feel after I take an exam?
- What do I want to major in? Why?
- Do I need a college degree to accomplish what I want out of life?
- What will a college degree do for me?
- What is my passion?

Take your time answering these questions. You may find that your discomfort about being in college is really a fear about a new beginning and the unknown. Being apprehensive about a new program or a new environment is perfectly normal and does not necessarily indicate that you are not right for college. On the other hand, you may know very clearly that you do not want to be in college at this point in your life. College may not be the best choice for you *right now,* which means that you should consider returning when you are certain it will be your top priority.

BENEFITS OF CONTINUING YOUR EDUCATION

If you are considering whether or not to continue your education next semester, it may be helpful to think about the benefits of going on. First, you will be that much closer to finishing a degree. More completed classes mean more degree requirements checked off the list. Second, if you have to take courses in a sequence (e.g., Writing I and Writing II), then you are more likely to remember what you learned in the first course. Staying out too long between courses that need to be taken close together may lead to forgetting important concepts, which could make that second course more difficult for you. Finally, staying in college now will mean you are more likely to stay friends with classmates. Even taking a semester break may result in losing touch with people you know and rely on now.

BENEFITS OF TAKING A BREAK

If you decide you need a break before completing your degree, be sure you make the most of the time away from college. Some students use that time to earn extra money, take care of personal issues, or work on their academic skills outside of college. A much-needed break can help you stay focused; instead of burning out by continuing a stressful pace, you may find yourself able to reenergize so that you can return with more focus and enthusiasm. A break can be a time to clarify your goals, and it can also help you recommit to the degree path you started on. Of course, during your break, if you decide to change degrees or career directions, you can return with a renewed sense of purpose.

REFLECTION *exercise* 9.4

How do you feel about being in college? Have you had any thoughts about quitting? If so, what is keeping you motivated to continue? If not, what would have to happen for you to consider seriously not continuing your education? What can you do to help stay motivated?

Your Terms of SUCCESS

WHEN YOU SEE . . .	IT MEANS . . .
Accelerated classes	Classes conducted at a faster pace than regular semester-long classes. May require more time per week to complete, but may also allow you to complete sequences of classes more quickly than if you took classes during a traditional term.
Cooperative learning	Arrangements in which students work in small groups or teams to complete class assignments. Goals of the group work will vary, but usually cooperative learning requires that all members contribute to the learning process.
Hybrid classes	Classes that are held on campus for part of the semester and that also use an online learning system to supplement teaching on the days students are not in class. Will require access to a computer and the Internet.
Intersession classes	Classes that are scheduled in between regular semesters. Sometimes offered in January or May before or after a spring semester or term. Usually faster-paced but limited to only one or two classes available to take.
Learning communities	Taking classes with a "cohort" or the same group of students for two or more classes. Classes often share similar assignments and course content.
Perkins Loan	Low-interest loan that helps students pay for undergraduate education.
PLUS loan	Parent Loan for Undergraduate Students.
Self-paced classes	Course requirements completed at student's own pace. If you need more time than a traditional semester, you are allowed to continue in the classes until you have successfully mastered the course content.
Service learning	Requirement to participate in a community project as part of a course. The project will reinforce the concepts and content of the course and may also include an opportunity for you to reflect on what you have learned.
Web-enhanced classes	Using the World Wide Web to supplement learning in a class. Will require access to a computer and the Internet. Sometimes *web-enhanced* is used interchangeably with *hybrid.*
Work-study	A financial aid program that allows students to earn money while working on campus. Depending on the position's job duties, you may be able to study when you are not engaged in a task.

Transfer Tips: FROM COLLEGE TO UNIVERSITY

Preparing for Unexpected Higher Costs

It is very likely that you will see a change in college costs when you transfer to a university. You may be paying twice as much for tuition at the four-year school as you did at your local community college. In addition to tuition, you may see added fees that you didn't have at your community college: Fees for athletic facility use, sporting events, campus organizations, and labs are possible additional expenses. Be sure to read the college catalog carefully and add the fees to the cost per credit hour to get an accurate picture of what you will be spending per class.

Despite the increase in tuition and fees, you may notice that your bookstore expenses stay the same. Although the price of books can be a significant portion of your overall college expenses, it is unlikely that you will experience an increase in cost. However, upper-level science and computer classes require weighty textbooks and additional software. These books can cost as much as $100 or more. Multiply that by four classes, and you will be paying at least $400 for the semester. An advantage, however, to transferring to a larger school is that there are more people from whom you can buy used books. Take notice of special discounts for used books in the bookstore and look for flyers on bulletin boards that announce books for sale.

Transfer Tips: FROM COLLEGE TO CAREER

The Benefits of Returning to Work before Continuing Your Education

There may be a time when you must interrupt your college career to return to your job full time. Balancing financial and educational goals may become too difficult to handle, which may mean that your financial needs take precedence. If this happens to you, there are some ways of dealing with the transition back to the world of work while still keeping your eye on returning to college.

First, realize that going back to work doesn't have to be forever. Just because you are unable to return for more than one semester doesn't mean you never will. Be sure to talk with your employer about your desire to get a degree. You may be surprised by his or her support of your goals. There may even be financial assistance for employees who take college classes. Remember to also discuss with your family and friends your need to further your education. Someone may be willing to help you with finances, scheduling, and family duties. Set a time line for returning to college. If you need to work a semester to earn more money to pay for tuition, then be sure to keep up with registration periods and college announcements.

Finances will be an important consideration, so be sure to save your money. Even if expenses were not the reason you returned to work, putting aside money in a "college fund" will make it easier to reenroll in college. You won't have any excuses for not being able to afford the increased costs. Look for scholarships and financial aid for working adults. Some states are creating grant programs for nontraditional students who work full time in order to increase the number of college graduates in their states. Finally, stay connected with former classmates and instructors. If you are aware of what is going on at the college, you are more likely to return because you will feel as though you had never completely left.

References and Recommended Readings

"Federal Financial Aid FAFSA." (2010). Retrieved April 7, 2010, from www.fafsa.ed.gov

"Federal Pell Grant Program." (2010). Retrieved April 7, 2010, from www2.ed.gov/programs/fpg/index.html

Lipphardt, D. (2008). *The scholarship & financial aid solution: How to go to college for next to nothing with short cuts, tricks, and tips from start to finish*. Ocala, FL: Atlantic Publishing.

Miller, C. A., & Frisch, M. B. (2009). *Creating your best life: The ultimate life list guide*. New York: Sterling.

"Scholarships." (2010). FinAid. Retrieved April 7, 2010, from www.finaid.org/scholarships

"Student Loans." (2010). FinAid. Retrieved March 25, 2010, from www.finaid.org/loans

U.S. Department of Education. (2010). "Types of Federal Student Aid." Retrieved March 25, 2010, from http://studentaid.ed.gov/students/publications/student_guide/2006-2007/english/typesofFSA_grants.htm

CHAPTER ten

PREPARING for a Career and a Life

IN THIS chapter Deciding where you want to go and what you want to do can be characterized by uncertainty. After reading this chapter, you will have a better understanding of your choices *after* you have taken courses at your community college. Even though you have just begun your journey toward a certificate or a degree, you may want to keep in mind your options and the different paths you can take. Ideally, you should read this chapter thoroughly and then refer to it as you complete each semester, ensuring that you are on the right track and reminding yourself of the different choices you have.

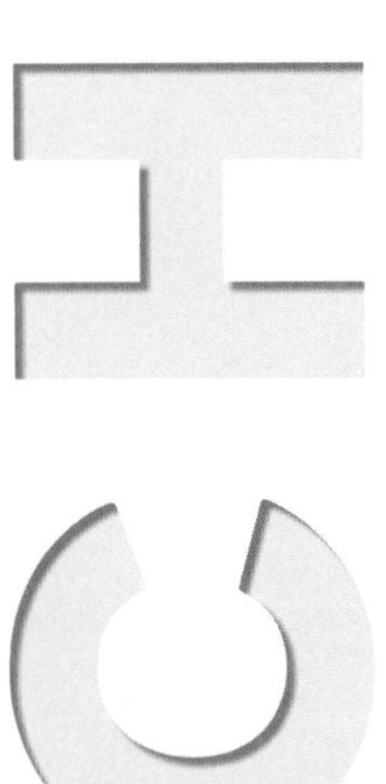

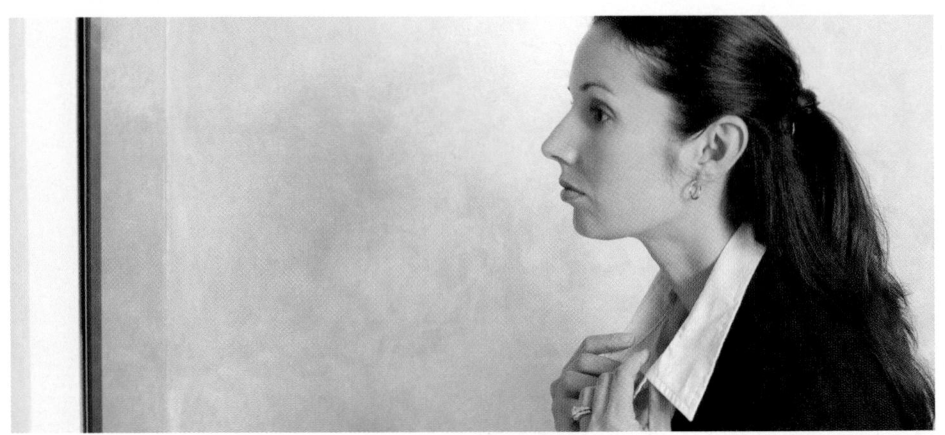

"My students need to know how to ask for a letter of recommendation letter properly. What can I do to help them?"
—Diane, 42, instructor
"Will people view me differently after I graduate? What will they expect of me?"
—Thomas, 28, student
"I want to be a teacher when I graduate. Is it okay that I have been blogging about what it is like to be a single parent and in college?"
—Rory, 24, student
"How can my college help me find a career that is right for me?"
—Rochelle, 19, student
"To go from having very little money to getting a regular paycheck is worrying me. What do I need to do not to blow it all?"
—Lynetta, 39, student
"When students write their résumés, they have a hard time coming up with additional information besides work history. What can I do to help them showcase their skills and experiences?"
—Larry, 33, career counselor

More specifically, after completing this chapter, you will be able to do the following:

- List the opportunities available for career exploration.
- Identify the steps to writing a résumé and cover letter.
- Discuss the importance of networking effectively.
- Explain how to create a budget and handle credit cards.
- Describe the processes for creating a life beyond college.

CAREER Exploration

Whether you know exactly what career you want or are still experimenting with what you want to do when you graduate, your college offers a variety of services, people, and information that will help you make a decision that is right for you. Take advantage of career centers, counselors, career readiness workshops, and even the faculty, who will be more than happy to talk to you about a career in the field that they teach. You may be surprised how helpful your college will be to see not only that you graduate, but also that you find a fulfilling career afterward.

CAREER VALUES AND GOALS

Before you begin delving into the resources and services available at your college, take some time to reflect on your career values and goals. They may not be much different than the ones you recorded when you read Chapter 2. However, it is worth considering what you value in a career and what kinds of experiences you want to have. For example, do you value working with others on projects with strict deadlines or would you prefer to work alone with little supervision? Your answer to that question and others can help you determine what you value and what careers work best for you. If, for instance, you have a strong interest in writing, but you prefer working with others, you may decide to choose a career that has many opportunities for collaboration when writing.

In addition to considering your values as they relate to your career, you may also want to consider your career goals—it is never too soon to think about them! For example, is your goal to move up quickly in a company or would you rather find a business that will allow you to indulge in a preferred lifestyle, such as traveling and meeting a diverse group of people? For sure, when you get to the point of creating clear, realistic, and reachable career goals, your values will inform what you write down or tell others, just as values and goals will influence your discussions with a career counselor or your search for a job and the resulting interviews.

If you are not sure where to start when considering your career values and goals, then you may want to check out the various career assessment programs, such as DISCOVER or Kuder, at your career counseling center.

CAREER COUNSELING

Long before you think about graduating and finding a job, you should visit the career counselors at your college. Preparing for a career takes longer than a few weeks, and the more planning you do, the smoother the process will be. Each college offers different services in its career center, but most provide access to interest inventories, which can help you pinpoint which fields you are best suited for. Most career services also provide "career libraries" that include information about different occupations as well as their responsibilities and pay potential. In addition, career centers may offer help with writing a cover letter and résumé and tips for interviewing for a job. Spend some time in your college's career library to learn more about potential opportunities instead of hitting all of the employers at a career fair.

Don't forget that your professors can also be great career counselors because they often have connections with people in the field (or have friends or relatives working in different industries). You never know when your welding instructor may have a contact at an accounting firm or a biology instructor may have a connection with the human resources department at an advertising firm. Tell professors what you want to do as a career whenever you have a chance. They may be likely to remember you and your goals when they meet someone in your field of study.

CAREER FAIRS

Career fairs are another way to get information about jobs and employers in your area. If your college sponsors a fair off campus or provides one to students on campus, then be sure to take advantage of it. Whether or not you are graduating next month or next year, it will pay to approach a career fair with the goal of making contacts and learning more about area businesses.

When you attend a career fair, there are several steps you can follow to make the most of your visits with potential employers. This list is just a start; you can get even more tips from your college counselors about how to maximize your time at a career fair:

- *Dress professionally.* Also, carry a professional-looking bag (no backpacks!) and a folder with copies of your résumé. Neatness counts.
- *Do your homework.* Find out what companies will be present at the fair and research the ones that interest you. You can find out more about them through their websites or through searching in the library.
- *Avoid asking what a company does.* Your research should tell you what the company does.
- *Choose a few booths to attend.* Instead of blanketing the fair and hitting every representative, be selective and limit yourself only to companies that you would like to work for.
- *Write and practice a standard introduction.* Then use it when you meet someone at the fair. Make sure the introduction is brief (state your name, your interests, and any relevant experience you may have) so that you maximize your time at the fair.
- *Be energetic and positive.* Recruiters and employers want to meet eager, exciting potential employees.

If you cannot make your college's career fair, you may be able to participate in a virtual career fair, which allows job seekers to "meet" participating companies and send résumés. Virtual career fairs are usually linked to a college's website and coincide with the actual fair. For example, the Virtual Career Fair link may only be available while the on-campus fair is open. Some colleges and organizations, however, provide a continual virtual career fair so that students can investigate potential careers and companies at any time. One such website is www.careersinoilandgas.com, which offers an abundance of information and resources for anyone interested in a career in the oil or gas industries. Other sites, such as www.collegegrad.com/careers, offer more general information about careers as well as advice and preparation for job seekers.

INTERNSHIPS

Another work option for community college students is an internship. This is a supervised position that allows a student to receive on-the-job training. Usually, internships are unpaid, which makes them less attractive to students who need to work. However, even if you need to make money while attending college, think about an internship anyway. Your college may offer course credit for internships, or you might even get paid for your work. This may be a good way to get closer to your degree *and* explore careers. Another idea is to volunteer once or twice a week at a place of business. If you have a few extra hours a week or can trade college credit for an internship, then you should investigate the benefits of interning.

"I was an intern at an advertising firm and learned so much about the industry. I highly recommend internships if you want some experience."
—Xian-ti, 21, student

Why are internships such a good opportunity for college students? One reason is that they allow you to work closely in a field that you may be interested in pursuing. In addition, internships can help you explore different ways that a major can be used in the workforce. For example, an English or journalism major may want to participate in an internship at a newspaper or as a proofreader at a company. A networking major may want to intern at a small business to get practical experience with computer networking issues on a small scale. These opportunities can give you firsthand experience with using your degree.

Internships also allow you to network with others who can help you find a job once you graduate. Even if you decide that you don't want to work in the same area as your internship, you will have contacts who may help you find a job in other fields. If you decide to intern, you should treat it as a job. Some employers rely on interns to complete certain projects each year, and they will expect you to be serious about the position, even if you don't get paid. Keeping a good attitude and being self-motivated are excellent ways to shine during

Your Terms of SUCCESS

WHEN YOU SEE . . .	IT MEANS . . .
Career fair	An event that brings various employers together into one place to meet job seekers.
Cover letter	A letter that "covers" a résumé and provides a more detailed description of a job applicant's qualifications.
Internship	A supervised position that allows a student to receive on-the-job training.
Networking	Creating connections among people for the purpose of helping them or having them help you.
Objective	A statement in a résumé that explains your career goals.
Recommendation letter	A letter written to provide a recommendation of your abilities and skills.
References	People listed on a résumé who can provide a recommendation of your abilities and skills.
Résumé	A document that provides information about you, your education, and your work experience.
Résumé padding	The act of exaggerating or lying about educational or work experience on a résumé.
Social networking	Creating connections, usually through websites, for the purpose of communicating with others.

your internship. In addition, you should meet regularly with your supervisor to ask questions and get guidance on projects. Most of all, make the best of your unique opportunity, and add that experience to your résumé—you never know, when the time comes to find someone to fill a position, your name may be at the top of the list because you were an intern.

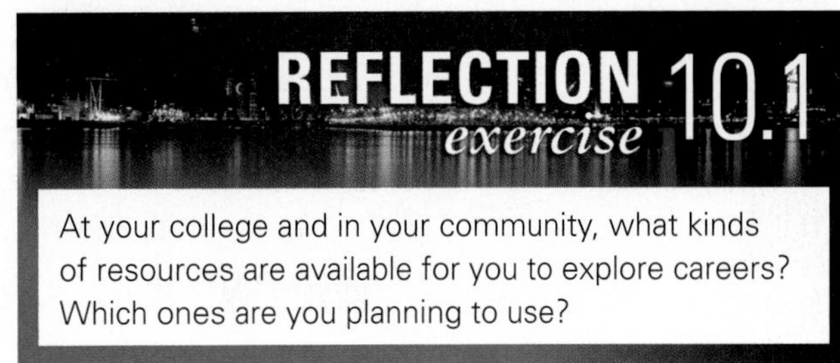

At your college and in your community, what kinds of resources are available for you to explore careers? Which ones are you planning to use?

JOB Preparation

In addition to educating or training you for a career, your college may also include services that help you land the job you want. Many specialized programs, such as nursing, culinary arts, and welding, provide job placement as well as a degree or certificate. Other degree programs, such as fine arts or health sciences, may offer fewer career services, but the instructors and advisors in those programs can still be valuable resources as you prepare for the workforce. At the very least, you will need to know the basics for finding a job after you graduate.

INTEGRITY MATTERS

Although you may be excited to include accomplishments on your résumé, you will need to be sure that you do not go overboard in describing what you have done in the past. A good rule to follow is to always provide accurate, truthful information in your résumé and cover letter. Highlight your accomplishments without overexaggerating them.

Lying on a résumé is called "résumé padding," and it can get you in serious trouble. At the very least, you may not get the job; at the very worst, you could be fired after being hired if the company finds out that your résumé contains false information.

YOUR TURN Where is the line between making your accomplishments noteworthy and exaggerating them? ■ What steps will you take to ensure that all of your information for a résumé or a cover letter is accurate?

____

____

____

____

____

Writing résumés and cover letters, as well as polishing your interviewing skills, will be necessary for you to move into your career of choice. As you get more education, the jobs you apply for will require that you present yourself more professionally.

WRITING A RÉSUMÉ

Learning to write a résumé is an essential skill for new graduates, and there is no time like the present to begin honing that skill. According to John J. Marcus (2003) in his book *The Résumé Makeover: 50 Common Résumé and Cover Letter Problems—and How to Fix Them,* a résumé is "no place to be modest. Prospective employers and recruiters will be looking for exciting accomplishments, and if they don't see them, your résumé will pale in the face of the competition" (p. 9).

There are actually two parts to an effective résumé: the résumé and the cover letter. A résumé is a page or two that lists your qualifications and accomplishments. A cover letter, on the other hand, provides information to a specific person that highlights your strengths that may not be apparent in the résumé. Both should be printed on high-quality paper using a good printer. A résumé, as well as any other document you send to a potential employer, should be carefully proofread for errors.

When writing a résumé, the first item you will include is your name, address, phone number, and email address. Make sure your voicemail has an appropriate message on it and that your email is professional as well: ejcantu@abcmail.com is preferred over bananafreak72@chunkymonkey.com. Double-check that there are no errors in your address, phone number, or email address—one misplaced number or letter can cost you an interview because you won't get the message. Michael's résumé (see Figure 10.1) contains a new email address to replace his more personal one that he uses for friends and family because he wants to separate career email from more casual correspondence.

"I volunteer at my son's school and I coach a community cheerleading team. I didn't realize that I could use both on my résumé as community service. Both things allow me to be a leader, which is good experience."

—Juanita, 25, student

A successful résumé will also contain a clear objective, or statement, that tells others what your career goals are. Think of it as a mini mission statement for your career! Objectives are not always written in a complete sentence. For example, your objective may be "To join an aircraft maintenance team at a highly rewarding company" or "To use my knowledge and skills to manage employees in the retail industry effectively." Writing a good objective takes time and consideration, and you may need to develop more than one if you plan to apply for different types of jobs or jobs in different industries. At least, be sure that your objective matches the job for which you are applying. If, for example, your objective is "To have a fulfilling career working with infants and toddlers in an accredited daycare" and you are applying to teach classes at a nursing home, then you may not get a second glance, much less an interview. Counselors and professors can help you craft an appropriate objective as you build your résumé.

FIGURE 10.1 Sample Résumé

Michael Cook
1234 Broadway Street
Anyplace, US 01234
555-555-1234
mrcook@anyplace.edu

Objective	To use my experience and education to work as an accounting manager.
Education	Associate of Applied Science in Accounting, Juno Community College, May 2011
Experience	Bookkeeper, Mays and Associates, August 2010–present • Send invoices to clients • Pay invoices from clients • Maintain general ledger • Supervise one staff member Work-Study, Financial Aid Office, Juno Community College, January 2009–July 2010 • Filed financial aid applications • Maintained communication with students through newsletter
Honors and Awards	Accounting Award for Outstanding Student, May 2012 President's Scholarship, August 2009–May 2011 Volunteer of the Year, Humane Society, October 2008
	References Available Upon Request

Once you include an appropriate objective, you will need to include information about your educational accomplishments and job history. If you have not completed your degree at this point, you can write down the anticipated date: "Associate of Arts, May 2012." Be sure to include any other certificates or degrees that you have earned. The most recently earned certificate or degree should be listed first. Information about your work history may be placed either before or after the information about your education. Again, list most recent job first and include the date you worked, your position title, the name of the company and location, and a bulleted list of job responsibilities. The following is a very basic format for reporting your work experience on a résumé. Depending on what kind of format you use, the order of the information may vary.

2008–2010 Dental Assistant No Worry Dental Group Tacoma, WA

- Cleaned clients' teeth and identified problem areas.
- Took x-rays of clients' teeth and updated their charts.
- Provided guidance for preventing tooth decay and improving gum health.

Depending on how much experience you have had, the first few parts of a résumé may be easy to complete. Many students have previous or current work experience and know what educational experiences they have had. However, a part of the résumé that is sometimes more difficult is the section on extracurricular activities, organizations, or awards. If you are early in your college career, you may not feel as though you have been able to participate in extracurricular activities worthy to add to your list of accomplishments. Nonetheless, with just a little creative thinking, you may be able to create a list of activities and endeavors. For instance, if you received a college scholarship, you can list it as an award. If you volunteer regularly with your child's school, you can list that. If you have participated in a fundraising event, organized a community meeting, coached a sport, or sat on a committee at your church or synagogue, you can list those accomplishments. You may not realize all the ways you have been involved with others that can show you have other interests than college and work.

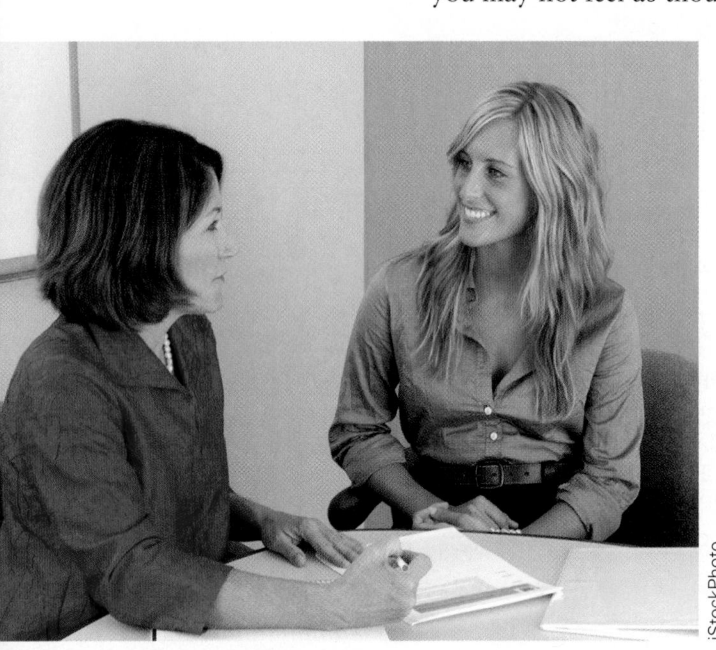

iStockPhoto

Take advantage of career services on your campus when you are writing your résumé and searching for a job.

Your college will also provide you with future opportunities to add to a résumé, so be sure to keep your eyes and ears open for chances to participate in a one-day event or a semester-long program. The key is to get involved at any level and record your involvement so that you can remember it when you need to develop your résumé. Here are just a few opportunities for students to get involved that colleges often provide:

- Dean's list or president's list for specified grade point averages
- Student ambassadors organization for promoting the college in the community
- Student government association for representing the voice of students
- Honor societies for community colleges such as Phi Theta Kappa as well as honor societies for specific disciplines such as Sigma Kappa Delta, an English honor society
- Special events such as fundraisers, cultural events, political or community rallies, or celebrations

One last part of the résumé that you will want to include is a list of references or a statement that says references are available upon request. As you meet people in college, you may want to create a list of potential references. A professor whom you got to know well, your advisor whom you see each semester as you plan your degree, or a campus official with whom you have worked closely on a project are good candidates for letters of recommendation or references. People you have worked with—either on the job or through a community project—are other excellent possibilities for references. Make sure these people know you well enough to speak of your strengths and potential in the workplace. Getting their permission before you list them is essential to getting a good reference.

Figure 10.1 is an example of a résumé showing you one way you can list the information. There are many ways to grab an employer's attention, and résumé books will provide you with examples of the various formats. However, a format that is concise, easy to read, and professional is usually best.

Working in a group, discuss and list all the types of activities and events your college provides for students to get involved with that could be included on a résumé.

CREATING A COVER LETTER

A cover letter accompanies a résumé and explains in detail how your qualifications match what the employer is looking for. As with a résumé, keep a cover letter brief and to the point, usually no more than a page unless you have enough work experience that you believe needs to be detailed in the letter. Often, the reason that cover letters should be short and to the point is that many employers simply scan these documents to see whether candidates meet the minimum qualifications and then decide, pretty quickly, whether or not to interview them. The more concise your résumé and cover letter, the easier it will be for potential employers to determine whether you are right for the job.

When writing a cover letter, be sure to address a specific person. Avoid starting your letter with "Dear Sir or Madam" or "To Whom It May Concern." If you do not know to whom to address the letter, call the company and ask for the appropriate person's name, along with the correct spelling. If you are responding to several different job advertisements, double-check that you have correctly matched each letter with its corresponding addressed envelope and that all material in the cover letter applies to the specific job for which you are applying.

The basic format of a cover letter is simple; once you type in your address, the date, and the potential employer's name, company name, and address, follow this outlined format:

1. Introduction Paragraph
   a. Introduce yourself
   b. Tell where you learned about the job (Internet, newspaper, person at the company)

2. Background Paragraph
   a. Tell more about yourself and how you are qualified
   b. Relate your education and skills to what the company is looking for
3. Closing Paragraph
   a. Tell potential employer how to contact you
   b. Thank the person for her time and say you are looking forward to hearing from her

Figure 10.2 is an example of an effective cover letter that could accompany the résumé in Figure 10.1.

FIGURE 10.2 Sample Cover Letter

1234 Broadway Street
Anyplace, US 01234

June 1, 2011

Dr. Judy Pile
Ingram Enterprises
6789 Levi Lane
Anyplace, US 09876

Dear Dr. Pile,

I am responding to your advertisement in the *Tonitown Times* for an accounting specialist at your company Ingram Enterprises. As you will see from my résumé, I have earned an Associate of Applied Science degree in accounting from Juno Community College, and I have experience working as a bookkeeper for a local company.

My additional experience as a work-study in the financial aid office at Juno has allowed me to improve my people skills as well as to understand how an organized and efficient office works. I have also learned to use the following computer programs effectively: Microsoft Word, Microsoft Excel, and QuickBooks.

I am sure that you will find both my education and experience fit the position that was advertised. If you would like to interview me, I can be reached during the day at 555-555-1234. I look forward to hearing from you.

Sincerely,

Michael Cook

Self-Regard

Emotionally intelligent people acknowledge their feelings in a situation, stop and think about what is involved, and then choose an act that will help resolve any problems. Read the following common situation and work through the three steps in the boxes.

What emotions do you have in this situation?

FEEL

What is the optimal outcome of the situation for you?

THINK

What attitude and positive action will help you achieve the outcome you want?

ACT

SITUATION

Your dream job is to work with teenagers at a rehabilitation program in your community. You have experienced some of the same challenges as the teenagers in the program, and you feel that you can relate to them because of your background. In fact, on your résumé, you have a three-month gap in your work history because you were enrolled in a treatment program for anger management. You also know that the competition for the job is intense—it is a great entry-level position in an award-winning facility—but you have proven that you can achieve: You have a 3.8 GPA and will graduate with an associate of arts degree in a few months. Before you interview, what should you do?

INTERVIEWING

Another important component to a successful career, if not the most important, is interviewing for a job. If your winning résumé gets you an interview, you are about halfway to getting a job. The tips in this section will help you maximize your performance at the interview. Do your research by checking out the company's website or search for other company information that may have appeared with the job advertisement. The goal is to find out what the company does and where it is going.

Don't forget to practice interview questions with your friends or family. Try to simulate the interview process by sitting across from the person who is practicing with you. Ask that person to make note of any fidgety habits and unclear answers. When you interview, you will want to dress professionally and pay attention to the details. Keep your fingernails clean and short. Check out hems and cuffs for tears. Make sure your clothes are clean and pressed and your shoes are polished. For women, be sure that there are no runs in your hose and that your heels are not scuffed.

When you score an interview, be sure to arrive early. Introduce yourself to the receptionist and prepare to wait. If you are offered a drink, decline; you may end up spilling it on your clothes. During the interview, listen carefully to the interviewer's questions, pause before answering, and speak slowly and carefully. Be sure, too, to look all of the interviewers in the eye when speaking, sit up, and lean forward slightly. Show by your body language that you are interested and relaxed, even if you are nervous. And speaking of nervous, if you are that is normal, but be sure to avoid fidgeting with a pencil or paper and tapping your fingers or feet.

When you are speaking of what you can do, be sure to highlight your strengths. Even if you don't meet all of the job's qualifications, you may be able to persuade the employer that you can do the job. Most experts agree that you should avoid inquiring about the salary during an initial interview. Instead, ask about the job responsibilities and benefits—the interviewer may provide a salary range as part of the information and he or she will most likely give you all of that information at some point during the interview process. As a last question, ask about the time line for filling the position. Knowing when the company will be making the final decision will help you prepare for the next step and reinforces your interest.

As you leave, thank everyone you meet and follow up with a thank-you letter to each interviewer (see Figure 10.3). If you do not know how to spell their names, call the receptionist the next day to get the correct spellings.

Interviewers want to hire people who are energetic, polite, professional, and appreciative. Put your best face forward and try to relax and enjoy the process.

CYBER CONSIDERATIONS

The Internet has made it much easier to find and apply for jobs, communicate with potential employers, and network to improve your contacts and connections. However, it can also be a potential hazard if it is not used appropriately and professionally. Most people are aware that posting messages, information, and photos can be risky—even dangerous—to your professional "health," but they may not be aware how much potential employers look for—and find—before they interview candidates. Many employers and company recruiters search for potential candidates online to see what kinds of information and images are out there. In some career fields, the more a candidate exposes (literally and figuratively) himself, the less likely he will get the job.

"Never post anything that could be considered inappropriate to a future employer. If you wouldn't want to see it on the front pages of the newspaper, don't post it."
—Ricardo, 39, career counselor

What can you do to protect yourself? Deleting your accounts is your best defense, but you can also change your account settings to private. Remember that material posted on the Internet is never completely deleted. In addition, be aware that if you have a large network of "friends," people who want to find out about you may still be able to do so. It is best not to post or put into writing anything that you think may be questionable to a potential employer, and if you have posted

FIGURE 10.3 Sample Thank-You Letter

Michael Cook
1234 Broadway Street
Anyplace, US 01234
555-555-1234
mrcook@anyplace.edu

July 12, 2011

Dr. Judy Pile
Ingram Enterprises
6789 Levi Lane
Anyplace, US 09876

Dear Dr. Pile,

Thank you for interviewing me yesterday. I enjoyed meeting you and your colleagues and learning more about how your company works.

After speaking with you, I am more firmly convinced that I would be a good person for the job. My education and experience would be a great match for what the position demands. I enjoy professional challenges, and I think your company provides the type of opportunities I am looking for.

Please feel free to contact me at 555-555-1234 or mrcook@anyplace.edu. I look forward to hearing from you.

Sincerely,

Michael Cook

anything, delete it if you feel it may jeopardize your ability to get the job you want.

STAY FLEXIBLE

All college career counselors want students to walk into high-paying jobs the day after graduation, but the reality is much different. Students who major in sought-after fields, such as information technology and health services, sometimes do not find the jobs that they thought were plentiful. Fluctuations in the economy are usually the cause for changes in the job market. Being prepared in case the job market has changed is your best defense.

To keep yourself grounded, formulate a plan for what you will do if you don't waltz into a dream job immediately. When writing your plan, be sure to answer the following questions:

- Are you willing to take less money if the opportunity is good?
- Are you willing to relocate for a better job?
- Are you willing to take a job in a different field than you expected?
- Are you willing to repackage your skills and knowledge to be considered for different types of work?

In addition, start building up your network of friends, family, coworkers, classmates, and acquaintances, if you have not already been working on it. Let them know that you are about to graduate and will be looking for a job.

Finally, consider the process that you must go through if you are to be successful in finding the right job for you. Getting a job requires you to prepare in the following ways:

- Consider which field best suits your skills, personality, and dreams.
- Attend workshops and information sessions that provide assistance with résumé writing, interviewing, and networking.
- Prepare a solid résumé.
- Network with friends, family, and acquaintances.
- Actively look for work.
- Respond to job advertisements by sending out your résumé and cover letter.
- Follow up job interviews with a thank-you letter.
- Remain positive and flexible but stick to your goals.

NETWORKING

Diane Darling, in her book *The Networking Survival Guide* (2003), defines *networking* as "sharing of knowledge and contacts; getting the help you need when you need it from those from whom you need it . . . ; [and] building relationships *before* you need them" (p. 16). Now, even more than ever, networking is an essential part of staying connected with others, especially because social networking sites on the Internet have made it so easy (and addictive) for us to keep up with each other.

Networking Online

One of the largest trends in networking is using online websites such as LinkedIn and Facebook to create networks of friends, family, and special-interest groups. The possibilities seem endless as to how you can use the Internet to connect with others who have special interests and activities or problems to solve. With this said, if you decide to join a network that focuses on an interest of yours, such as auto body repair, be sure to investigate who runs the group, what kinds of information are shared, and how active the group is. Some networks will be more active than others, which will make it easier to connect with people and get involved; networks or groups that are less active won't help you if you are using them to get to know others as potential contacts in the future. Still others may not be legitimate. Because creating networks of your own is so easy, you may want to consider creating an interest group if you cannot find one that relates to the kind of job you want. Networking sites such as Facebook and LinkedIn allow you to set up groups that can be used for professional, educational, or social purposes.

Networking Face to Face

Another way to get to know others is to network with them face to face. Finding active groups who share similar interests may be easier than you think. Look to clubs on campus that share your interests. Even if they are not career related, such as a drama club, you will meet people who may be future contacts for jobs. You can also get involved with your community through volunteer programs or civic groups such as your city's chamber of commerce. They may sponsor community-building, fundraising, and social events that allow you to meet other people in career fields that you are interested in. Additionally, involvement in such groups can provide you with more experience to record on your résumé. The more people you get to know, the more likely you will be able to use those contacts when you need them—in finding a career or in anything else.

TECH TACTICS

Using Technology to Get Ahead

Numerous resources on the Internet can help you prepare for stepping out into the workforce. Video sites such as YouTube provide examples of interviewing techniques (and probably many examples of what *not* to do) that you can practice on your own; résumé writing sites offer examples of winning résumés; and networking sites, especially the ones designed for professional networking, can connect you with other people in your career field or your community.

RECOMMENDED SITES

- http://career-advice.monster.com Monster's career advice site provides numerous links to tips including how to highlight military service and how to show holes in work experience.
- www.bestcoverletters.com Cover Letters provides over 40 examples of cover letters to suit any field, any situation.
- www.symsdress.com Dress to Achieve gives college graduates the basic information they need to make the best first impression.

REFERENCES AND RECOMMENDATION LETTERS

Recommendation letters and letters of reference are part of the job-finding process. If you have taken the time to cultivate a good relationship with a professor or an administrator at your community college, you will have an easier time asking for and receiving a recommendation letter that is full of specific information about the quality of your work and your character. Asking an instructor, advisor, or counselor to be a reference is simple. Email, call, or ask in person whether the person does not mind being used as a reference. Give them information about the job you are applying for and about when they may expect a phone call or email from a potential employer.

When considering someone to ask for a recommendation letter, choose a person who has had the chance to see you at your best. If you worked closely with a professor or spent many hours talking with a counselor, ask him or her to write a recommendation letter for you. The better the person knows you, the better the recommendation letter will be. In addition, give this person plenty of time to think about the quality of your work or recall specific examples in order to write a polished letter. If you are on a tight deadline, such as a week, be honest with the person and give him or her a chance to decline the opportunity. If the person does agree to write a recommendation letter on such short notice, be sure to provide him or her with all the necessary materials to complete it properly, including an addressed, stamped envelope and the correct forms. You may want to include a brief résumé so that the person can speak specifically about your accomplishments.

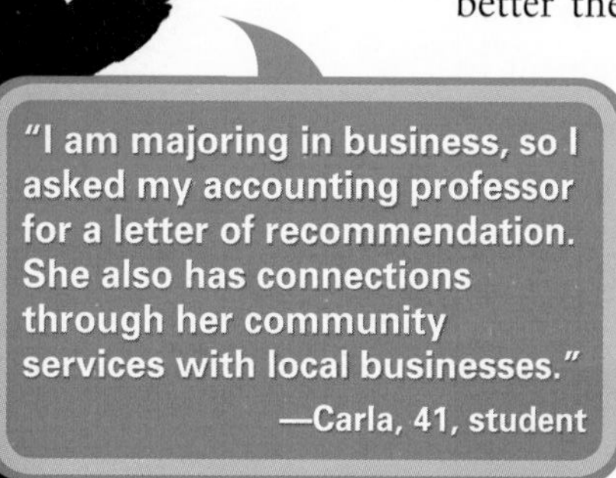

"I am majoring in business, so I asked my accounting professor for a letter of recommendation. She also has connections through her community services with local businesses."
—Carla, 41, student

Once your recommendation letter has been written, write a thank-you note and show your appreciation for the favor. Consider a handwritten note that expresses your gratitude rather than a verbal or email message of thanks. Finally, when requesting a recommendation, you should take the necessary steps to ensure that you do not read the recommendation letter. If you must hand deliver the letter, ask that it be sealed in an envelope first. Maintaining the confidentiality of the recommendation ensures a more honest appraisal from the individual who has written it. Committees that evaluate recommendation letters want truthful descriptions of your abilities and strengths; if they know that you have seen the recommendation letter, they may doubt the accuracy of the description.

CRITICAL THINKING *exercise* 10.3

What are the benefits and drawbacks to networking online? How do those benefits and drawbacks compare with networking face to face?

YOUR Finances

Even before you enter the workforce as a college graduate, you will need to get your finances in shape—if they are not already in good condition. Financial fitness, or the ability to use the money you are receiving to pay bills, eliminate debt, and save for the future, will be a crucial component to your overall success.

CREATING A BUDGET

Numerous financial experts say that the first step to getting your finances in shape is to create a budget that will help you meet your financial and personal goals. No matter how much money you make, it is relatively easy to create a budget. The hard part is following it.

First, you need to create a customized budget sheet. Figure 10.4 shows a sample budget form that you can start with. In the first column, you will estimate

FIGURE 10.4 Sample Budget Form

Category	Estimated Amount per Month	Actual Amount per Month	Difference
Income			
Source 1 (wages/salary)			
Source 2 (scholarship, financial aid, etc.)			
Source 3 (alimony, employee tuition reimbursement, child support)			
Total Income			
Expenses			
Mortgage/rent			
Utilities			
Car payment/transportation			
Insurance			
Groceries			
Household items			
Clothing			
Gas			
Car maintenance			
Cellular phone/pager			
Eating out			
Entertainment			
Health care (medications, doctor's visits, etc.)			
Credit cards or loans			
Total Expenses			
Net Income (Total Income minus Total Expenses)			

your income and expenses. The middle column will be used to record actual amounts for income and expenses. Record any differences in the marked column by subtracting the actual amount from the estimated amount. For example, if you estimate that you earn about $1000.00 a month, but this month you earn $1092.56, the difference is $92.56. If you earned $997.36, then the difference is –$2.64.

Once you determine the categories that fit your lifestyle, you will need to gather all the bills and paystubs that you have and add up your expenses and income. It is a good idea to review at least three months' worth of bills to get an accurate picture of your expenditures. If you have any bills that are paid less frequently than once a month, then you will need to convert them to a monthly expense. For example, if you pay $240 for car insurance every six months, your monthly expense is $40 ($240 divided by six months).

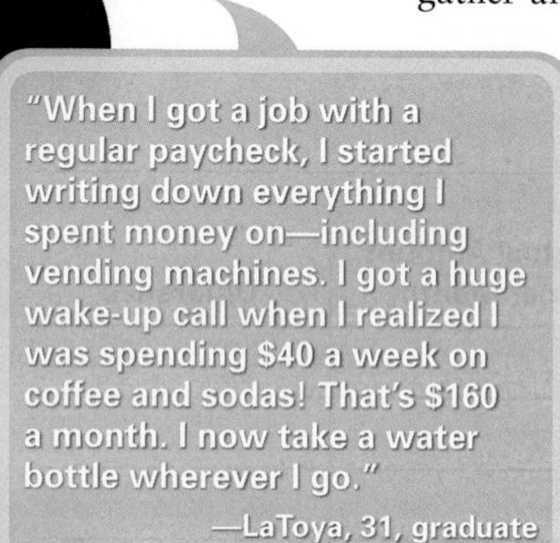

"When I got a job with a regular paycheck, I started writing down everything I spent money on—including vending machines. I got a huge wake-up call when I realized I was spending $40 a week on coffee and sodas! That's $160 a month. I now take a water bottle wherever I go."
—LaToya, 31, graduate

One key to an accurate budget that helps you track your spending is to be honest about your expenses. That means you must write down everything you spend, even the money for snacks or supplies. You may find that you spend $25 a week ($100 a month) on items that are unnecessary. The more you can track unnecessary items, the better you can control your spending.

After you get an accurate picture of your income and expenses, you can start setting short-term and long-term financial goals. Because you are in college and probably trying to keep expenses to a minimum, you may think that creating and working toward financial goals will be a difficult undertaking until you have a job with a steady income and secure future. However, you can start setting small, short-term goals now. For example, your first short-term goal could be keeping a monthly budget and making adjustments periodically. Another short-term goal could be to gather all the documents about your financial aid and keep them organized until after you graduate. Meeting these two goals will help you reach larger goals down the road.

You should also write down your long-term financial goals. One of these goals could be financial freedom and security. However, in order to reach that long-term goal, you will need to make a list of other goals and start working toward them. Be sure to include long-term goals that prepare you for retirement and the unlikely event of disability and unemployment.

HANDLING CREDIT CARDS

Credit cards can be very tempting when you are in college because they are so easy to use and the offers pour in just about every day. The reality of credit cards, however, is that they can cause big financial problems, leading to debts that are sometimes difficult to pay off. Think about this: You don't want to start a new career after college that pays a good salary only to send a substantial portion of it to a credit card company. Although it may seem easy, try to avoid paying your college tuition with a credit card. The interest rate will be more than double (possibly even five times higher) than you can get with a student loan. Additionally, avoid as many unnecessary expenses as you can. Use the rule that if it is not vital

TABLE 10.1 Credit Card Payments

Month	Previous Balance	Interest	Balance + Interest	Payment	Remaining Balance
Month 1	$1,000.00	$14.17	$1,014.17	$20.00	$994.17
Month 2	$ 994.17	$14.08	$1,008.25	$20.00	$988.25
Month 3	$ 988.25	$14.00	$1,002.25	$20.00	$982.25
Month 4	$ 982.25	$13.92	$ 996.17	$20.00	$976.17
Month 5	$ 976.17	$13.83	$ 990.00	$20.00	$970.00
Month 6	$ 970.00	$13.74	$ 983.74	$20.00	$963.74

to your life, then it can wait until you have the cash—even if it is a one-of-a-kind, super-duper deal.

In case you are still enticed to use a credit card, think about this sobering information. If you were to charge $1000 on a credit card that charges 17% interest and only pay $10 a month, you will be accruing more in interest than you will be paying each month. And that is only if you do not charge anything else!

Table 10.1 shows that paying twice as much—$20—each month for six months only reduces the balance by $36.26—after paying $120. Unfortunately, some students have many more thousands of dollars of credit card debt, and with the current interest rates, it is no wonder that students can find themselves in an endless cycle of charging and paying minimums. If it is at all possible, put the cards away until you are out of college, and then use them wisely.

CREATING a Life

It is now a cliché to say that "commencement"—the ceremony marking graduation—means "a beginning" rather than "an ending." Many graduation speakers address that point each year: When you graduate from college, you are not just ending your academic career; you are beginning the rest of your life. For community college students, however, the difference between being in college and going off to a career may not be that clear. In fact, career and college, for most community college students, are very much intertwined. Therefore, it may seem that there is no distinct beginning and ending for you. However, once you do graduate with a certificate or degree or even a group of credits, you can think about a brighter future as a beginning.

What will be left for you once you graduate? Beyond transferring to a four-year university, there is always graduate school or a professional school. Why not go as far as you can with your degree? With each semester, you are getting closer. Once you meet your goal of graduating with an associate's degree or certificate, you will see that what it mostly takes is goal setting, time management, and a desire to meet your goals.

Starting a new career or going back to the same career with more education and a new outlook on your abilities can be another way to start a new life. Some community college students entered college to achieve a skill set to do their jobs better or to be promoted. Other community college students will move directly from graduation into a new career. Either way, the students entering the workforce will be able to use the knowledge they have learned and skills they have sharpened to excel on the job.

Another "beginning" as you complete a degree at your community college is lifelong learning. Not only will you be able to use the research and information literacy skills that you have learned in college, but you will also have access to materials through alumni borrowing privileges at the library. In addition, you may be more interested in and informed about guest speakers and community events that are sponsored by your college. At the very least, you will have a network of instructors, counselors, and advisers to call on when you need advice and information.

MISSION, VALUES, AND GOALS REVISITED

In Chapter 2, you wrote down your values, goals, and mission statement. Do you still have that information in a convenient location? If so, get it out and reflect on how well you have met your original short-term goals and how far you have come to reaching your long-term goals. Have your values changed any? Or have they been strengthened by your achievements? Have you followed your mission statement? Is there anything that you would change about it?

To answer these questions, you will need to reflect on your achievements over the past semester. Your mission and values should not have changed much in the past weeks, but if they have, you can make a new list of values and rewrite your mission statement. Most definitely, some of your short-term goals should be met, and you have no doubt moved on to a new list as you make your way to your long-term goals. Now is the time, then, to revisit your long-range plans and make adjustments if you need to. Keeping up with what you have accomplished will serve as a reminder of your success if you ever feel unsure about your progress. Figure 10.5 is an example of a new list you can make.

"I never realized how many of my friends and family now look up to me because I am in college. I am a role model! I have already encouraged two friends to enroll."

—Toby, 23, student

Once you revise your short-term goals, you may notice that your time line for reaching your long-term goals needs adjusting as well. Keeping your list in a convenient location and looking at it every day or week will help you stay on track.

ENGAGING IN THE COMMUNITY

Although your focus during college will be on yourself and either moving on to another degree or to a new job, consider looking for opportunities to enhance your community. One of the purposes of higher education is to improve the lives

FIGURE 10.5 Goal Achievement and Goal Setting

Goals I Have Met

1. Completed my courses with above-average grades.
2. Created a study group with classmates.
3. Kept up with my commitments on the job.
4. Paid my tuition.

New Short-Term Goals

1. Get registered for next semester.
2. Speak with a counselor about career possibilities.
3. Make at least two A's in my classes.
4. Take more time to relax.

of individuals so that the community benefits as well, and it is essential that educated community members give back and make improvements.

Professional clubs, social and civic groups, churches, and volunteer organizations are other ways you can get involved in the community after college, if you have not done so already. The people you meet in these groups and the connections you make, both professional and personal, can enrich your life and career. If you are not part of a community group, seek out one whose interests are similar to yours; also, look for ways to participate in events in your community, whether a 5K run or a recycling drive. Participating in strengthening your community will allow you to give back to those in need, improve your surroundings, and gain friendships and business connections that may last a long time.

Jeff Greenberg/PhotoEdit

Life after college can mean using your education to make a difference in your community.

Now may not be the time to encourage you to help financially, but think about how you can continue to support your school after you have left. In order for a college—or any educational institution—to be successful in improving the lives of the people in its community, it must depend in part on its graduates to make a good name for themselves and to give back with their time, talent, and financial resources. There are a variety of ways that you can contribute to the education of those who will surely follow in your footsteps.

By being a productive, educated member of society, you are already giving back to your college. Because higher education's mission is to improve a community by increasing the knowledge of its population, we all benefit from students who complete graduation requirements for degree and certificate programs and go on to lead productive, happy lives. The skills and knowledge you

REFLECTION exercise 10.4

In what ways have you already mentored others who want to attend college or are just starting their college careers? How have you influenced others to value education?

have obtained in college are a good advertisement for the school. Alumni who make a difference in the lives of others through their jobs and community service fulfill the college's mission to not only provide education to strengthen the local economy, but to also graduate people who demonstrate the ideals of higher education.

Transfer Tips: FROM COLLEGE TO UNIVERSITY

Hold Off on Starting Your Career until You Have Met Your Educational Goals

It may be very tempting to head back to work before you have completed your certificate or degree because of changes in your family or financial situation. However, remember that if you can hang in there and go further toward your ultimate education goal, the better opportunities you will have in the workforce and the easier it will be to go back if you do find yourself "stopping out" of college for a while as you work.

Another idea for helping you stay in college before returning to work is to look for ways to break your ultimate educational goal into achievable, realistic shorter-term goals that will move you in the right direction. For example, if you need to return to work before completing your registered nursing (RN) degree, which is often a two-year degree, you may be able to complete a licensed practical nursing (LPN) program in a shorter amount of time. Completing a shorter program first, working in the field, and then returning to complete a longer program may be a good fit for your educational and financial needs. Be sure, though, that you speak with an advisor to make sure you avoid taking too many classes that will not fit into your longer-term educational goal.

Transfer Tips: FROM COLLEGE TO CAREER

Practicing What You Have Learned to Earn the Job Will Help You Progress

Time management, goal setting, and long-term planning are all skills that you have learned during your college career, and these skills will take you far in the workplace. If anything, knowing that you can juggle multiple responsibilities, such as taking care of family, job, and college, as well as yourself, should give you the confidence to tackle other challenges that you will face in the workforce. For sure, practice those skills on the job, but also know that you may need to improve on those skills as you complete new tasks and take on more projects at work and change positions.

Don't forget that your college, even long after you have graduated, can help you while you are in the workplace. You may still have, for example, access to their career services as a graduate of the college. You may also be able to use the library to do research. For sure, you will have the connections that you made while in college, people you can call on for advice and friendship. Look into what services they offer for you before you graduate, services that you can utilize as a successful graduate.

References and Recommended Readings

Darling, D. (2003). *The networking survival guide: Get the success you want by tapping into the people you know.* New York: McGraw-Hill.

Farr, M. J. (2004). *Same-day résumé: Write an effective résumé in an hour.* Indianapolis, IN: Jist Publishing.

Leider, R. J. (2005). *The power of purpose: Creating meaning in your life and work.* San Francisco: Berrett-Koehler Publishers.

Marcus, J. J. (2003). *The résumé makeover: 50 common résumé and cover letter problems—and how to fix them.* New York: McGraw-Hill.

Safko, L., & Brake, D. (2009). *The social media bible: Tactics, tools, and strategies for business success.* San Francisco: Wiley & Sons.

APPENDIX A

VARK Learning Styles

The VARK inventory uses the following categories: Visual, Aural, Read/write, and Kinesthetic. This system has been developed by Neil D. Fleming and Charles Bonwell. The inventory helps you determine your learning style preference; they also provide learning strategies based on your strengths based on information that you provide about how you would best act or react in certain situations. If you have strong preferences in more than one mode, you are considered multimodal (MM).

VARK Inventory*

Choose the answer which best explains your preference and circle the letter. Please select more than one response if a single answer does not match your perception.

Leave blank any question that does not apply.

1. You are helping someone who wants to go to your airport, town centre or railway station. You would:
   a. go with her.
   b. tell her the directions.
   c. write down the directions.
   d. draw, or give her a map.
2. You are not sure whether a word should be spelled "dependent" or "dependant." You would:
   a. see the words in your mind and choose by the way they look.
   b. think about how each word sounds and choose one.
   c. find it in a dictionary.
   d. write both words on paper and choose one.

3. You are planning a holiday for a group. You want some feedback from them about the plan. You would:
   a. describe some of the highlights.
   b. use a map or website to show them the places.
   c. give them a copy of the printed itinerary.
   d. phone, text or email them.
4. You are going to cook something as a special treat for your family. You would:
   a. cook something you know without the need for instructions.
   b. ask friends for suggestions.
   c. look through the cookbook for ideas from the pictures.
   d. use a cookbook where you know there is a good recipe.
5. A group of tourists want to learn about the parks or wildlife reserves in your area. You would:
   a. talk about, or arrange a talk for them about parks or wildlife reserves.
   b. show them internet pictures, photographs or picture books.
   c. take them to a park or wildlife reserve and walk with them.
   d. give them a book or pamphlets about the parks or wildlife reserves.
6. You are about to purchase a digital camera or mobile phone. Other than price, what would most influence your decision?
   a. Trying or testing it.
   b. Reading the details about its features.
   c. It is a modern design and looks good.
   d. The salesperson telling me about its features.
7. Remember a time when you learned how to do something new. Try to avoid choosing a physical skill, e.g. riding a bike. You learned best by:
   a. watching a demonstration.
   b. listening to somebody explaining it and asking questions.
   c. diagrams and charts—visual clues.
   d. written instructions—e.g. a manual or textbook.
8. You have a problem with your knee. You would prefer that the doctor:
   a. gave you a web address or something to read about it.
   b. used a plastic model of a knee to show what was wrong.
   c. described what was wrong.
   d. showed you a diagram of what was wrong.
9. You want to learn a new program, skill or game on a computer. You would:
   a. read the written instructions that came with the program.
   b. talk with people who know about the program.
   c. use the controls or keyboard.
   d. follow the diagrams in the book that came with it.

10. You like websites that have:
    a. things you can click on, shift or try.
    b. interesting design and visual features.
    c. interesting written descriptions, lists and explanations.
    d. audio channels where you can hear music, radio programs or interviews.

11. Other than price, what would most influence your decision to buy a new non-fiction book?
    a. The way it looks is appealing.
    b. Quickly reading parts of it.
    c. A friend talks about it and recommends it.
    d. It has real-life stories, experiences and examples.

12. You are using a book, CD or website to learn how to take photos with your new digital camera. You would like to have:
    a. a chance to ask questions and talk about the camera and its features.
    b. clear written instructions with lists and bullet points about what to do.
    c. diagrams showing the camera and what each part does.
    d. many examples of good and poor photos and how to improve them.

13. Do you prefer a teacher or a presenter who uses:
    a. demonstrations, models or practical sessions.
    b. question and answer, talk, group discussion, or guest speakers.
    c. handouts, books, or readings.
    d. diagrams, charts or graphs.

14. You have finished a competition or test and would like some feedback. You would like to have feedback:
    a. using examples from what you have done.
    b. using a written description of your results.
    c. from somebody who talks it through with you.
    d. using graphs showing what you had achieved.

15. You are going to choose food at a restaurant or cafe. You would:
    a. choose something that you have had there before.
    b. listen to the waiter or ask friends to recommend choices.
    c. choose from the descriptions in the menu.
    d. look at what others are eating or look at pictures of each dish.

16. You have to make an important speech at a conference or special occasion. You would:
    a. make diagrams or get graphs to help explain things.
    b. write a few key words and practice saying your speech over and over.
    c. write out your speech and learn from reading it over several times.
    d. gather many examples and stories to make the talk real and practical.

Scoring. For each question, mark your answer below and then add up how many V's, A's, R's, and K's you have. The largest number of V, A, R, or K indicates your learning style preference. For example, if you marked "A" for question number 2, your learning style preference for that question is V. If you have more V's than any other letter, your learning style preference is Visual.

Question	Choice A	Choice B	Choice C	Choice D
1	K	A	R	V
2	V	A	R	K
3	K	V	R	A
4	K	A	V	R
5	A	V	K	R
6	K	R	V	A
7	K	A	V	R
8	R	K	A	V
9	R	A	K	V
10	K	V	R	A
11	V	R	A	K
12	A	R	V	K
13	K	A	R	V
14	K	R	A	V
15	K	A	R	V
16	V	A	R	K

Calculating Your Score

Add the number of each letter and write the totals in the spaces below.

Total Number of V's circled _____

Total Number of A's circled _____

Total Number of R's circled _____

Total Number of K's circled _____

Look at your calculated score. If you have more V's than any other letter, then you have a strong visual learning preference. You may also have another learning style preference that is the same or close to your dominant learning style preference. For example, if you recorded 8 R's and 7 K's, you have both a read/write learning style preference as well as a kinesthetic learning style preference. Record your preference(s) in the space below.

My VARK Learning Style Preference is ________________.

Now that you know your learning style preference, you have made that first step. May the rest of the journey move you closer to your educational and personal goals.

APPENDIX B

Plagiarism Guide

OVERVIEW

The following guide is intended to supplement the information in Chapter 7 about avoiding plagiarism. Because understanding plagiarism—and how to avoid it—is a key component of college success, it is worth exploring the issue in depth. Think of this part of the book as a quick guide to plagiarism: what it is, why it happens, what colleges expect, and what you can do to prevent it.

WHAT Is It?

Plagiarism is the act of using someone else's words, images, and ideas without properly and accurately acknowledging them. This definition can also cover artwork and computer programming code. Basically, any material, besides information that is considered common knowledge, that you use within an assignment must be properly and accurately acknowledged. That means you must be familiar with and use the correct documentation format that your professor requires. Common documentation formats include MLA (Modern Language Association), APA (American Psychological Association), and CBE (Council of Biology Editors). Your professors will expect you to learn how to use a documentation format consistently in your work.

Anytime that you are creating, writing, or producing an assignment either as an individual or as part of a group, you will need to document the information and sources you use. If your professor wants the assignment to be completely original—without the use of sources—then you will need to adhere to those guidelines. If you are completing an assignment as part of a group, you may be asked to document which group members completed which parts of the assignment.

The following is a list of specific instances of plagiarism to avoid in all of your assignments:

- Buying or otherwise downloading a paper from the Internet and turning it in as your own.

- Copying and pasting material from the Internet or print sources without documenting or properly documenting.
- Allowing someone else to write all or part of your paper.
- Creating a "patchwork" of unacknowledged material in your paper by copying words, sentences, or paragraphs and changing only a few words.
- Including fictitious references.

The simplest rule to remember when it comes to plagiarism is that if you had to look up the information or you used part or the whole of someone else's idea, image, or exact words, you must let your professor or reader know. As in every unclear situation you may encounter, always ask for clarification. Your professor will be able to help you determine what you need to do if you are unsure.

WHY DOES It Happen?

Plagiarism happens for many reasons, but some of the most common include the following:

- Students do not understand the expectations of the college.
- Students do not know the rules of quotations, paraphrases, and summaries.
- Students do not care or do not see the importance of learning the rules.
- Students do not think they will get caught.
- Students do not make the time to check sources and acknowledge their sources.
- Students do not do their own work and allow or ask others to complete it for them.

Whatever the reason, students who do commit plagiarism will find that none of them will be excusable if they are caught. As you will read in the following section, colleges expect you to understand the rules and code of conduct. Professors also expect that you will make the time to do the assignment correctly and with integrity.

WHAT DO Colleges Expect?

Plain and simple, colleges and college professors expect that you already know what plagiarism is. In fact, many colleges outline their expectations, sometimes called *academic integrity,* in their catalogs, student handbooks, and on their websites and assume that you have read the information before you even step foot into a classroom, much less complete an assignment. Most colleges, too, do not distinguish between intentional plagiarism, or willingness to deceive by passing off work that is not original, and unintentional plagiarism, or forgetting to document or incorrectly documenting someone else's material. What that means for you is that you will most likely have very little chance of pleading that you didn't know or forgot to document if you are accused of plagiarizing. Colleges and professors take plagiarism very seriously; often, the most minimal penalty is an F on the assignment with no chance of doing it over or completing an additional assignment.

The following policy comes directly from the Pulaski Technical College's Web page that contains material from the student handbook. Notice that the policy defines plagiarism without reference to intent:

> Plagiarism Defined: Offering the work of another person as one's own without proper acknowledgment is plagiarism. Therefore, any student who fails to give appropriate credit for ideas or material he/she takes from another, whether fellow student or a resource writer, is guilty of plagiarism. This includes downloading or buying papers from the Internet and cutting and pasting from the Internet without proper acknowledgment. ("Code of Student Conduct," 2010)

What is not explicitly included in this definition, but is expected in every class, is that students do not plagiarize themselves or recycle papers from previous classes. Self-plagiarism or recycling is a less well-known form of plagiarism that is still considered cheating the system. When a professor assigns a paper, she assumes that her students are creating original writings for that class. She does not merely want her students to turn in assignments they may have written months or even years ago. Sometimes new students find this kind of definition of plagiarism troublesome since they are not plagiarizing someone else. However, they must understand that the purpose of the assignment is to learn something new, not to circumvent the learning process by handing in something old.

In addition to understanding your college's policies regarding plagiarism, it is worth also knowing that as a student you have a right to appeal any disciplinary decision that you think is not right. This is part of your rights to due process as a student. What this means is that if you have been accused of plagiarism and have spoken with your instructor, but you do not agree with the outcome, you may appeal the decision. Each college's process is different, so be sure to review the information in your catalog, student handbook, or on the website. The following is an example of information from Pulaski Technical College's website:

> Students have due process rights with regard to cheating and plagiarism violations. Students wishing to appeal a grade related to cheating or plagiarism should follow the Academic Due Process procedures outlined in the Academic Catalog. Students wishing to appeal disciplinary sanctions should follow procedures outlined in the Disciplinary Procedures section of the Academic Catalog. Once an instructor has determined that academic dishonesty has occurred, the accused student may not withdraw from or drop the course. The student must appeal the grade given by the instructor by completing the Academic Due Process procedures. ("Student Code of Conduct," 2010)

Knowing your college's policies and procedures is important whether or not you are accused of plagiarism.

WHAT CAN YOU DO to Prevent It?

The very reasons students plagiarize can be, if turned around, good reasons to prevent it. First of all, know what your college expectations are and be sure you know what the policies for plagiarizing are. If you may receive an F for the course for plagiarizing, that may be a great incentive to make sure you avoid it at all costs. Second, learn what kind of documentation is expected of you. Your professors and the college's tutors are great resources for learning how to format and document your papers correctly. Ask someone if you are unsure of what to do. Third, realize that acknowledging your sources and creating original work is an expectation of the professional community. Employers, colleagues, and most members of the workforce value those who recognize the thoughts and ideas of those who have influenced their own work. It's not just a bothersome practice in college alone—it is a professional expectation. Finally, do your own work and give yourself plenty of time to do it. Waiting to the last minute to complete a ten-page paper can produce anxiety and desperation, both of which can be triggers to short-cutting expectations by downloading a paper or using something you have written for another class.

Reference

"Student Code of Conduct." (2010). Retrieved June 6, 2010, from www.pulaskitech.edu/admission/web_catalog/student_life.asp#Code%20of%20Student%20Conduct

GLOSSARY

Academic calendar—A list of important dates. Included are vacation breaks, registration periods, and deadlines for certain forms.

Academic probation—A student whose GPA falls below a designated number can be placed on academic probation. If the GPA does not improve, then the student may be prohibited from registering for classes for a designated number of semesters.

Articulation agreement—A signed document stating that a college will accept the courses from another college.

Associate of Applied Science—A degree that consists of about 60 credit hours of courses. Not intended to serve as a transferable degree to a four-year university.

Associate of Arts—A degree that consists of about 60 credit hours of general education courses. Often considered as the equivalent of the first two years of a four-year degree.

Audience—In essay writing, the audience is the person or persons whom you are addressing.

Catalog—A book that provides students with information about the college's academic calendar, tuition and fees, and degree/certificate programs.

Corequisite—A course that you can take at the same time as another course. For example, if intermediate algebra is a corequisite for physical science, then you can take both courses during the same semester.

Cornell System—A note-taking system in which a student draws an upside-down "T" on a sheet of paper and uses the space to the right for taking notes, the space to the left for adding questions and highlighting important points, and the space at the bottom for summarizing the material.

Course objective—A goal that the instructor has identified for the student to meet once the course is completed. For example, a course objective could be to use MLA documentation properly.

Cover letter—A letter accompanying a résumé that describes how a person's qualifications match the advertised requirements for the job.

Creative thinking—Thinking that creates or generates ideas.

Critical thinking—The ability to use specific criteria to evaluate reasoning and make a decision.

Curriculum—A term used to refer to the courses that a student must take in a particular field, or it can refer to all the classes that the college offers.

Developmental classes—Sometimes referred to as remedial classes, developmental classes focus on basic college-level skills such as reading, writing, and math. Students who earn scores below a certain number on standardized tests such as the ACT and COMPASS exams may be required to take developmental classes before enrolling in college-level courses.

Family Educational Rights and Privacy Act (FERPA)—A federal law that ensures that a student's educational records, including test grades and transcripts, are not accessed or viewed by anyone who is not authorized by the student to do so.

Full-time student—A student who is taking at least 12 credit hours of courses per semester.

Full-time worker—A person who is working at least 40 hours per week.

Grade point average (GPA)—The number that is used to determine a student's progress in college. It refers to the number of quality points divided by the number of credit hours a student has taken.

Knowledge—The product created from taking in information, thinking about it critically, and synthesizing one's own ideas about what one has read or seen.

Long-term goal—A goal that takes a long time to complete (within a year or more).

Major—The area that a student is focusing on for his or her degree. If a student wants to teach third grade, his or her major can be elementary education. (*See also* Minor.)

Matching question—A test question that provides one column of descriptors and another column of words that must be matched with the appropriate descriptor.

Minor—A second area that a student can emphasize in his or her degree. A minor usually requires fewer classes and is not as intensive as a major. For example, if a student majors in marketing but also wants to learn more about running his or her own business, the student may want to minor in business or accounting.

Mission statement—A declaration of what a person or an institution believes in and what that person or institution hopes to accomplish.

Multiple-choice question—A type of test question in which an incomplete sentence or a question is given and the correct response must be chosen from a list of possibilities.

Objective question—A question that presents a limited number of possible answers.

OK5R—A reading strategy that was developed by Dr. Walter Pauk and stands for Overview, Key Ideas, Read, Record, Recite, Review, and Reflect.

Part-time student—A student who is taking less than 12 credit hours per semester.

Prerequisite—A required course or score that must be completed or achieved before enrolling in a course.

Priority—Something that is important at a particular moment.

Purpose—What a student hopes to accomplish with his or her writing assignment.

Quality points—The number that is assigned each grade. For example, an A is worth four quality points and a B is worth three quality points.

Remedial classes—*See* Developmental classes.

Résumé—A page or two that provides a person's educational and work experience, career objective, and contact information.

Short-term goal—A goal that can be accomplished in a short period of time (within a week or a few months).

SQ3R—A reading method that consists of the following elements: survey, question, read, recite, and review.

Stress—A physical and psychological response to outside stimuli.

Student handbook—A publication of the college that outlines what the college expects of the student.

Subjective question—A test question that requires a student to provide a personal answer. Usually, there are no "wrong" answers to subjective questions.

Syllabus—A document that contains an overview of the course, including objectives, assignments, and required materials as well as the instructor's policies for attendance, exams, and grading. It may also contain the college's policies on disability accommodations and academic dishonesty.

Time management—Strategies for using time effectively.

Topic—The subject of a piece of writing.

Transcript—A record of the courses a student has taken and the grades the student has earned. Transcripts also note the student's grade point average.

Transfer—Refers to moving from one school to another. Students who transfer must apply for admission to the second school and must request that their transcripts be sent to the new school.

T system—*See* Cornell System.

Values—Part of a person's belief system that provides the foundation of what the person does and what the person wants to become. If a person values financial stability, then the person will look for opportunities to earn money and provide a secure future.

Work-study—A federal program that allows students to work at their college while taking classes. Students must qualify for work-study money and must meet college department requirements for work.

INDEX